Mabon

GUIDE TO FOLKLORE,
HISTORY, AND
CELEBRATIONS OF THE
AUTUMN EQUINOX

ROBIN GINTHER VENNERI

KIPS Publishing LLC
Rochester, PA

Mabon: Guide to Folklore, History, and Celebrations of the Sabbat Season
© 2024 by Robin Ginther Venneri

Print ISBN 13: 979-8-9875591-6-1
First Edition, 2024
10 9 8 7 6 5 4 3 2 1
KIPS Publishing LLC
Rochester, PA
www.kipspublishingllc.com

LEGAL DISCLAIMER

We, KIPS Publishing, and the author, Robin Ginther-Venneri, are not herbal experts by any means and are not medical professionals. The products available, along with statements, opinions, views expressed, ideas, notes, procedures, and suggestions in this book, on the blog, on the website, in e-books, on Facebook, Pinterest, and Twitter pages, and any follow-up comments on-site or by email, are opinions and are meant for informational purposes only. They are not meant to be used to diagnose, treat, prescribe, prevent, or cure any disease or to administer in any manner to any physical ailments. They are not intended as a substitute for the medical advice of a trained health professional. We cannot be held liable for your decisions and choices and the outcome of those decisions and choices. You are encouraged to do your own research and consult your healthcare professional before treating yourself or anyone else.

The information in this book, on the blog, on the website, in e-books, on Facebook, Pinterest, and Twitter pages, and any follow-up comments on-site or by email are general and not specific to individuals and their circumstances. You must study herbs thoroughly and talk with a healthcare practitioner before you treat yourself or anyone else. I would like you to know that all matters regarding your health require medical supervision. Please consult your health care professional before adopting the statements, opinions, views expressed, ideas, notes, procedures, and suggestions in this book, on the website, in e-books, on Facebook, Pinterest, and Twitter pages, and any follow-up comments on-site or by email, as well as about any condition that may require diagnosis or medical attention.

Herbs are very powerful, and if they are misused, they can be harmful. Herbs can also cause allergic reactions and interfere with traditional medications by blocking their effectiveness, increasing their effectiveness, or reacting with them harmfully. Always check with your health care professional before using herbs or herbal products!

Do not use herbal products of any kind if you are nursing, pregnant, taking medications, or undergoing treatment for any medical condition without consulting your health care professional.

Any plant substance, whether used as food or medicine, externally or internally, can cause an allergic reaction in some people. Neither KIPS Publishing nor the author Robin Ginther-Venneri can be held responsible for claims arising from the mistaken identity of any herbs or the use of any remedy or healing regime or because you did not first seek the advice of a trained healthcare professional as recommended. Do not try self-diagnosis or self-treatment for serious or long-term problems without consulting a healthcare professional. Do not undertake self-treatment while undergoing a prescribed course of medical treatment without seeking professional advice. Always seek medical advice if symptoms persist.

We, KIPS Publishing, and Robin Ginther-Venneri disclaim any liability arising directly or indirectly from using this book, on the website, on the blog, in e-books, a class, class notes, follow-up email contacts, or of any products available or mentioned herein.

Additionally, the FDA has not evaluated the statements on the website, blog, e-books, Facebook, Pinterest, and/or Twitter pages, and any follow-up comments on these sites or by email. The information on this site is not intended to diagnose, treat, or cure any disease.

Thank you,
KIPS Publishing LLC

Expressing Gratitude and the Value of Mistakes in Research

Robin understands that making mistakes is an integral part of the learning process. They are grateful for the valuable lessons they have learned and the infinite knowledge yet to be discovered.

As you read Robin's work, it's important to acknowledge the effort put into it while also understanding that it is the result of a rigorous yet imperfect process. Robin is excited to share both the final polished research and the raw, unrefined process that led to it. Together, we can appreciate the evolution of ideas and the remarkable journey of seeking knowledge.

With humility and gratitude,
KIPS Publishing LLC

Acknowledgments

First and foremost, a huge thank you goes out to my amazing husband, Jeff. His support, from reading initial drafts to designing the cover and keeping me on track, was just as vital to finishing this book as my own efforts. Thank you, hon.

To my children, Caitlan and Kenan, your love and encouragement were instrumental in inspiring me to write this series. Watching you both grow into wonderful, caring individuals fills me with immense pride.

And to my adorable grandchildren - you know Mimi loves you!

To my closest friends, thank you for your unwavering friendship, lending an ear, and offering a shoulder to lean on. Your support has been invaluable on this journey. 🤍

A heartfelt appreciation to my mentors for standing by me since the start. Your kindness and motivation have touched me deeply.

I am grateful to all the businesses that took a chance on me and carried my books in their stores. Your generosity knows no bounds.

I want to thank EVERYONE who ever said anything positive to me or shared knowledge with me. Every bit of encouragement and wisdom has made a difference. I see you 🥰

Lastly, to you, the reader, who believed in me and invested in my book —thank you from the depths of my heart. Your support leaves me truly humbled. 😁

As always
Blessings to You and Yours

Book Blessing and Protection Spell

Supplies:
The book you wish to bless and protect
A small white candle
A sprig of Rosemary
Clear quartz crystal or amethyst (optional)
A quiet and sacred space

Preparation: Choose a time when you can be undisturbed and when you feel calm and focused. Place the book, the candle, the Rosemary, and any optional crystals on a clean and sacred surface.

Cleanse the Space: Light the white candle. As it flickers, visualize its flame clearing and purifying the energy around you. Pass the book and the Rosemary through the candle flame, visualizing any negative or stagnant energies being cleansed.

Invoke Divine Energy: Close your eyes and take a few deep breaths to center yourself.
If you work with specific deities, call upon them for blessings. Otherwise, you can invoke the universal energies of light, wisdom, and protection.

Blessing the Book: Hold the book in your hands and visualize a warm, golden light surrounding it.

Say aloud or in your mind: "By the light of this flame and the wisdom it contains,
I bless and protect this book and its knowledge to sustain. May it be a source of insight, growth, and grace, Guarded by the energies of this sacred space."

Infuse with Rosemary: Take the sprig of Rosemary and gently wave it over the book. Feel the protective energies of Rosemary infusing the book.

Say: "Rosemary, herb of wisdom and protection. Guard this book with your magical reflection. Shield it from harm, keep its pages pure, Infuse it with the knowledge that will endure."

Optional Crystal Blessing: If you have a clear quartz crystal or amethyst, hold it in your hands.
Visualize the crystal radiating a protective energy field around the book.

Say: "Crystal clear, amplify this protective sphere, Guard this book, keep it ever dear. May its energies be enhanced and pure, Infusing it with magic to endure."

Closing: Thank the divine energies, deities, or universal forces you invoked. Blow out the candle, visualizing the protection lingering around the book.

Placement: Keep the book in a safe and sacred space. For continued protection, you may choose to keep the rosemary sprig with it.

Remember to perform this spell with respect, intention, and a focused mind. The energies you infuse into the book will contribute to its positive atmosphere and long-lasting protection.

Mabon

During Mabon, the autumnal equinox, there is a brief moment when darkness and light are in perfect harmony across the Earth. As summer draws to a close, take this time to honor the rewards of your hard work.

Show gratitude for Mother Gaia's blessings. Embrace the transitional phase between beginnings and endings; it's a time to welcome new opportunities and let go of what no longer serves you. Your tasks are complete; the cycle has reached its conclusion. Today marks the beginning of a season focused on balance, acceptance, tranquility, and liberation.
Amen, Aho, and may it be so.

Mabon Blessings
"Equal dark, equal light Flow in Circle, deep insight Blessed Be, Blessed Be The transformation of energy! Let it flow, let it go Three-fold back it shall be Blessed Be, Blessed Be The transformation of energy."

Embrace the Mabon Blessing
This season brings a shift in light, with shorter days and longer nights. The wheel has turned; time will rearrange, while the darker side of the earth will stay unchanged. The lunar light holds enchantment, Heightening our intuition. Mother Earth's alchemy, from birth to end, brings forth rebirth. The unbroken and authentic cycle of nature offers peace of mind and well-being to you.

Blessings To You and Yours
Robin

Mabon

September 21st / 22nd

In the balance of Mabon's equinox, where day and night are equal,
As the leaves begin to turn, and the air is crisp and regal,
We gather 'round the autumn's hearth, where the apples hang low and sweet,
Bless this altar with your harvest as we gather what we reap.

By the apple's crimson skin, by the vine's ripe grape,
May this space be filled with abundance as we celebrate Mabon's sacred shape.

With balance and harmony to the cycles of the earth,
We bless this sacred space as we honor nature's worth.

Mabon Affirmation
Embracing Mabon, I embrace the flow of time without hindrance. I open my hands, once in the soil, now ready to reap the bounty of my inner harvest.

In harmony with nature's transformations, I find perfect equilibrium. Gratefully acknowledging life and respectfully honoring what has passed.

My words carry kindness, embracing love for myself and those sharing this harvest journey.

CHAPTER 1

Wheel of the Year

The Wheel of the Year Explained

The Wheel of the Year, also known as the Wheel of Life, symbolizes the Earth's cycles and the cycle of life itself. Our ancestors used it to mark the turning of the seasons and years, for farmers to plan their work, and for modern pagans to reconnect with nature's rhythms.

The Wheel of the Year consists of eight holidays or festivals, also known as holy days. These festivals follow the cyclical calendar of the sun and moon and the natural world's rhythms. Four are solar festivals or lesser Sabbats, associated with the sun and God. The other four are season-change festivals, or Grand Sabbats, related to the Earth and Goddess.

The Wheel of the Year has two halves: a dark half marking Autumn/Winter and a light half marking Spring/Summer. Each half has two lesser Sabbats and two Grand Sabbats. The lesser Sabbats are Yule, the Winter Solstice; Ostara, the Spring Equinox; Litha, the Midsummer Solstice and Equinox; Litha, the Midsummer Solstice, and Mabon, the Autumn Equinox. The two annual equinox solstices are the solar festivals or lesser Sabbats. The equinoxes occur when we have a day and night of almost equal length because the sun is directly over the equator. The solstices occur when we have the shortest day (June) and the longest day (December), related to the Earth's tilt. The exact date varies each year by a few days due to the Earth's rotation around the sun in 365.25 days, while our calendar is set for 365 days. Hence, we have a leap year every four years to balance the calendar.

Wheel of the Year

Mabon
September 23rd
Autumn Equinox

Lughnasadh
August 1st
First Harvest

Samhain
October 31st
New Year

Litha
June 21st
Summer Solstice

Yule
December 21st
Winter Solstice

Beltane
May 1st
May Day

Ostara
March 20th
Spring Equinox

Imbolc
February 2nd
Spring Begins

KIPS Publishing LLC

Pagan Sabbats

A pagan sabbat is a seasonal festival celebrated by some pagan and Wiccan traditions. There are eight sabbats in a year, marking key points in the solar cycle. These include Samhain, Yule, Imbolc, Ostara, Beltane, Litha, Lammas, and Mabon. Each sabbat has its own significance, rituals, and traditions. For example, Samhain is often associated with honoring ancestors and the thinning of the veil between worlds, while Beltane is a celebration of fertility and the coming of summer. These festivals allow practitioners to connect with nature, celebrate the changing seasons, and honor spiritual beliefs.

Light and Dark

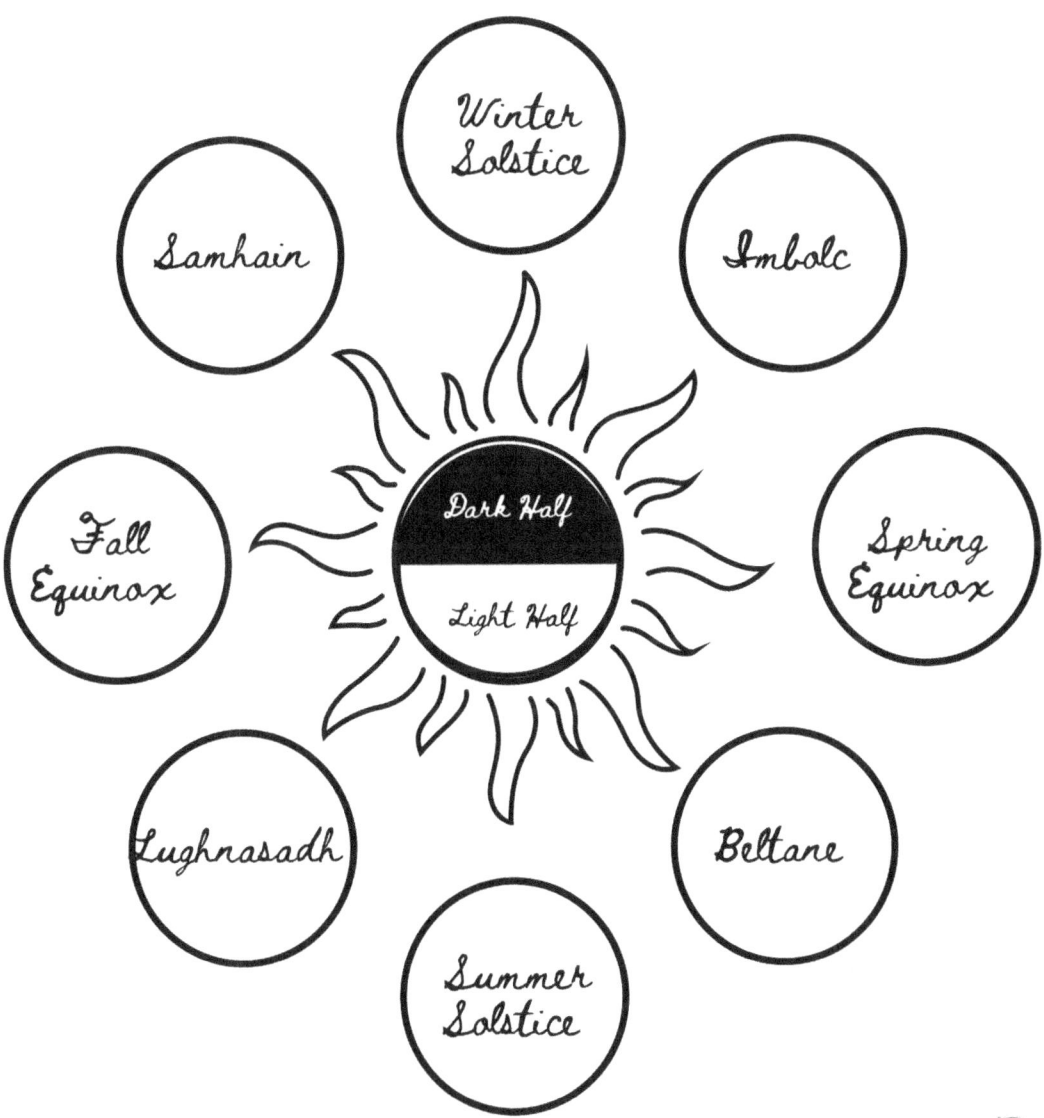

Sabbat Dates

Sabbat	Northern Hemisphere Date	Southern Hemisphere Date
Imbolc	February 1-2	August 1-2
Ostara	March 19-21	September 20-23
Beltane	May 1	October 31
Litha	June 20-22	December 20-23
Lammas	August 1-2	February 1-2
Mabon	September 21-24	March 20-22
Samhain	October 31	April 30
Yule	December 20-23	June 20-22

CHAPTER 2

Mabon at a Glance

Mabon at a Glance

Mabon - September 21 - 24

Northern Hemisphere: September 21 - 24
Southern Hemisphere: March 20 - 23
Pronounced: MAH-bawn, MAH-bun, MAY-bun, or MAY-vhon
Themes: harvest, gratitude, abundance, balance, preparation, welcoming the dark

Also Known As Autumnal Equinox, Fall Equinox, September Equinox, Harvest Tide, Harvest Home, Harvest Festival, Wine Harvest, Feast of Avalon, Alben Elfed, Meán Fómhair, Gwyl canol Hydref

The holiday of the Autumnal Equinox is known variously among neopagans as Harvest Home, Mabon, the Feast of the Ingathering, Meán Fómhair, An Clabhsúr, or Alban Elfed (in neo-druidry). It is a neopagan festival of thanksgiving for the fruits of the Earth and a recognition of the need to share them to secure the blessings of the Goddess and the Gods during the coming winter months. The name Mabon was coined by Aidan Kelly around 1970 as a reference to Mabon ap Modron, a character from Welsh mythology.

Mabon is the autumn harvest festival that marks the year's turning point. With equal days and nights, Mabon balances the changing seasons. While traditionally celebrated on Sept 22, the exact timing varies due to the Earth's rotation around the Sun. Embrace the transition from summer to fall as nature's vibrant colors and cooler evenings set the stage for the impending darkness. As the God prepares for his symbolic death at Samhain, Mabon reminds us of the fleeting nature of all things and the continual cycle of light and dark. Experience the beauty and wisdom of this moment in time, symbolizing the eternal dance of balance in our lives.

There is no right or wrong way to celebrate any of the Sabbats. Pagans base their celebrations on cultural traditions, historical practices, and inclinations.

So live and let live!

Archaeoastronomical Timing and Associated Planets

Astronomical equinox marking the waning point of the sun;
Sun enters 0 degrees of Libra in the Northern Hemisphere, Sun at 0 degrees of Libra in the Southern Hemisphere. The alignment of planets changes from year to year.

Archetypes
Female
The Grieving Widow
Harvest Lady
Harvest Queen
Kern Baby
The Warrior Woman

Male
The Divine King
The Dying King
The Harvest Lord
The Warrior Man

Heroes, Deities, and Goddesses
Demeter (Greek)
Epona (Celtic)
Ereshkigal (Sumerian)
Inanna (Sumerian)
Juno (Roman)
Minerva (Roman)
Modron (Celtic)
the Muses (Greek)
Persephone (Greek)
Osun (Yoruba).
Yemaya (Yoruba)
Oya (Yoruba)

Heroes, Deities, and Gods
Apollo (Greek)
Dionysus (Greek)
Green Man (Celtic)
Hermes (Greek)
Jupiter (Roman)
Mabon (Celtic)
Thor (Norse)
Thoth (Egyptian)
Vulcan (Roman)

Flowers
Carnation, chrysanthemum, marigold, and sunflower

Trees
Ash, alder, maple, and oak

Crystals
Amber, golden topaz, and hematite

Metals
Gold and iron

Scents
Aloe, benzoin, burning leaves, cinnamon, cedar, clove, frankincense, myrrh, and pine

Herbs
Acorns, bay, benzoin resin, echinacea, hyssop, ivy, myrrh, Solomon's seal, tobacco, and yarrow

Animals, Totems and Mythical Creatures
Blackbird, eagle, goose, horse, owl, salmon, squirrel, and stag

Symbols and Tools
Cornucopia, baskets, effigies, scarecrows, garlands and wreaths, scythes, bolines, and sickles

Food
Apples, barley, bread, carrots, corn, gourds, grapes, melon, nuts, oats, onions, potatoes, rye, and wheat

Drinks
Beer, cider, mead, water, and wine

Colors
Brown, green, orange, red, and yellow

Activities and Traditions of Practice
Communal feasting (corn roast barbecues, shared dinners) effigy burning dancing,
dunk tank games, music parades/processionals, target games

Acts of Service
Food drives, nursing home and hospice visits, park, and highway cleanups, public school service and booster projects, and veterans' care

Alternate Names for Mabon in Other Pagan Traditions

Aequinoctium Auctumnale (Hellenic, celebrates agriculture and end of military campaign season)

Alban Elfed (Druid, celebrates the final harvest and balance of light and dark)

Equinozio di Autunno (Stregha)

Feast of Avalon (Welsh Celtic)

Mein Fomhair (Gaelie, "middle of autumn" and the modern Irish word for September)

Holidays or Traditions Occurring During Mabon in the Northern Hemisphere:

Religious

Ampelia (Hellenic, honoring harvest and sacrifice, August 19th)

Vinalia (Nova Romans, celebrating wine harvest, August 19th)

Eleusinian Mysteries (Hellenic, approximately September 11th-20th)

Feast of Jupiter, Juno, Minerva (Nova Romans, September 13th)

Boedromion (Hellenic festival honoring the dead, September 19th)

Harvest Home (Scottish Celts, celebrating final harvest around the end of autumn)

Michaelmas (Catholic Christian, honoring archangel Michael, strength of will, September 29th)

Mimneskia (Hellenic, Roman suppression of the Bacchanalia, October 7th)

Winter Finding (Heathen/Norse, from Equinox to October 15th)

Secular

Second Harvest Festival (Autumn Equinox in mid-September)

Thanksgiving (Last Thursday in November in the United States)

Holidays or Traditions Occurring During Mabon in the Southern Hemisphere:

Religious

Dionysus or Bacchus Day (Greco-Roman, March 16th-17th)

Annunciation of the Blessed Virgin Mary or Lady Day (Catholic, March 25th)

Palm Sunday (Christian, the Sunday before Easter)

Good Friday (Christian, the Friday before Easter)

Easter (Christian, the first Sunday after the first full moon after the Spring Equinox)

Passover (Jewish, fifteenth day of Nisan, which begins on the night of the full moon after the northern Vernal Equinox)

Secular

St. Patrick's Day (while originally the Catholic Feast Day of a Saint, it is celebrated more as a secular holiday of Irish culture around the world, March 17th)

HAPPY Equinox

CHAPTER 3

Mabon

Mabon

Mabon is a pagan holiday and one of the eight Sabbats celebrated by modern pagans, particularly those who follow Wicca and other neopagan traditions. It marks the autumnal equinox, which occurs around September 21st in the Northern Hemisphere and around March 21st in the Southern Hemisphere.

The Facts:
Harvest Festival: Mabon is a festival that celebrates the second harvest, also known as the harvest of fruits and vegetables. It is a time to give thanks for the earth's bounty and acknowledge the harvest season's abundance.

Balance of Light and Dark: Mabon is observed at the autumnal equinox when day and night are equal in length. It symbolizes the balance between light and dark and the transition from the warmth and brightness of summer to the cooler, darker days of autumn.

Mythological and Spiritual Significance: In Neopagan traditions, Mabon is associated with mythological and spiritual themes. It is often linked to the story of the god and goddess, with the god descending into the underworld or sacrificing himself to ensure the fertility of the land.

Connection to Nature: Mabon is a time to connect with the rhythms of nature and the changing seasons. It encourages practitioners to observe the natural world around them, appreciate the beauty of the autumn landscape, and reflect on their inner balance and growth.

Rituals and Celebrations: Mabon is celebrated with rituals, ceremonies, and festivities that reflect its themes of gratitude, balance, and abundance. These may include making offerings to deities or spirits associated with the harvest, performing rituals to honor the changing seasons, and sharing meals made from seasonal foods.

Symbols and Traditions: Common symbols associated with Mabon include apples, grapes, pumpkins, corn, and other fruits and vegetables harvested at this time of year. Traditions may include decorating altars or homes with autumnal colors and symbols, creating cornucopias or wreaths, and participating in outdoor activities such as apple picking or nature walks.

Community and Connection: Mabon is often celebrated in the community with other pagans and neopagans. It allows practitioners to come together, share their experiences, and support one another in their spiritual practices.

Mabon

Reflecting on Mabon, the pagan observance marks the changing seasons as we approach the autumn equinox. It is a time for contemplation, acknowledging nature's rhythms and the onset of transition. Prepare for the autumn harvests by caring for the soil, nurturing seeds indoors, and envisioning a flourishing herb garden. Embrace the balance between light and darkness as the sun sets, signaling the season's abundance. Take moments to wander outdoors, witnessing nature's transformations. Consider the perpetual cycle of the Wheel of the Year and find comfort in the beauty of seasonal changes.

May the gentle embrace of autumn bring serenity during Mabon, harmonizing light and darkness for inner peace. As nature evolves, may your spirit find joy and resilience. Embrace the season's fertile energy, and may your endeavors thrive like the fields' crops. Wishing you a bountiful Mabon with abundance, warmth, and the enchanting rhythm of the ever-turning Wheel of the Year.

On this autumn equinox, as daylight and darkness find harmony, may your life be touched by equilibrium's gentle hand. May renewal and growth imbue your days with hope and potential. Like ripening fruits and changing leaves, may your aspirations flourish. May autumn's energy bring tranquility to your soul, and may you welcome the seasons' beauty with gratitude—a blessing for the autumn equinox, where balance and transformation intertwine in life's dance.

Autumn Equinox Blessing
The light and the dark are the same in length, They have equal time and equal strength. But soon the darkness will prevail, And the light and warmth will begin to pale. But do not be afraid, do not dismay, For this is the rhythm of nature's way. Rejoice in the abundance that this year bears, Breathe deep in the coolness and change in the air. Have gratitude and blessing, keep toll, And may this shift of nature enlighten your soul.

Druids

Druids, modern practitioners of Druidry, often celebrate Mabon as one of their eight seasonal festivals, known as the Wheel of the Year. Mabon also called the autumnal equinox, marks the point in the year when day and night are of equal length, symbolizing the balance between light and dark. While Druidic practices can vary among individuals and groups, there are some common elements to how Mabon is celebrated.

Druids have a deep reverence for nature and the cycles of the seasons. Mabon is seen as a time to honor the changing landscape, the harvest's bounty, and the wisdom of the earth.

Druidic celebrations of Mabon often include rituals and ceremonies performed in natural settings, such as forests, groves, or meadows. These rituals may involve invocations, prayers, and offerings to honor the deities, spirits, and ancestors associated with the harvest and changing seasons.

Altars may be set up with symbols and decorations representing the autumn season, such as leaves, acorns, nuts, apples, and seasonal flowers. Offerings of food, drink, or other gifts may be placed on the altar as offerings to the spirits of the land.

Mabon is often celebrated with communal feasting and sharing, where Druids gather to enjoy seasonal foods and drinks in the company of friends and fellow practitioners. Dishes may include locally sourced produce and ingredients, reflecting a connection to the land and its abundance.

Druids may engage in activities related to the harvest, such as foraging for wild foods, harvesting fruits and vegetables from gardens or orchards, or participating in community harvest festivals and events.

Mabon celebrations may include music, poetry, and storytelling to express gratitude for the harvest, honor the spirits of the land, and connect with the wisdom of the ancestors.

Mabon is a time for reflection and contemplation on balance, abundance, and transition themes. Druids may use meditation, guided visualization, or journaling to explore these themes and deepen their connection to the natural world.

Mabon celebrations provide opportunities for Druids to come together in the community, strengthen bonds, and support one another on their spiritual paths. These gatherings foster a sense of belonging and shared purpose among practitioners.

Neo-Pagans

Neo-pagans, including various modern pagan traditions such as Wicca, Druidry, and eclectic pagan practices, celebrate Mabon as one of their eight Sabbats, marking the autumnal equinox. While practices can vary among different neo-pagan groups and individuals, there are some common elements to how Mabon is celebrated.

Neo-pagans often mark Mabon with rituals and ceremonies that honor the changing of the seasons and the themes of balance, gratitude, and abundance. These rituals may take place outdoors in natural settings, such as forests, parks, or gardens, to connect with the energies of the earth.

Altars are often adorned with symbols and decorations representing the harvest season, such as autumn leaves, gourds, pumpkins, apples, and grains. Candles in colors associated with autumn, such as orange, yellow, and brown, may also be used.

Many neo-pagan rituals begin with casting a sacred circle, creating a space separate from the mundane world and conducive to spiritual practice. This may be done using a wand, athame (ritual knife), or simply by visualizing energy forming a protective boundary around the ritual space.

Invocations may be made to deities associated with the harvest and the changing of the seasons, such as Demeter, Persephone, Dionysus, or the Green Man. These invocations may express gratitude for the earth's abundance and seek blessings for the coming months.

Food, drink, or other gifts may be offered to honor the deities and spirits of the harvest. These offerings are often placed on the altar or at a designated outdoor space as a gesture of thanks and reciprocity.

Mabon is often celebrated with a feast, where participants gather to share food, drink, and conversation. Seasonal foods such as apples, squash, pumpkins, grains, and nuts are commonly enjoyed during these gatherings.

Many neo-pagans choose to celebrate Mabon outdoors, connecting with nature and the changing landscape. Activities may include hiking, camping, foraging for wild foods, or simply spending time in natural settings to appreciate the season's beauty.

Some practitioners may use Mabon as a time for divination or seeking guidance for the coming months. This can involve various methods such as tarot readings, scrying, or other forms of divination.

Heathens

Heathens, also known as followers of Heathenry or Germanic Heathenry, typically do not celebrate Mabon as it is a modern pagan holiday primarily observed by Wiccans and Neo-Pagans. Instead, Heathenry encompasses a variety of traditions inspired by the pre-Christian beliefs and practices of Germanic peoples, such as the Norse and Anglo-Saxons. However, there are some general facts about Heathen practices and beliefs that can be shared:

Heathenry is a decentralized religious movement with diverse practices and beliefs. There is no central authority or standardized set of rituals, so practices can vary widely between individuals and groups.

While Heathens may not specifically celebrate Mabon, they often observe seasonal changes and agricultural festivals that align with their cultural and historical roots. These may include celebrations of harvests, such as the Anglo-Saxon holiday of Hlæfmæst (Loaf Feast), which marks the beginning of the harvest season.

Blót is a central ritual in Heathenry, involving offerings and feasting to honor deities, ancestors, and spirits. During seasonal observances, Heathens may perform blóts to give thanks for the harvest's bounty and seek blessings for the coming months.

Heathen celebrations often involve communal feasting and gatherings, where participants share food, drink, and camaraderie. These gatherings provide opportunities for socializing, storytelling, and strengthening bonds within the community.

Heathenry strongly emphasizes a connection to the natural world and the cycles of the seasons. Practices may include spending time outdoors, engaging in activities such as foraging or gardening, and honoring the land and its spirits.

Ancestor veneration is an important aspect of Heathenry, and seasonal celebrations may include rituals or offerings to honor the spirits of deceased relatives and forebears. This can consist of setting places at the table for ancestors or making offerings at ancestral gravesites.

Heathens may engage in personal rituals and practices to mark the changing seasons and honor their beliefs in addition to communal celebrations. These may include meditation, divination, or solitary rituals performed in nature.

Wiccans

Wiccans celebrate Mabon as one of the Sabbats, seasonal festivals that mark significant points in the year's cycle. Mabon, also known as the autumnal equinox, occurs when the day and night are of equal length, symbolizing the balance between light and dark. It typically falls around September 21st in the Northern Hemisphere, though the exact date may vary slightly each year.

The celebration of Mabon reflects Wiccan beliefs in the cyclical nature of the seasons and the interconnectedness of all life. It is a time to give thanks for the abundance of the literal and metaphorical harvest and prepare for the introspective time of winter.

Wiccans may celebrate Mabon with rituals that honor gratitude, balance, and transition themes. These rituals often occur outdoors, where practitioners can connect with nature and the changing landscape. The following are some common elements of Mabon rituals:

The altar is typically adorned with seasonal decorations such as autumn leaves, gourds, pumpkins, and harvest symbols. Candles in colors associated with autumn, such as orange, yellow, and brown, may also be used.

Wiccans often begin rituals by casting a sacred circle, creating a space separate from the mundane world and conducive to spiritual practice; this may be done with a wand, athame (ritual knife), or the practitioner's hand.

Food, drink, or other gifts may be offered to honor the deities and spirits of the harvest. These offerings are often placed on the altar or at a designated outdoor space as a gesture of thanks and reciprocity.

Mabon is a time for introspection and reflection on the balance between light and dark within ourselves and the world around us. Practitioners may engage in meditation, guided visualization, or journaling to explore these themes.

Mabon is often celebrated with a feast, where participants gather to share food, drink, and conversation. Seasonal foods such as apples, squash, pumpkins, grains, and nuts are commonly enjoyed during these gatherings.

Some practitioners may use Mabon as a time for divination or seeking guidance for the coming months. This can involve various methods such as tarot readings, scrying, or other forms of divination.

After the rituals and festivities, Wiccans typically close the sacred circle, thanking the deities and spirits for their presence and energy. It may involve walking the circle's perimeter counterclockwise, symbolizing the winding down of the ritual energy.

CHAPTER 4

Other Holidays

Mabon Around the World

Many people in North America celebrate Mabon by participating in apple picking, corn mazes, and harvest festivals. Thanksgiving in Canada, typically celebrated in October, also aligns with autumn.

In the UK, Mabon is acknowledged through the Harvest Festival, where churches and communities come together to give thanks for the land's bounty. Traditional customs include making corn dollies and displaying harvested produce in churches.

In China, the Mid-Autumn Festival, also known as the Moon Festival, is celebrated during the autumn equinox. Families gather to appreciate the full moon, share mooncakes, and express gratitude for the harvest.

Chuseok, the Korean harvest festival, falls around the autumn equinox. Families pay respects to ancestors, share food, and participate in traditional dances and activities.

Japan celebrates Tsukimi, a moon-viewing festival, during the autumn equinox. People gather to view the full moon, make offerings of seasonal fruits and rice dumplings, and express gratitude for the harvest.

In Germany, the Erntedankfest (Harvest Thanksgiving Festival) is observed. Communities come together for parades, feasts, and church services to express gratitude for the harvest.

In Greece, the Thesmophoria, an ancient festival honoring the goddess Demeter, is linked to the harvest season. Women would participate in rituals to ensure fertility and a successful harvest.

In the Southern Hemisphere, where the autumn equinox occurs around March, Mabon is celebrated in a similar manner. Its focus is on giving thanks for the harvest and preparing for the coming winter.

Mabon is a significant festival in Neopagan and Wiccan traditions. During it, practitioners celebrate the balance of day and night, give thanks for the harvest, and perform rituals to connect with the changing seasons.

Many individuals and families worldwide celebrate Mabon in unique ways. These may include creating altars with autumnal symbols, enjoying seasonal foods, and expressing gratitude for nature's abundance.

While the specific customs vary, the common thread in Mabon celebrations is the acknowledgment of the harvest season and the expression of gratitude for the bounty of the Earth. The festival brings people together to reflect on the changing seasons and the cyclical nature of life.

In France, the Autumnal Equinox is marked by regional harvest festivals. People gather to enjoy local produce and wines and participate in various agricultural fairs.

Italians celebrate the harvest season with the Vendemmia, a grape harvest festival. Wine regions host events where people can participate in grape stomping and enjoy freshly pressed wines.

In Australia, where the seasons are reversed, some may celebrate a spring equinox around Mabon time. To welcome the warmer weather, people engage in outdoor activities, picnics, and gardening events.

The Swedish celebrate the harvest with the Mårten Gås (Martinmas) feast. This includes enjoying a festive meal centered around roast goose and participating in lantern processions.

Russians celebrate the Autumn Equinox by observing the traditional Russian Tea Day. This event involves sharing tea and treats with friends and family, celebrating the changing season.

While there isn't a specific equinox celebration, India observes various regional harvest festivals, such as Pongal in the south and Baisakhi in the north.

Various Native American tribes hold harvest ceremonies during the autumn equinox. These ceremonies involve giving thanks, dancing, and honoring the Earth's gifts.

In Ireland, communities come together for harvest fairs and markets, celebrating the richness of the land with music, dance, and traditional Irish foods.

In the Netherlands, the people celebrate the Autumn Equinox with various local events, including harvest markets and agricultural showcases, which focus on showcasing the season's bounty.

In New Zealand, where the equinox aligns with spring, some communities celebrate the changing season with outdoor events, flower festivals, and activities that welcome the warmer weather.

Festivals and Celebrations

Several holidays and festivals occur around the time of Mabon, the Autumn Equinox. These celebrations are observed by various cultures and traditions, each with its own unique significance.

Alban Elued, also known as the Light of the Water, is a Druidic celebration that aligns with the Autumn Equinox. Druids may honor the balance of light and dark during this festival.

Michaelmas, or the Feast of Saint Michael and All Angels, is a Christian festival observed on September 29th. It honors the archangel Michael and marks the beginning of autumn in the Northern Hemisphere.

Chuseok, also known as Korean Thanksgiving Day, is a major harvest festival celebrated in Korea. It typically occurs around the time of the Autumn Equinox and involves family gatherings, ancestral rites, and traditional games.

Tsukimi, or Otsukimi, is the Japanese Moon-Viewing Festival. It occurs in September or early October, coinciding with the full moon. People gather to appreciate the moon's beauty and make offerings.

Harvest Home is a traditional English harvest festival celebrated in late September. It involves bringing in the last sheaf of the harvest and decorating homes and churches with the fruits of the season.

The Mid-Autumn Festival, also known as the Moon Festival, is a Chinese celebration that usually occurs in September. Families gather to view the moon, share mooncakes, and express gratitude for the harvest.

Navaratri is a Hindu festival dedicated to the goddess Durga. It lasts nine nights and usually occurs in September or October. It involves various rituals, fasting, and dance performances.

Sukkot, or the Feast of Tabernacles, is a Jewish festival that begins five days after Yom Kippur and usually falls in September or October. It involves building temporary sukkahs (booths) and celebrating the harvest.

Pagan Pride Day events often occur around Mabon. These gatherings celebrate Pagan and nature-based spiritualities, fostering community, education, and awareness.

Oktoberfest is a traditional German beer festival that usually starts in late September and continues into October. It originated as a celebration of the fall harvest.

Durga Puja is a Hindu festival dedicated to the goddess Durga. It typically occurs in September or October and involves elaborate decorations, cultural performances, and rituals honoring the goddess.

Some Christian denominations hold Blessing of the Animals ceremonies on October 4th, the feast day of St. Francis of Assisi. Pets and animals are brought to churches for blessings.

Yom Kippur, the Day of Atonement, usually occurs in September or October, following Rosh Hashanah. In Jewish tradition, fasting, prayer, and reflection is a solemn day.

Maha Navami is the ninth day of Navaratri in Hinduism, celebrated to honor the goddess Durga. It typically falls around September or October and involves rituals, fasting, and cultural events.

In Norse Heathenry, practitioners may celebrate a Midharvest Blót around the equinox, offering thanks for the harvest and seeking blessings for the coming winter.

Erntedankfest, or German Thanksgiving, is celebrated in late September or early October. It involves giving thanks for the harvest with religious services, parades, and feasts.

Buddhist traditions celebrate the Day of the Orange around September 23rd. It marks when Buddhists offered robes and other supplies to monks as part of their practice.

Cherry Esplanade Harvest Festival is held at the Brooklyn Botanic Garden. This festival celebrates the Japanese tradition of moon viewing with cultural performances, tea ceremonies, and family-friendly activities.

Pitru Paksha, also known as Shraaddh or Mahalaya Paksha, is a Hindu fortnight for honoring ancestors. It typically occurs in September and involves rituals and offerings to deceased family members.

Manifest Abundance

Tonight I release all energies that do not belong to me and ask that karma clears.
I let go of old belief systems, unhealthy habits, obsessive thoughts, irrational fears, regret, anger, disappointment, harmful behaviors, and generational trauma.
I am magnetically attracting all that I vibrationally align with. I invite new magical energy into my life, I welcome transformational change and I am worthy of deep love, miracles, and magnificence.
With gratitude, I accept the blessings, good fortune, and opportunities that are meant for me.

Dożynki

Dożynki is a Polish harvest festival celebrated annually to give thanks for the harvest and to pray for continued abundance and prosperity.

The word "Dożynki" in Polish translates to "harvest festival" or "harvest home." The tradition dates back centuries and has roots in rural agrarian communities where agriculture played a central role in people's lives.

Dożynki is typically celebrated around the harvest season in late summer or early autumn. The exact date varies depending on local customs and traditions, but usually between August and September.

Dożynki is a time-honored tradition with deep cultural and religious significance in Polish society. It celebrates the fruits of the earth and expresses gratitude to God for the blessings of the harvest.

Harvest Blessing: The festival begins with a special Mass or religious service, during which a priest blesses the newly harvested crops. Farmers, villagers, and members of the community attend this ceremony.

Following the religious service, there may be parades and processions through the village or town, with participants dressed in traditional folk costumes and carrying banners, flags, and sheaves of wheat or other grains.

Homes, churches, and public spaces are decorated with flowers, garlands, and agricultural produce such as fruits, vegetables, and grains. Colorful displays of corn, wheat, and barley are common, symbolizing the bounty of the harvest.

Dożynki is celebrated with feasting, music, dancing, and cultural performances. Traditional Polish dishes made from freshly harvested ingredients are served, including pierogi (filled dumplings), kielbasa (sausage), kapusta (cabbage), and various types of bread and pastries.

Some Dożynki celebrations feature pageants, competitions, and contests to showcase agricultural skills and craftsmanship. These may include beauty pageants, talent shows, baking contests, handicraft displays, and traditional folk art.

Dożynki is a community-wide celebration that brings people together from all walks of life. It is a time for neighbors, friends, and families to gather, socialize, and share in the joy of the harvest season.

Erntedankfest

Erntedankfest, also known as the Harvest Thanksgiving Festival, is a traditional German harvest festival celebrated to give thanks for the blessings of the harvest season.

Erntedankfest translates to "harvest thanksgiving festival" in German. The festival has its roots in ancient agricultural practices and has been celebrated in various forms throughout German-speaking regions for centuries.

Erntedankfest is typically celebrated in autumn, around the harvest season. The exact date varies depending on local customs and traditions, but it is usually between late September and early October.

Erntedankfest is an important cultural and religious festival in Germany, Austria, and Switzerland. It is a time for communities to come together to give thanks for the bounty of the harvest and to pray for continued abundance and prosperity.

The festival often begins with a special church service or Mass, during which prayers are offered for the harvest's success and blessings are given to farmers and agricultural workers.

Homes, churches, and public spaces are adorned with decorations made from fruits, vegetables, grains, and flowers. Colorful displays of corn, pumpkins, gourds, and wheat sheaves are common, symbolizing the fruits of the earth.

Some Erntedankfest celebrations feature parades and processions through the streets, with participants dressed in traditional folk costumes and carrying banners, flags, and harvest symbols.

Erntedankfest is celebrated with feasting, music, dancing, and cultural performances. Traditional German dishes made from locally grown ingredients are served, including hearty soups, roasted meats, sausages, potato dishes, and freshly baked bread.

In the spirit of giving thanks and helping those in need, some Erntedankfest celebrations include charitable activities such as food drives, donations to food banks, and fundraising for agricultural charities.

Erntedankfest is a community-wide celebration that brings people from all walks of life. It is a time for neighbors, friends, and families to gather, socialize, and share in the joy of the harvest season.

Sukkot

Sukkot, also known as the Feast of Tabernacles or the Feast of Booths, is a Jewish festival celebrated to commemorate the harvest and to remember the Israelites' journey through the wilderness during the Exodus from Egypt.

Sukkot is observed on the 15th day of the Jewish month of Tishrei, which usually falls in September or October in the Gregorian calendar. The festival lasts for seven days, with an additional eighth day called Shemini Atzeret.

Sukkot is one of the three pilgrimage festivals commanded in the Torah (the Jewish holy scriptures), along with Passover and Shavuot. It is mentioned in the Book of Leviticus (Leviticus 23:33-43) as a time for dwelling in temporary shelters (sukkot) and rejoicing before the Lord.

The word "Sukkot" means "booths" or "tabernacles" in Hebrew, referring to the temporary dwellings that Jews are commanded to live in during the festival. These sukkot symbolize the temporary shelters used by the Israelites during their 40-year journey through the desert after the Exodus from Egypt.

One of the central rituals of Sukkot is the construction of a sukkah, a temporary structure with a roof made of branches or thatch and walls made of natural materials such as wood or canvas. Jews are commanded to dwell in the sukkah for the festival, eating meals and spending time with family and friends.

Another important ritual of Sukkot is the waving of the Four Species (arba minim) – the lulav (palm branch), etrog (citron), hadass (myrtle branches), and aravah (willow branches). These plants are held together and waved in all directions during prayers, symbolizing the Jewish people's unity and the harvest's bounty.

During Sukkot, some Jewish communities perform a special water pouring ceremony called Simchat Beit Hashoeva, commemorating the water libation ceremony that took place in the Temple in Jerusalem in ancient times.
Hoshana Rabbah: The seventh day of Sukkot is known as Hoshana Rabbah, which is considered the final sealing of judgment for the coming year. It is marked by special prayers and rituals, including circling the synagogue with the Four Species and reciting additional prayers for divine mercy and forgiveness.

Sukkot is a joyous and festive time in the Jewish calendar, marked by singing, dancing, and rejoicing. Many communities hold communal meals, called "sukkah parties," where friends and neighbors gather to eat, drink, and celebrate together.

The eighth day of Sukkot is known as Shemini Atzeret, which is considered a separate festival with its own significance. It is followed immediately by Simchat Torah, a joyous celebration marking the completion of the annual cycle of Torah readings and the beginning of a new cycle.

Simchat Torah

Simchat Torah, which translates to "Rejoicing of the Torah" in Hebrew, is a Jewish holiday celebrated to mark the completion of the annual cycle of Torah readings and the beginning of a new cycle.

Simchat Torah is observed on the 22nd day of the Jewish month of Tishrei, immediately following the seven-day festival of Sukkot. In Israel, where Sukkot is observed for one day less, Simchat Torah is celebrated on the 23rd day of Tishrei.

While Simchat Torah is not explicitly mentioned in the Torah (the Jewish holy scriptures), it is rooted in the biblical commandment to read the Torah continuously throughout the year. The practice of completing the annual cycle of Torah readings and immediately beginning a new cycle dates back to ancient times.

Simchat Torah is a time of great joy and celebration in the Jewish calendar. It is a day to express gratitude for the gift of the Torah, considered the spiritual and moral foundation of Jewish life, and to rejoice in the eternal wisdom and teachings contained within it.

Hakafot is the central ritual of the Simchat Torah the hakafot, or procession, during which the Torah scrolls are carried in a joyous parade around the synagogue. Participants, often including children, dance and sing traditional songs as they circle the sanctuary with the Torah scrolls held aloft.

The final portion of the Torah (Parashat V'Zot HaBerachah) is read, followed immediately by the opening portion (Parashat Bereishit), marking the seamless transition from the end of one cycle to the beginning of the next. This symbolic act represents the cyclical nature of Torah study and the perpetuation of Jewish learning from generation to generation. During the Torah reading, congregation members are called up to the bimah (the platform where the Torah is read) to receive aliyot (blessings) and participate in the reading. It is considered a great honor to be called up for an aliyah on Simchat Torah.

Simchat Torah is a joyous and festive occasion marked by singing, dancing, and exuberant expressions of joy. Many synagogues hold lively celebrations, with music, flags, and colorful decorations adorning the sanctuary.

Simchat Torah is a family-friendly holiday; children are actively involved in the festivities. They may be given flags or miniature Torah scrolls to carry during the hakafot, and special activities and programs are often organized to engage and educate young participants.

Simchat Torah is a communal celebration that brings Jews of all ages together to rejoice in the gift of the Torah. It is a time for unity, camaraderie, and spiritual renewal as communities unite to affirm their commitment to Jewish learning and tradition.

Sh'mini Atzeret

Sh'mini Atzeret, which translates to "Eighth Day of Assembly" in Hebrew, is a Jewish holiday celebrated on the eighth day of the Sukkot festival.

Sh'mini Atzeret is observed on the 22nd day of the Jewish month of Tishrei, immediately following the seven-day festival of Sukkot. In Israel, where Sukkot is observed for one day less, Sh'mini Atzeret is celebrated on the 21st day of Tishrei.

Sh'mini Atzeret is mentioned in the Torah (the Jewish holy scriptures) as a special assembly day, distinct from Sukkot. Leviticus 23:36 describes it as a day of rest and solemn assembly, during which no regular work is to be done.

Sh'mini Atzeret is considered a separate holiday from Sukkot, although it is often grouped together with Sukkot in Jewish tradition. It serves as a transitional day between Sukkot and the following holiday of Simchat Torah, marking the conclusion of the annual cycle of Torah readings and the beginning of a new cycle.

Prayers and Blessings: On Sh'mini Atzeret, special prayers and blessings are recited in the synagogue, including prayers for rain (Tefillat Geshem) and prayers for the well-being of the Jewish people. The holiday is a time to seek divine blessings for the upcoming year.

In some Jewish communities, the custom of reciting hoshanot (supplicatory prayers) continues on Sh'mini Atzeret. During the hoshanot ceremony, worshippers circle the bimah (the platform where the Torah is read) with their lulav and etrog (the Four Species) while chanting special prayers for salvation and redemption.

In many synagogues, preparations for the celebration of Simchat Torah, which follows immediately after Sh'mini Atzeret, begin on this day. Torah scrolls may be taken out of the ark and displayed prominently in the sanctuary, anticipating the upcoming joyous festivities. Sh'mini Atzeret is a time for spiritual reflection, renewal, and gratitude. It is a day to appreciate the harvest season's blessings, seek divine guidance and protection, and reaffirm one's connection to the Jewish community and tradition.

Sh'mini Atzeret is observed as a full holiday in Jewish tradition, with many of the same restrictions and observances as other major Jewish holidays. Jewish law prohibits work on Sh'mini Atzeret, and special meals and festive gatherings are held in observance of the holiday.

Thanksgiving

Thanksgiving is a national holiday celebrated primarily in the United States and Canada. It originated as a harvest festival, during which people gave thanks for the blessings of the harvest and the preceding year.

In the United States, Thanksgiving is celebrated on the fourth Thursday of November. President Abraham Lincoln officially set this date in 1863.
In Canada, Thanksgiving is celebrated on the second Monday of October. It was first observed as a holiday in 1879.

Thanksgiving's origins in North America can be traced back to early European settlers, particularly the Pilgrims, who settled in Plymouth, Massachusetts, in 1620.

The Pilgrims held a celebratory feast in the autumn of 1621 to thank God for their successful harvest and express gratitude for the help they received from Native American allies, particularly the Wampanoag tribe.

The event is often cited as the first Thanksgiving in North America, although similar harvest festivals were held by Indigenous peoples long before the arrival of European settlers.

Family Gatherings: Thanksgiving is traditionally celebrated with family and friends gathering for a festive meal. Roast turkey, stuffing, mashed potatoes, cranberry sauce, and pumpkin pie are among the classic dishes served.

In the United States, the Macy's Thanksgiving Day Parade in New York City is a famous tradition featuring giant balloons, floats, marching bands, and performances.

Football games, both professional and amateur, are a popular Thanksgiving tradition in the United States, with many families watching games together.

Some people choose to volunteer at food banks, shelters, or community organizations on Thanksgiving to give back to those in need.

Thanksgiving is considered a time to express gratitude for blessings and to reflect on the importance of family, community, and unity.

Many people also pause to give thanks for the privileges and opportunities they enjoy and to remember the holiday's historical and cultural significance.

Michaelmas

Michaelmas is a Christian feast day observed in honor of the Archangel Michael and all angels.

Michaelmas is celebrated on September 29th each year. It falls near the autumn equinox and is one of the four traditional quarter days in the Christian calendar.

Michaelmas has its roots in Christian tradition and is named after the Archangel Michael, who is mentioned in the Bible as an influential angelic figure associated with protection, justice, and victory.

The feast of Michaelmas was first observed in the 5th century in Rome, and its celebration gradually spread throughout the Christian world.

Michaelmas is a time for Christians to honor and give thanks for the intercession and protection of the Archangel Michael and all angels.

The feast day is also associated with the change of seasons, notably the transition from summer to autumn in the Northern Hemisphere. It is a time to reflect on nature's cycle and the spiritual significance of the changing seasons.

Church Services: Many Christian denominations observe Michaelmas with special church services, including Mass or liturgies dedicated to the Archangel Michael and the angelic hosts.

In some traditions, Michaelmas is celebrated with festive meals featuring seasonal foods such as goose ("Michaelmas goose"), apples, and blackberries. It is also a time for community gatherings and social events.

The Michaelmas daisy, a late-flowering perennial plant with purple or pink flowers, is associated with the feast day and blooms around Michaelmas. It is sometimes used as a decorative element in churches and homes during the celebrations.

Michaelmas was an important quarter day in medieval Europe's legal and agricultural calendar. It marked the end of the harvest season, the beginning of the agricultural year, and the settling of debts and contracts.

Michaelmas was also associated with various customs and traditions, including hiring fairs, where farm laborers and servants would seek employment for the coming year, and the payment of rents and dues to landlords.

Onam

Onam is a traditional Hindu festival celebrated primarily in the Indian state of Kerala and by Malayali communities worldwide. It is one of Kerala's most significant cultural festivals and holds great importance in Malayali culture.

Onam is typically celebrated in the month of Chingam, the first month of the Malayalam calendar, which corresponds to August or September in the Gregorian calendar. The festival usually lasts ten days, with the main celebrations occurring on the last day, Thiruvonam.

Onam commemorates the annual return of the mythical King Mahabali, a legendary ruler of Kerala known for his righteousness, generosity, and benevolence. According to Hindu mythology, Mahabali was granted the boon of visiting his kingdom and people once a year during the festival of Onam.

Onam is primarily a harvest festival, celebrating the bountiful harvest season and Kerala's agricultural prosperity. It marks the end of the monsoon season and the beginning of the harvest season when farmers reap the fruits of their labor.

Onam is celebrated with various cultural traditions and customs that reflect the rich heritage of Kerala. These may include:

Pookalam, one of the most iconic aspects of Onam, is the creation of intricate floral carpets, known as pookalam, made from a variety of colorful flowers laid out in beautiful patterns. New designs are created each day of the festival, and homes are adorned with these vibrant decorations.

The Onam feast, known as Onasadya, is a grand vegetarian meal served on banana leaves. It typically consists of a wide array of traditional Kerala dishes, including rice, sambar, avial, olan, thoran, and various payasam (desserts). The feast symbolizes abundance and unity.

Vallamkali is a traditional boat race that takes place during Onam in the backwaters of Kerala. Teams of rowers compete in long, narrow boats called snake boats adorned with colorful flags and banners. The races are accompanied by cheering crowds and traditional music.

Pulikali, or tiger dance, is a colorful folk art form performed during Onam. Participants paint their bodies to resemble tigers, leopards, or other animals and dance through the streets to the beat of drums and other musical instruments.

Yom Kippur

Yom Kippur, also known as the Day of Atonement, is one of the holiest and most solemn days in the Jewish calendar. It is observed on the 10th day of Tishrei, the seventh month of the Jewish lunar calendar, typically falling in September or October.

Yom Kippur is a day of fasting, prayer, and repentance, during which Jews seek forgiveness for their sins and strive to make amends for any wrongdoings committed in the past year. It is considered the culmination of the Ten Days of Repentance, which begins with Rosh Hashanah, the Jewish New Year.

The observance of Yom Kippur dates back to biblical times and is described in the Torah, the central religious text of Judaism. According to tradition, Yom Kippur was established by Moses after the Israelites' sin of the Golden Calf as a day of atonement and reconciliation with God. Yom Kippur is characterized by several themes and practices that reflect its solemn nature and spiritual significance:

Observant Jews abstain from food and drink, as well as from other physical comforts such as bathing and wearing leather shoes, for a period of approximately 25 hours, from sunset on the eve of Yom Kippur until nightfall the following day. Fasting is seen as a form of self-denial and purification, allowing individuals to focus their minds and hearts on spiritual matters.

Yom Kippur is marked by intensive prayer services held in synagogues throughout the day and evening. These services include the recitation of special prayers, liturgical readings, and the chanting of biblical passages, such as the Book of Jonah and the Vidui (confessional prayer). Jews also engage in private prayer and introspection, reflecting on their actions and seeking forgiveness from God and from those they have wronged.

The evening service on the eve of Yom Kippur begins with the recitation of the Kol Nidre prayer, a solemn declaration that nullifies any vows or oaths made unintentionally or under duress in the past year. This ritual symbolizes the desire to start the new year with a clean slate and a renewed commitment to honesty and integrity.

The concluding service of Yom Kippur is known as Ne'ilah, meaning "closing" or "locking." It is a climactic and emotional moment in which the gates of heaven are said to be closing, and final prayers for forgiveness and redemption are offered. The shofar (ram's horn) is sounded at the conclusion of Ne'ilah, signaling the end of the fast and the beginning of a new year.

Oktoberfest

Oktoberfest is the world's largest and most famous beer festival, annually in Munich, Germany. It is a significant cultural event that attracts millions of visitors from around the globe.

Oktoberfest originated as a public celebration of the royal wedding of Crown Prince Ludwig (later King Ludwig I) and Princess Therese of Saxe-Hildburghausen on October 12, 1810. The citizens of Munich were invited to join in the festivities, which included horse races, parades, and various entertainments. The event proved so popular that it was repeated in subsequent years, eventually evolving into the modern-day Oktoberfest.

Oktoberfest typically lasts 16 to 18 days, beginning in late September and ending on the first Sunday in October or occasionally extending to the German Unity Day holiday on October 3. The festival dates are adjusted each year to include at least two weekends.

Oktoberfest takes place on the Theresienwiese, a large open space in the heart of Munich commonly known as the "Wiesn" by locals. The festival grounds feature numerous large beer tents, amusement rides, carnival games, and food stalls.

The centerpiece of Oktoberfest is its famous beer tents, each operated by one of Munich's traditional breweries. These tents are massive structures capable of accommodating thousands of revelers. They are elaborately decorated, featuring live music, dancing, and a lively atmosphere. The beer served at Oktoberfest must adhere to strict Bavarian purity laws and is typically a strong, malty lager known as Märzen.

Oktoberfest is renowned for the staggering amount of beer consumed during the festival. Each year, millions of liters of beer are served to attendees, who enjoy the festive atmosphere while indulging in traditional Bavarian cuisine such as pretzels, roast chicken, sausages, and sauerkraut.

Many attendees of Oktoberfest choose to wear traditional Bavarian clothing, such as Lederhosen (leather breeches) for men and Dirndls (traditional dresses) for women. These garments add to the festive atmosphere and are a source of pride for many Bavarians.

Oktoberfest features a variety of parades, processions, and special events throughout its duration. These may include the opening ceremony, the traditional riflemen's parade, the costume and riflemen's parade, and various cultural performances and folk dances.

Canadian Thanksgiving

Canadian Thanksgiving is a national holiday celebrated in Canada on the second Monday in October. It is a time for Canadians to give thanks for the blessings of the harvest and the preceding year.

The origins of Canadian Thanksgiving can be traced back to European harvest festivals and religious observances, particularly those of the Christian tradition. The first recorded Thanksgiving celebration in North America occurred in 1578 when English explorer Martin Frobisher held a ceremony to give thanks for his safe arrival in what is now Newfoundland. However, the modern observance of Canadian Thanksgiving is rooted in traditions brought by European settlers to Canada.

Canadian Thanksgiving falls on the second Monday in October, which is earlier than the American Thanksgiving celebrated in the United States. The earlier date is due to Canada's shorter growing season and the earlier onset of winter in northern regions.

Canadian Thanksgiving is primarily a harvest festival, marking the end of the agricultural season and the gathering of crops. It is a time to celebrate the harvest's abundance and give thanks for the past year's food, blessings, and prosperity.

While Canadian Thanksgiving has its roots in Christian and European traditions, it is celebrated by people of all religious and cultural backgrounds in Canada. It is a secular holiday emphasizing gratitude, family gatherings, and community spirit.

Canadian Thanksgiving is celebrated with various traditions and customs among families and regions. Common customs include:

Canadian Thanksgiving is typically celebrated with large family gatherings and festive meals. Families come together to share a traditional Thanksgiving dinner, which often includes roast turkey, stuffing, mashed potatoes, cranberry sauce, gravy, and pumpkin pie.

Many Canadians take advantage of the long weekend to enjoy outdoor activities such as hiking, camping, or scenic drives to admire the fall foliage.

Some cities and communities in Canada hold Thanksgiving parades featuring floats, marching bands, and other festive attractions.

Thanksgiving is also a time for Canadians to give back to their communities by volunteering, donating to food banks, or participating in charitable events.

Canadian Thanksgiving provides an opportunity for reflection and gratitude. Individuals and families take stock of their blessings and express thanks for the people and experiences that enrich their lives.

Diwali

Diwali, also known as Deepavali, is a major Hindu festival celebrated by millions of people worldwide. It is one of the most significant and widely observed festivals in Hinduism.

Diwali is celebrated on the 15th day of the Hindu lunar month of Kartika, which typically falls in October or November in the Gregorian calendar. The festival lasts for five days, with each day having its own significance and rituals.

Diwali holds deep spiritual significance in Hinduism. It symbolizes the victory of light over darkness, good over evil, and knowledge over ignorance. It commemorates several mythological events and legends associated with Hindu deities and historical figures.

Diwali commemorates Lord Rama's return to the kingdom of Ayodhya, along with his wife Sita and brother Lakshmana, after 14 years of exile and the defeat of the demon king Ravana. The people of Ayodhya welcomed them back by lighting rows of oil lamps, symbolizing the victory of righteousness and the triumph of good over evil.

In some regions of India, Diwali marks Lord Krishna's victory over the demon king Narakasura. According to legend, Krishna freed 16,000 captive princesses and restored peace and prosperity to the world.

Diwali is also associated with the worship of Goddess Lakshmi, the Hindu goddess of wealth, prosperity, and good fortune. Hindus believe Goddess Lakshmi visits homes during Diwali to bless them with wealth and prosperity. Therefore, the festival is marked by cleaning and decorating houses, lighting oil lamps, and making offerings to Goddess Lakshmi.

Diwali is often called the "Festival of Lights" because of the traditional practice of lighting oil lamps (diyas), candles, and decorative lights to symbolize the victory of light over darkness and dispelling ignorance. Homes, temples, and public spaces are illuminated with colorful lights and decorations during the festival.

Diwali is celebrated with various rituals, customs, and traditions that vary among different regions and communities. Common customs include:

Before Diwali, homes and surroundings are thoroughly cleaned and decorated with rangoli (colorful designs made with colored powders or flower petals), flowers, and traditional decorations.

Diwali is a time for prayer, worship, and religious rituals. Families visit temples, perform puja (prayer rituals), and offer prayers to Hindu deities for blessings and prosperity. Diwali is also a time for exchanging gifts and sweets with family members, friends, and neighbors as a gesture of goodwill and affection.

Fireworks and firecrackers are an integral part of Diwali celebrations, symbolizing the joy and excitement of the festival. Communities come together to enjoy fireworks displays, cultural performances, and festive gatherings.

Chuseok

Chuseok, also known as Korean Thanksgiving Day, is a major harvest festival celebrated in South Korea and by Korean communities worldwide.

Chuseok is celebrated on the 15th day of the 8th month of the lunar calendar, which usually falls in September or October in the Gregorian calendar. The festival lasts three days, including the day before and after Chuseok.

Chuseok is primarily a harvest festival. It marks the end of the autumn harvest season and gives thanks for the bountiful crops of the year. Along with Seollal (Korean New Year), it is among the most important and widely celebrated holidays in Korean culture.

Chuseok has deep cultural and historical significance in Korea, dating back to ancient times. It is a time for Koreans to honor their ancestors, express gratitude to their families, and reaffirm bonds of kinship and community.

One of the central rituals of Chuseok is the memorial service (charye) held in honor of ancestors. Families gather at their ancestral homes or gravesites to pay respects to their ancestors by offering food, wine, and incense and performing ceremonial bows and prayers.

Chuseok is celebrated with various traditional foods and dishes that hold symbolic significance. Some of the most common Chuseok foods include:

Songpyeon are half-moon-shaped rice cakes filled with sweet fillings such as sesame seeds, honey, or red beans. They are traditionally made and eaten during Chuseok as a symbol of abundance and prosperity.

Fresh fruits such as apples, pears, and persimmons are often displayed and consumed during Chuseok as offerings to ancestors and as symbols of the harvest season.

Jeon are savory Korean pancakes made with various ingredients such as vegetables, seafood, or meat, and they are often enjoyed as part of the Chuseok feast.

Japchae is a traditional Korean dish with stir-fried glass noodles, vegetables, and meat. It is a popular Chuseok dish that symbolizes longevity and prosperity.

Chuseok is a time for families to come together and celebrate with feasting, games, and traditional activities. Families may travel long distances to reunite with relatives, share meals, exchange gifts, and participate in cultural traditions. Chuseok is also marked by various folk games and performances that reflect Korean cultural heritage. These may include traditional dances, music, storytelling, folk games such as ssireum (Korean wrestling), yutnori (a traditional board game), and archery competitions.

Ganesh Chaturthi

Ganesh Chaturthi, also known as Vinayaka Chaturthi, is a Hindu festival celebrated in honor of Lord Ganesha, the elephant-headed deity of wisdom, prosperity, and remover of obstacles.

Ganesh Chaturthi is observed on the fourth day (Chaturthi) of the Hindu lunar month of Bhadrapada, which typically falls in August or September in the Gregorian calendar. The festival lasts ten days, with the main celebrations culminating on the final day, Anant Chaturdashi.

Ganesh Chaturthi traces its origins to the Maratha ruler Chhatrapati Shivaji Maharaj, who initiated public celebrations of the festival in Maharashtra in the 17th century. However, the festival became more widespread and popular in the 19th century during the time of Indian freedom fighter Lokmanya Tilak, who promoted it to foster unity and national pride.

The centerpiece of Ganesh Chaturthi celebrations is the installation of clay idols of Lord Ganesha in homes, temples, and public pandals (temporary structures). Skilled artisans meticulously craft these idols, and they come in various sizes, ranging from small household idols to giant statues displayed in public pandals.

Throughout the 10-day festival, devotees offer prayers, chant mantras, and perform rituals honoring Lord Ganesha. Offerings such as flowers, fruits, sweets, and modaks (a dumpling considered Lord Ganesha's favorite) are made to the deity as a symbol of devotion and gratitude.

The festival begins on the first day with the installation of the Ganesh idol, known as Ganesh Chaturthi. This is followed by daily rituals and prayers, including reciting Vedic hymns and singing devotional songs (bhajans). The Ganesh Puja culminates on the tenth day with the Visarjan, or immersion, of the idols in water bodies such as rivers, lakes, or the sea.

On the final day of Ganesh Chaturthi, devotees participate in elaborate processions to accompany the idols to the immersion sites. The streets come alive with music, dancing, and chanting as people bid farewell to Lord Ganesha with heartfelt prayers and offerings. The immersion ceremony symbolizes Lord Ganesha's departure and the promise of his return the following year.

In recent years, there has been growing awareness about the environmental impact of Ganesh Chaturthi celebrations, particularly regarding the immersion of idols made from non-biodegradable materials such as plaster of Paris and chemical paints. Efforts are being made to promote eco-friendly alternatives such as clay idols and natural colors to minimize pollution and protect the environment.

Rosh Hashanah

Rosh Hashanah, also known as the Jewish New Year, is one of the most significant holidays in the Jewish calendar.

Rosh Hashanah is observed on the first two days of the Jewish month of Tishrei, which usually falls in September or October in the Gregorian calendar. It marks the beginning of the High Holy Days, a 10-day period of reflection, repentance, and renewal that culminates with Yom Kippur, the Day of Atonement.

Rosh Hashanah holds deep spiritual significance in Judaism. It symbolizes the anniversary of the world's creation and the beginning of the new year in the Jewish calendar. It is a time for introspection, repentance, and renewal as Jews reflect on their actions and seek forgiveness for any wrongdoings committed in the past year.

Rosh Hashanah is marked by special prayer services held in synagogues. Jews gather to recite liturgical prayers, hymns, and biblical passages about repentance, judgment, and redemption.

One of the central rituals of Rosh Hashanah is the blowing of the shofar, a ram's horn trumpet, which is sounded throughout the prayer services. The shofar is blown in a series of distinctive blasts, symbolizing the call to repentance and awakening the soul to spiritual renewal.

On the afternoon of the first day of Rosh Hashanah, many Jews participate in a ritual called Tashlich, in which they gather near a body of water to symbolically cast away their sins by emptying their pockets or tossing bread crumbs into the water. This act represents the casting off of past mistakes and the commitment to a fresh start in the new year. Rosh Hashanah is also a time for festive meals and celebrations with family and friends. Special foods with symbolic significance are served, such as apples dipped in honey (to signify a sweet new year), round challah bread (to represent the cyclical nature of life), and foods made with sweet ingredients like honey or dates.

Rosh Hashanah is not only a religious holiday but also a cultural and communal celebration for Jews around the world. It is a time for families to come together, share meals, exchange blessings, and engage in traditions passed down through generations.

On Rosh Hashanah, Jews greet one another with special blessings and wishes for the new year. The traditional greeting is "Shanah Tovah," which means "a good year" in Hebrew. Other common greetings include "L'shanah tovah tikatevu" (may you be inscribed for a good year) and "Ketivah v'chatimah tovah" (may you be written and sealed for a good year).

Assumption of Mary

The Assumption of Mary, also known as the Feast of the Assumption, is a Christian feast day commemorating the belief that the Virgin Mary, the mother of Jesus, was taken up body and soul into heaven at the end of her earthly life.

In the Western Christian tradition, the Assumption of Mary is celebrated on August 15 each year. In the Eastern Orthodox Church, the feast is known as the Dormition of the Theotokos and is observed on August 28.

The Assumption of Mary is not explicitly mentioned in the Bible, but it is based on early Christian traditions and beliefs about Mary's fate. The doctrine of the Assumption teaches that Mary, having completed her earthly life, was assumed body and soul into heaven by God. This belief is rooted in the reverence and honor accorded to Mary as the mother of Jesus and her unique role in Christian salvation history.

The belief in the Assumption of Mary dates back to the early centuries of Christianity and was gradually developed and accepted by the Church over time. The earliest written accounts of Mary's Assumption can be found in apocryphal texts and early Christian writings, although the doctrine was not formally defined until much later in Church history.

Pope Pius XII formally proclaimed The Assumption of Mary as a dogma of the Catholic Church on November 1, 1950, through his apostolic constitution "Munificentissimus Deus." In this document, Pope Pius XII declared that "the Immaculate Mother of God, the ever Virgin Mary, having completed the course of her earthly life, was assumed body and soul into heavenly glory."

The Assumption of Mary is celebrated with special liturgical services and devotions in Catholic and Orthodox churches worldwide. These may include Masses, processions, prayers, hymns, and readings from scripture that highlight the significance of Mary's role in salvation history and her exaltation in heaven.

Various cultural traditions and customs in different countries and regions also mark the Feast of the Assumption. In many Catholic-majority countries, it is a public holiday, and communities may hold religious processions, festivals, and other celebrations in honor of Mary's Assumption.

The Assumption of Mary is significant for Catholics and Orthodox Christians as it reflects their belief in the resurrection of the body and the hope of eternal life. It affirms Mary's special role in God's plan of salvation and underscores her unique status as the Mother of God and the first among the redeemed.

Raksha Bandhan

Raksha Bandhan, also known as Rakhi, is a Hindu festival celebrated primarily in India and among the Indian diaspora worldwide. It celebrates the bond of love and protection between brothers and sisters.

Raksha Bandhan is observed on the full moon day (Purnima) of the Hindu lunar month of Shravana, which usually falls in August. The exact date varies each year according to the Hindu calendar.

"Raksha Bandhan" translates to "the bond of protection" in Sanskrit. It is a compound word consisting of "Raksha," which means protection, and "Bandhan," which implies bond or tie. The festival symbolizes the sacred bond of love and duty between brothers and sisters.

The central ritual of Raksha Bandhan involves the sister tying a decorative thread or bracelet called a "rakhi" around her brother's wrist. The rakhi is typically adorned with colorful threads, beads, and decorative motifs, symbolizing the sister's love and prayers for her brother's well-being and protection. After tying the rakhi, the sister performs aarti (a worship ritual) and applies tilak (a mark of vermilion) on her brother's forehead. She then offers prayers for her brother's prosperity, happiness, and long life, and the brother reciprocates by giving his sister blessings and gifts.

The exchange of gifts is an integral part of Raksha Bandhan celebrations. Brothers give gifts, money, or other tokens of appreciation to their sisters as a gesture of love and gratitude. Sisters also prepare special sweets and delicacies for their brothers during the festivities. Raksha Bandhan is often celebrated with family gatherings, where relatives come together to tie rakhis, exchange gifts, and share meals. It is a time for bonding, laughter, and joyous festivities as families reaffirm their bonds of love and unity.

The tradition of Raksha Bandhan dates back to ancient times and has its roots in Hindu mythology and historical events. Some of the stories associated with Raksha Bandhan include Draupadi and Krishna: In the Mahabharata, the epic Hindu mythological text, Draupadi tied a rakhi to Lord Krishna, who reciprocated by protecting and coming to her aid during her time of need. According to another legend, Yama, the god of death, was deeply moved when his sister Yamuna tied a rakhi on his wrist and granted her immortality and eternal protection. In medieval India, Rani Karnavati of Chittor sent a rakhi to Emperor Humayun of the Mughal Empire, seeking his help and protection against an impending invasion. Touched by her gesture, Humayun rushed to her aid to honor the sacred bond of rakhi.

Raksha Bandhan is a religious festival and a cultural celebration that transcends religious boundaries. It is a time for strengthening familial bonds, expressing love and gratitude, and fostering community unity and harmony.

Krishna Janmashtami

Krishna Janmashtami, also known as Janmashtami or Gokulashtami, is a Hindu festival celebrated to commemorate the birth of Lord Krishna, an avatar of the Hindu deity Vishnu. It is one of the most significant and widely observed festivals in the Hindu calendar.

Krishna Janmashtami is observed on the eighth day (Ashtami) of the Hindu lunar month of Bhadrapada, which usually falls in August or September in the Gregorian calendar. Hindus across India and around the world celebrate the festival with great enthusiasm and devotion.

According to Hindu mythology, Lord Krishna was born in Mathura to Devaki and Vasudeva on the auspicious day of Janmashtami. He is believed to be the eighth avatar (incarnation) of Lord Vishnu, sent to Earth to restore righteousness (dharma) and protect the virtuous. Lord Krishna is said to have been born at midnight in a prison cell, where his parents were imprisoned by Devaki's brother, the tyrannical King Kansa. Upon his birth, miraculous events occurred, including the sudden appearance of divine light and the opening of prison doors.

Devotees observe fasting and engage in prayers, hymn chanting, and scripture recitation throughout the day and into the night in honor of Lord Krishna's birth. Abhishekam: Many temples conduct abhishekam, a ritual bathing ceremony in which the deity of Lord Krishna is bathed with various auspicious liquids such as milk, honey, yogurt, ghee, and water, followed by an offering of fruits and flowers.

The highlight of Krishna Janmashtami celebrations is the midnight puja and arati (ritual of worship) performed at the moment of Lord Krishna's birth. Devotees gather in temples and homes to offer prayers, sing devotional songs (bhajans), and participate in cultural programs and religious discourses.

In some parts of India, especially in Maharashtra, a widespread tradition known as Dahi Handi is observed. Young men form human pyramids to reach and break pots (handis) filled with curd or butter hung high above the ground. This tradition symbolizes the playful and mischievous nature of Lord Krishna, who was fond of stealing butter as a child.

In temples and homes, swings decorated with flowers and leaves are set up to depict the cradle of baby Krishna. Devotees take turns swinging the cradle while singing devotional songs and recounting stories of Krishna's childhood exploits.

Krishna Janmashtami is a religious festival and a cultural celebration that brings communities together in joyous festivities. It is a time for devotees to express their devotion, seek blessings, and immerse themselves in the divine love and grace of Lord Krishna.

CHAPTER 5

Mabon
Activities

Ways to Celebrate Mabon

Harvest Feast: Prepare a meal using seasonal fruits, vegetables, and grains to share with friends or family.

Apple Picking: Visit an orchard and pick apples. You can use them for baking, making cider, or enjoying them as a healthy snack.

Nature Walk: Take a leisurely walk in nature to appreciate the changing colors of the leaves and the autumn landscape.

Create a Gratitude List: Reflect on what you're grateful for and create a list. Share your gratitude with others.

Autumn Decor: Decorate your home with symbols of the season, such as acorns, pinecones, and autumn leaves.

Bonfire: If possible and safe, have a bonfire. Use it for rituals, storytelling, or simply enjoying the warmth of the flames.

Make a Wreath: Craft a wreath using autumn leaves, twigs, and other natural elements. Hang it on your door to welcome the season.

Divination: To gain insights for the coming months, practice divination methods like tarot readings, scrying, or using runes.

Pumpkin Carving: Carve or decorate pumpkins with symbolic designs. Use them to add a festive touch to your home.

Community Service: In the spirit of giving, volunteer your time for a community service project or donate to local food banks.

Candle Magic: Use candles in your rituals or light them to create a cozy and magical atmosphere.

Organize a Potluck: Host a Mabon potluck with friends and family. Everyone can bring a dish to share.

Star Gazing: Spend an evening stargazing and contemplating the cosmos, appreciating the vastness of the universe.

Crafting: Engage in autumn-themed crafts. Create decorations, artwork, or homemade gifts.

Meditation: Meditate on balance, reflecting on the equilibrium of light and darkness during the equinox.

Autumn Equinox Ritual: Develop your Mabon ritual, incorporating elements like candles, crystals, and seasonal offerings.

Bake Seasonal Treats: Use seasonal ingredients like apples, pumpkins, or cinnamon to bake pies, cookies, or bread.

Renewal Rituals: Focus on personal renewal and letting go of what no longer serves you through rituals or symbolic acts.

Craft a Cornucopia: Create a symbolic cornucopia filled with fruits, nuts, and symbols of abundance.

Cider Tasting: Sample different types of apple cider or make your own—experiment with adding spices for a seasonal twist.

Outdoor Picnic: Have a picnic in a park or your backyard, celebrating the outdoors and the season.

Seed Planting: Plant seeds or bulbs symbolizing intentions or goals for the coming season.

Make Herbal Infusions: Experiment with herbal teas or infusions using seasonal herbs and spices.

Yoga in Nature: Practice yoga outdoors, connecting with the earth and embracing the changing energy.

Ancestor Altar: Set up an altar with photos, candles, and offerings to honor your ancestors.

Fall Cleaning: Declutter and clean your living space, creating room for new energy and intentions.

CHAPTER 6

Intro to Deities

Introduction to Deities

Worshiping and dedicating to gods and goddesses is an important aspect of many pagan traditions, including those celebrating the Litha Sabbat. The honored and revered deities can vary greatly depending on the individual or group's beliefs and practices. Some may worship a pantheon of gods and goddesses, while others may focus their devotion on a single deity. Regardless of the approach, dedicating oneself to these powerful spiritual forces can be a significant and transformative experience.

Many pagans see their relationship with the divine as a two-way street. They believe they can receive blessings, guidance, and protection by offering devotion and reverence to the gods and goddesses. This energy exchange is often seen as a way to maintain balance in the world and one's life. Some also view the deities as archetypes or personifications of natural forces, such as the sun or the moon, and may seek to align themselves with these energies through worship.

There are many ways to worship and dedicate oneself to the gods and goddesses. Some may perform rituals or ceremonies, make food or drink offerings, or create sacred spaces in their homes or outdoor areas. Others may meditate, pray, or engage in personal acts of devotion. Whatever form it takes, this connection with the divine can be a source of inspiration, comfort, and spiritual growth for those who seek it.

A prayer to remove the blocks in your life:

Dear God / Goddess / The Universe,
I ask that you gently remove anything
which is preventing me from loving myself
fully and unconditionally. That which is
preventing me from believing in myself
wholeheartedly and consistently, and
that which is keeping me from my joy,
peace, blessings, and success.
Remove those barriers that I placed
around myself and my blessings in moments
of fear, and the blocks that I created
when I pushed down my pain.
Allow me to know and accept my worth
and greatness. I am open and ready for
more. Release anything that's not built
upon love, and do it all through feelings.
of peace, joy, and love. Amen!

Apollo (Greek)

Apollo is a major deity in Greek mythology, associated with the sun, light, music, prophecy, healing, archery, and more. Apollo is the son of Zeus, the king of the gods, and Leto, a Titaness. His twin sister is Artemis, the goddess of the hunt.

Apollo is often depicted as a handsome young man with a lyre, representing his association with music and the arts. Other symbols include the laurel wreath, the bow and arrow, and the sun chariot. One of Apollo's significant roles is as the patron of the Oracle of Delphi. The priestess, known as the Pythia, delivered prophecies believed to be inspired by Apollo.

Apollo is a master musician and is credited with inventing the lyre. He is associated with the Muses and often depicted with the instrument. A famous myth involves Apollo's unrequited love for the nymph Daphne. To escape Apollo's advances, Daphne was transformed into a laurel tree. Apollo adopted the laurel wreath as a symbol in her memory.

Another myth tells of Apollo's close relationship with the mortal youth Hyacinth. Tragically, Hyacinth died, and Apollo created the hyacinth flower from his spilled blood.

Apollo is associated with healing and medicine. His son, Asclepius, became the god of medicine, and Apollo himself was often invoked to cure diseases and avert plagues.

Apollo is depicted slaying the monstrous serpent Python, which Hera sent to persecute his mother, Leto. This event symbolizes Apollo's victory over darkness and chaos.

Apollo was known for engaging in various competitions, such as music contests with Pan and Marsyas and athletic competitions like the discus throw. In the Trojan War, Apollo supported the Trojans. He guided Paris' arrow to Achilles, leading to the hero's demise.

As punishment for his role in Python's death, Apollo served a period of exile as a shepherd. During this time, he performed acts of purification and redemption.

Apollo's influence extends beyond mythology to literature, art, and philosophy. His characteristics of reason, harmony, and artistic inspiration contributed to the idealized image of Apollo in classical Greek culture.

In Roman mythology, Apollo is essentially equated with the sun god Sol. However, the multifaceted aspects of Apollo's character persist in the Roman context.

Osun (Yoruba)

Osun is a prominent deity in Yoruba mythology and is recognized as the goddess of rivers, fertility, love, and prosperity.

The Osun River in Nigeria is considered sacred to the goddess Osun. Pilgrimages and ceremonies are held along the river to honor her.

In Yoruba cosmology, Osun is often regarded as one of the many children of Olodumare, the Supreme Deity. She is a sibling to other Yoruba deities and spirits.

Osun is associated with love, sensuality, and motherhood. The river often symbolizes her, as do attributes like the mirror, fan, and peacock feathers.

In Yoruba mythology, Osun is believed to have played a role in creating the world. Different myths describe her involvement in shaping human destinies and the natural world.

Osun is revered for her healing abilities. Pilgrims seeking blessings and healing frequently visit her shrines, particularly the Osun-Osogbo Sacred Grove, a UNESCO World Heritage Site.

The annual Osun-Osogbo Festival is a major celebration in honor of Osun. It involves rituals, processions, and ceremonies held at her sacred grove in Osogbo, Nigeria.

Devotees of Osun express their devotion through prayers, offerings, and rituals. Many seek her blessings for fertility, protection, and general well-being.

Due to the transatlantic slave trade, Yoruba religious practices, including the worship of Osun, were carried to the Americas. She is often syncretized with Catholic saints in places like Brazil and Cuba, blending African and Christian elements.

The worship of Osun has had a lasting impact on Yoruba culture, influencing art, music, dance, and literature. The Osun-Osogbo Festival, in particular, attracts both locals and tourists.

There are priests and priestesses dedicated to serving Osun. The Arugba, a virgin chosen annually, carries the sacrificial materials during the Osun-Osogbo Festival.

Demeter (Greek)

Demeter is a prominent figure in Greek mythology, primarily associated with agriculture, fertility, and the harvest. Demeter is the daughter of Cronus and Rhea, making her one of the Olympian gods and goddesses.

She is the sister of Zeus, Hades, Hera, Poseidon, and Hestia. Demeter is the goddess of agriculture, grain, and fertility. She is often depicted holding sheaves of wheat or barley, symbolizing the harvest.

Demeter is the mother of Persephone, who is a central figure in the myth associated with the changing seasons.

The most famous myth involving Demeter involves Hades, the god of the underworld, abducting her daughter Persephone. Demeter's grief and despair over the loss of her daughter led to a prolonged period of barrenness on Earth, causing a devastating winter.

Demeter searched tirelessly for her daughter and, in her grief, withdrew her blessings from the Earth, causing crops to wither and die.

A compromise was eventually reached between Demeter and Hades, facilitated by Zeus. Persephone was allowed to spend part of the year in the underworld with Hades and the other with Demeter. Demeter's joy during the months Persephone was with her is reflected in the bounty of spring and summer, while her sorrow during Persephone's absence corresponds to the fall and winter when the Earth becomes barren.

Demeter was widely worshipped in ancient Greece, and her cults often involved agricultural rituals and festivals. The most notable festival dedicated to Demeter was the Eleusinian Mysteries, a religious ceremony held at Eleusis that promised initiates a more favorable afterlife.

Demeter is often represented with agricultural symbols, such as a sheaf of wheat, a cornucopia, or a poppy flower.

In Roman mythology, Demeter is identified with Ceres, a goddess with similar attributes and associations.

Dionysus (Greek)

Dionysus is a significant god in Greek mythology, associated with wine, revelry, fertility, theater, and ecstasy. Dionysus is the son of Zeus, the king of the gods, and Semele, a mortal princess. His dual parentage reflects both divine and mortal aspects.

Dionysus had an unusual birth. Zeus rescued him from the pregnant Semele's burning body and sewed him into his thigh until he was ready to be born.

Ecstatic rituals, including festivals, processions, and wine consumption, characterized Dionysus's worship. His cult was central to Greek religious practices. Dionysus is associated with various animals, including the bull, serpent, and panther. These creatures symbolize the untamed and wild aspects of nature.

Dionysus is often depicted with a retinue of followers known as the Maenads or Bacchae, wild and frenzied female devotees. Silenus, a drunken and wise old satyr, is also a frequent companion.

Dionysus's myths often involve madness, transformation, and breaking boundaries. His presence can lead to ecstasy and liberation but also chaos and destruction.

In one myth, Dionysus was captured by pirates who did not recognize his divine nature. He transformed into a lion, causing panic, and turned the pirates into dolphins as punishment.

Dionysus is closely linked to Greek theater. The Dionysia festivals featured dramatic performances, tragedies, and comedies, celebrating the god's influence on serious and humorous aspects of life.

Dionysus fell in love with Ariadne, the abandoned princess of Crete. After helping her on Naxos, they became a divine couple, and she was later placed among the stars in the constellation Corona Borealis.

In some myths, Dionysus undergoes a symbolic death and resurrection, representing the cyclical nature of life, vegetation, and the grape harvest.

Dionysian mysteries and initiation rites were held secretly, often involving rituals, dances, and symbolic experiences that conveyed a deeper understanding of the god's mysteries.

Ereshkigal (Sumerian)

Ereshkigal is a prominent goddess in Sumerian mythology. She is primarily associated with the underworld, or the land of the dead. She is the sister of Inanna (Ishtar), the foremost goddess of love, fertility, and warfare.

Ereshkigal holds the title of Queen of the Underworld, ruling over the realm of the dead with authority.

One of the most well-known myths involving Ereshkigal is the Descent of Inanna. In this myth, Inanna descends into the underworld to visit her sister. As she passes through the seven gates, she must give up various aspects of her power and clothing.

When Inanna reaches Ereshkigal's throne room naked and vulnerable, Ereshkigal judges her and decides to kill her. During Inanna's absence, the world above falls into a lifeless state. Enki, the god of wisdom, sends beings to rescue Inanna. They revive her, but the rule of the underworld demands that someone take Inanna's place.

Inanna's husband, Dumuzid, is chosen to spend part of the year in the underworld as a substitute for Inanna. This myth reflects the cyclical nature of life and death, as Dumuzid's time in the underworld corresponds to the barren season.

Ereshkigal is often associated with symbols of death and the underworld. Her presence in Sumerian art may include imagery such as the lion-headed mace, an emblem of authority.

In a later part of the myth, Inanna can return to the world above but must find someone to take her place in the underworld. She encounters Dumuzid, her husband, who had not mourned her properly during her absence, and he becomes the one to spend part of the year in the underworld.

Ereshkigal was likely worshipped through rituals and ceremonies associated with death and the afterlife. However, the details of her cult practices are not as well-documented as some other deities in Sumerian mythology.

Hermes (Greek)

Hermes is a significant deity in Greek mythology associated with transitions, boundaries, communication, commerce, and travel. He is the son of Zeus, the king of the gods, and Maia, a Titaness. He was born in a cave on Mount Cyllene in Arcadia.

Hermes is often depicted wearing winged sandals (talaria) and a winged hat (petasos), emphasizing his role as a swift messenger. He also carries a caduceus, a staff entwined with two serpents, symbolizing commerce and negotiation.

Hermes serves as the messenger of the gods, facilitating communication between divine beings and mortals. He delivers messages, announcements, and commands for Zeus and other Olympian deities.

Hermes is known for his cleverness and wit. He is a trickster figure who uses his ingenuity to achieve his goals. He is also credited with inventing the lyre, the alphabet, and other cultural advancements.

Hermes steals Apollo's cattle in a famous myth shortly after his birth. Hermes plays the lyre to resolve the conflict, entertaining Apollo and eventually returning the stolen cattle.

Hermes has a crucial role as a psychopomp, guiding the souls of the deceased to the afterlife. He is often depicted leading souls to the underworld, particularly as a guide for initiates in the Eleusinian Mysteries.

Hermes is associated with trade, commerce, and financial transactions. His name often appears on ancient Greek dedications related to business.

Hermes was widely worshiped in ancient Greece, and numerous temples and sanctuaries were dedicated to him. His significance extended to various aspects of daily life, including travel, communication, and trade.

In some myths, Hermes is the parent of Hermaphroditus, a deity with both male and female attributes. This reflects Hermes's connection to diverse and fluid identities.

Festivals in honor of Hermes, such as the Hermaia, were celebrated in various Greek city-states. These festivals included offerings, sacrifices, and athletic competitions.

In Roman mythology, Hermes is identified with the god Mercury, and many of his attributes and functions are assimilated into the Roman context.

Jupiter (Roman)

Jupiter, also known as Jove, is the king of the Roman gods and the ruler of the heavens. He is considered the Roman equivalent of the Greek god Zeus. Jupiter is the son of Saturn (Cronus in Greek mythology) and Ops (Rhea in Greek mythology). He is part of the Capitoline Triad alongside Juno and Minerva. Jupiter is often depicted with a thunderbolt (similar to Zeus's lightning bolt) and an eagle. The eagle is considered his sacred animal and a symbol of his authority.

Jupiter is regarded as the guardian and protector of Rome. The Temple of Jupiter Optimus Maximus on the Capitoline Hill was dedicated to him and is considered the most important temple in ancient Rome.

Jupiter played a central role in the Roman religion. Public ceremonies, rituals, and triumphal processions often invoked his favor for the well-being and success of the Roman state.

Jupiter, Juno, and Minerva formed the Capitoline Triad, a primary group of deities venerated at the Capitoline Temple. Each deity represented different aspects of Roman life and governance.

Jupiter had several consorts and numerous offspring. His most famous son is Mars, the god of war, and his daughter is Bellona, the goddess of war. In some myths, Venus, the goddess of love, is also associated with Jupiter.

Jupiter's influence extended to the Roman calendar. The Ides of each month, particularly the Ides of March, were associated with ceremonies in his honor.

Jupiter appears in various myths, often resembling Zeus's roles in Greek mythology. He intervenes in mortal affairs, dispenses justice, and asserts his authority over other gods.

As Jupiter Elicius, he was invoked in rituals to avert lightning strikes, emphasizing his control over thunder and storms.

Jupiter's importance is evident in Roman art, literature, and religious practices. His enduring influence is seen in the continued reverence for the planet Jupiter, which was named after him.

Jupiter, the largest planet in our solar system, is named after the Roman god. Its prominent presence in the night sky contributed to the association with the king of the gods.

Mabon (Welsh)

Mabon ap Modron is a figure from Welsh mythology. He is primarily featured in the medieval Welsh tale "Culhwch and Olwen" within the Mabinogion, a collection of Welsh prose tales. The name "Mabon" translates to "son," while "Modron" is often interpreted as "mother," suggesting a maternal relationship. Mabon's mythology revolves around his role as a heroic figure sought after for his aid and strength.

Mabon is described as the son of Modron, often equated with the Celtic mother goddess. In "Culhwch and Olwen," King Arthur's nephew, Culhwch, seeks him to assist in his quest to win the hand of Olwen, the daughter of the giant Ysbaddaden. Mabon's importance in the tale lies in his prowess as a warrior and hunter, making him essential for overcoming various challenges and adversaries encountered during the quest.

Mabon is portrayed as a youthful and vigorous character, embodying the vitality and energy associated with youthfulness.

He is often associated with fertility, abundance, and the bounty of the Earth, particularly during the harvest season.

In modern pagan traditions, Mabon is celebrated as a deity associated with the autumn equinox, marking a time of balance between light and dark. His name is invoked during rituals and ceremonies to honor the changing seasons and express gratitude for the abundance of the harvest.

Mabon's attributes and roles are similar to those of other Celtic and Indo-European deities, such as Apollo, Lugh, and Maponus, who are also associated with youthfulness, fertility, and the harvest.

In contemporary pagan and neo-pagan practices, Mabon ap Modron is revered as a deity of the harvest and the autumnal equinox. Devotional practices, rituals, and offerings are dedicated to Mabon to seek blessings of fertility, abundance, and balance. While historical details about Mabon are limited, his mythology continues to inspire spiritual reverence and celebrations that honor the cycles of nature and the changing seasons.

Minerva (Roman)

Minerva is a Roman goddess who was adapted from the Greek goddess Athena. She is associated with wisdom, strategic warfare, and craftsmanship. Minerva is often considered the daughter of Jupiter (the Roman equivalent of Zeus) and Metis, a Titaness associated with wisdom.

Minerva is one of the virgin goddesses in Roman mythology. Like her Greek counterpart, Athena, she emphasizes her dedication to wisdom and strategic warfare rather than domestic roles.

Minerva is also known as a goddess of war, particularly strategic warfare. She is often depicted wearing armor, holding a shield, and carrying a spear.

Minerva is strongly associated with wisdom, intelligence, and strategic thinking. Temples dedicated to Minerva were places of learning and education.

In addition to her martial and intellectual attributes, Minerva is considered a patroness of the arts and crafts. She is associated with activities such as spinning, weaving, and embroidery.

The festival known as the Quinquatria was dedicated to Minerva and celebrated from March 19 to March 23; it included various activities, such as sacrifices, athletic contests, and theatrical performances.

Minerva's symbols include the owl, which represents wisdom, and the olive tree, symbolizing peace and victory.

In ancient Rome, Minerva had several temples and cult centers, with notable temples on the Capitoline Hill. Her worship was particularly associated with intellectual pursuits, arts, and military strategy.

In some Roman art, Minerva is depicted with the Gorgon's head (Medusa's) on her shield, symbolizing her protective aspect and ability to ward off enemies.

Many aspects of Minerva's mythology and attributes closely parallel those of the Greek goddess Athena, which resulted from the Romans identifying their deities with Greek counterparts.

The Muses (Greek)

The Muses are a group of nine goddesses in Greek mythology, each presiding over a specific domain of the arts and sciences. Traditionally, the Muses are considered the daughters of Zeus, the king of the gods, and Mnemosyne, the Titaness of memory.

Each Muse is associated with a particular domain:
1. Calliope - Epic Poetry
2. Clio - History
3. Euterpe - Music and Lyric Poetry
4. Thalia - Comedy and Idyllic Poetry
5. Melpomene - Tragedy
6. Terpsichore - Dance
7. Erato - Love and Erotic Poetry
8. Polyhymnia - Sacred Poetry
9. Urania - Astronomy and Astrology

Artists and writers often invoke the muses to inspire creativity and artistic endeavors. They are considered the sources of inspiration for humans in various artistic pursuits.

The Muses were believed to reside on Mount Helicon or Mount Parnassus in Greece. Their presence was invoked in artistic gatherings, festivals, and performances.

The Muses are sometimes depicted as companions of Apollo, the god of music, poetry, and the arts. They frequently accompany him, inspiring and guiding his artistic endeavors.

The Muses are typically represented with attributes related to their domains. For example, Calliope may be depicted with a writing tablet, while Thalia might carry a comic mask. In addition to inspiring artistic endeavors, the Muses were associated with education and learning. They were considered sources of knowledge and wisdom.

The concept of the Muses has had a profound impact on Western literature, art, and culture. The idea of seeking inspiration from divine sources is a recurring theme in artistic traditions.

Each Muse is often associated with a specific musical instrument. For example, the terpsichore is linked to the lyre, while the erato may be related to the aulos (double flute).

The Muses were sometimes credited with having mortal offspring who would carry on their creative legacies. One notable example is Orpheus, the legendary musician and poet.

Oya (Yoruba)

Oya is a powerful and dynamic deity in Yoruba mythology. She is associated with winds, storms, lightning, and rapid transformation. Oya is often considered one of the wives of Shango, the Yoruba god of thunder and lightning. Together, they are a formidable couple associated with natural forces.

The colors maroon, purple, and burgundy represent Oya. Her attributes include a machete or sword, a whip, and a mask. Oya is also considered the cemetery's guardian, overseeing the transition from life to death. She is associated with the ancestral realm.

Oya is known for her ability to bring about rapid and often dramatic transformations. She is linked to change, upheaval, and renewal. Oya is depicted as a fierce warrior who defends her devotees and is unafraid to challenge or confront obstacles. She is seen as a protective force during times of chaos.

Devotees of Oya celebrate her in various Yoruba festivals, including the Egungun festival, which pays homage to ancestors. They honor her with dances, rituals, and offerings. Oya is associated with specific animals, including the water buffalo and the ram, symbolically in her worship.

Like other Yoruba deities, Oya's worship has spread through the African diaspora, influencing religions such as Santería and Candomblé. In these syncretic traditions, Oya may be identified with various Catholic saints.

Oya is sometimes invoked in divination rituals, particularly for insights into significant life changes and challenges. Practitioners may seek her guidance and protection. Priests and priestesses dedicated to Oya play a vital role in conducting rituals, offering guidance, and maintaining the traditions associated with her worship.

Thoth (Egyptian)

Thoth is a prominent deity in ancient Egyptian mythology, associated with wisdom, writing, magic, and the moon.

Thoth is often depicted with the head of an ibis or a baboon, emphasizing his connections to these animals. He is also associated with the moon and is sometimes depicted holding a stylus and the ankh, a symbol of life.

Thoth is equated with the Greek god Hermes due to similarities in their roles as messengers, inventors of writing, and keepers of divine knowledge.

Thoth holds various titles, including "Lord of Divine Words" and "Scribe of the Gods." He is considered a mediator between gods and humans, recording divine judgments and maintaining balance in the universe.

Thoth is credited with writing the "Book of Thoth," a legendary and mysterious text that contains the secrets of magic and wisdom. The book is said to grant the ability to understand animals' language and control nature's forces.

In some Egyptian creation myths, Thoth maintains order and cosmic balance. He arbitrates disputes among the gods and assists in creating the world.

Thoth is present in the afterlife's judgment scene, where the deceased's heart is weighed against the feather of Ma'at, the goddess of truth and justice. He records the results of this judgment.

Thoth's influence extends beyond mythology to Egyptian culture, where he is revered as a patron of scribes, scholars, and those involved in intellectual pursuits.

In the city of Hermopolis, Thoth was a central figure in the worship of the Ogdoad, a group of eight primordial deities representing chaos and order.

Thoth is sometimes referred to as Djehuty or Tehuti in ancient Egyptian texts, and his name is associated with words related to wisdom, writing, and reckoning.

Thoth is invoked in magical practices for guidance, knowledge, and protection. His connection to language and writing aligns with the use of written spells and incantations in ancient Egyptian magic.

Thoth is depicted in various forms in Egyptian art and hieroglyphs, emphasizing his roles as a wise counselor, recordkeeper, and messenger of the gods.

Vulcan (Rome)

Vulcan, known as Hephaestus in Greek mythology, is the Roman god of fire, volcanoes, metalworking, and craftsmanship.

Vulcan is the son of Jupiter (Zeus in Greek mythology) and Juno (Hera in Greek mythology). His birth is associated with various myths, including Juno giving birth to him alone.

Vulcan is often depicted as a skilled blacksmith and craftsman. His symbols, which represent his association with metalworking, include the anvil, hammer, and tongs.

In some myths, Vulcan is described as having a lame or deformed leg. He is associated with imperfection and resilience, emphasizing his strength in overcoming challenges.

Vulcan's forge is located beneath Mount Etna, a volcanic mountain. He is said to use this forge to create weapons, armor, and various metal objects for the gods.

In Roman mythology, Vulcan is associated with the creation of Pandora, the first woman. He molded her from clay, and each god gave her unique gifts. This story is similar to the Greek myth of Hephaestus creating Pandora.

Despite his physical imperfections, Vulcan was married to Venus (Aphrodite in Greek mythology), the goddess of love and beauty. This union is often explained as Jupiter's strategic move to maintain harmony on Mount Olympus.

Mars, the god of war, is sometimes identified as Vulcan's son. This association connects Vulcan with craftsmanship and the creation of weapons for warfare.

Vulcan had dedicated temples and festivals in his honor, such as the Vulcanalia celebrated on August 23. Offerings were made to him, especially during periods of intense heat when volcanic activity was considered more prominent.

Vulcan's importance is reflected in Roman culture, where his attributes as a skilled artisan and his connection to fire were celebrated. His craftsmanship also symbolizes the transformative power of fire.

Vulcan is a recurring figure in Roman art and literature, often portrayed in scenes related to metalworking, forging, and his interactions with other gods.

The mythology of Vulcan closely aligns with the Greek god Hephaestus, and in some contexts, the two deities are considered interchangeable due to the Roman practice of syncretism.

Yemaya (Yoruba)

Yemaya, also known as Yemoja, is a prominent deity in Yoruba mythology. She is revered as the goddess of the Ogun River and the sea and is associated with motherhood, fertility, and the protection of children.

Yemaya is often considered one of the daughters of Olodumare, the Supreme Deity in Yoruba cosmology. She has various siblings, including other deities in the Yoruba pantheon.

The moon, the sea, and the color blue symbolize Yemaya. She is often depicted as a motherly figure, carrying a child and adorned with flowing garments.

In some Yoruba traditions, Yemaya is considered the mother of all Orishas (deities), emphasizing her maternal and nurturing role within the pantheon.

In some Yoruba traditions, Yemaya is closely associated with Olokun, the god of the deep sea. Together, they represent the vastness and mysteries of the ocean.

Yemaya is regarded as a protector of children. Mothers often invoke her to seek her blessings for their children's well-being and protection.

Due to the African diaspora, Yemaya's worship extended to the Americas, particularly in regions influenced by Afro-Caribbean religions. In Cuba, Brazil, and other places, Yemaya is often syncretized with Catholic figures, creating hybrid religious practices.

Yemaya is honored in various festivals and ceremonies. In Cuba, the "La Regla de Ocha" festival, or Santería, includes celebrations dedicated to Yemaya. In Brazil, she is venerated during the Lavagem do Bonfim festival.

Devotees make offerings to Yemaya, including flowers, fruits, and items associated with the sea. Rituals involve prayers, songs, and dances expressing reverence for her protective and nurturing qualities.

Yemaya has priests and priestesses dedicated to serving her. These individuals play a crucial role in leading rituals, providing spiritual guidance, and maintaining the traditions associated with her worship.

CHAPTER 7

Magic of the Months

January - beginnings, healing, money protection, and strength
February - astral realm, banish, beginnings, empowerment, fertility, and purification
March - fertility, innocence, prosperity, spirituality, and success
April - beginnings, fertility, growth, and spirituality
May - divination, enchantment, fertility, love, and well being
June - abundance, love, marriage, prosperity, and relationships
July - dream work, light, magic, purpose, and strength
August - abundance, magic (animal), prophecy, prosperity, and wisdom
September - confidence, the home, manifestation, and protection
October - courage, healing, inspiration, memory/memories, and stability
November - cooperation, darkness, divination, healing, and hope
December - dedication/devotion, love, peace, prosperity, and strength

Colors of the Month

January - gray, purple, and white
February - black, blue, and red
March - green and white
April - brown and green
May - pink
June - purple and red

July - green and yellow
August - green (dark) and yellow
September - brown
October - black and blue
November - blue (pale), green, and silver
December - black and red

Crystals of the Months

January - garnet (rhodolite), moonstone, rose quartz, ruby, tourmaline (red)
February - amethyst, moonstone, obsidian, onyx, topaz, zircon (red)
March - aquamarine, bloodstone, jasper, opal, topaz (blue)
April - beryl, diamond, malachite, sapphire, and zircon
May - agat, carnelian, emerald, garnet, rose quartz, tourmaline, and tsavorite
June - agate, alexandrite, cat's eye, chrysoberyl, emerald, garnet, moonstone, and ruby
July - carnelian, malachite, onyx, ruby, sapphire, spinel, tourmaline (red), and turquoise
August - carnelian, emerald, jade, moonstone, peridot, sardonyx, topaz, and tourmaline
September - carnelian, cat's eye, iolite, lapis lazuli, peridot, sapphire, and spinel (blue)
October - aquamarine, garnet, kunzite, morganite, opal, sapphire, and tourmaline
November - beryl, cat's eye, chrysoberyl, citrine, sapphire (yellow), and topaz
December - aquamarine, bloodstone, ruby, topaz (blue), turquoise, and zircon

Days of the Week for Spells and Rituals

Monday
Best for psychic endeavors, invoking power, creative ideas, divine/inspirational messages, and healing.

Tuesday
It is best for protecting and building the strength of mind, body, and confidence.

Wednesday
Best for career/job issues, intellectual pursuits, travel planning and research.

Thursday
Best for finances, legal matters, spirituality, and development.

Friday
Best for romantic attraction, all relationships, reconciliation, physical makeovers, and beautifying your environment.

Saturday
Best for home-related issues, brainstorming future projects, committing to personal goals, weight loss, releasing bad habits, and ending relationships.

Sunday
Best for healing (body, mind, soul), management/decision-making, insights into problem-solving, divine intervention/miracles, and unique friendships.

Do what makes you comfortable; waiting for the "right" day to perform rituals or divination is unnecessary. So you do you, Boo!

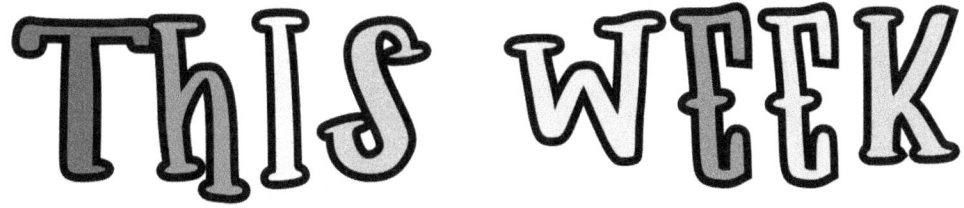

Monday

Zodiac: Cancer
Solar System: Moon
Rune: Lagu
Numbers: 2, 9
Colors: Blue (pale), Gray, Silver, White
Tarot: High Priestess, Moon
Trees: Birch, Elder, Myrtle, Willow
Misc. Plants: Moonwort, Wormwood
Herb and Garden: Bluebell, Chamomile, Gardenia, Jasmine, Poppy, Rose (white), Violet
Gemstones and Minerals: Emerald, Moonstone, Quartz (clear, white), Sapphire
Metal: Silver
From the Sea: Pearl
Goddesses: Hecate, Selene
Gods: Aegir, Thoth
Angel or Magical Beings: Gabriel
Issues, Intentions, and Powers: astral realm, clairvoyance, creativity, dream work, emotions, family, fertility, healing, the home, illumination, inspiration, intuition, love, magic (general, moon), prophecy, protection, psychic ability, travel, truth

Tuesday

Zodiac: Aries, Scorpio
Solar System: Mars
Rune: Tyr
Number: 5
Colors: Black, Orange, Red, Scarlet
Tarot: Strength, Wands (5, 6)
Trees: Cedar, Elm, Holly, Palm (dragon's blood)
Misc. Plants: Allspice, Ginger, Patchouli, Thistle
Herb and Garden: Basil, Garlic, Snapdragon
Gemstones and Minerals: Bloodstone, Emerald, Garnet, Ruby, Sapphire (star), Topaz
Metal: Iron
From the Sea:
Goddess:
God: Mars
Angel or Magical Beings: Elves
Issues, Intentions, and Powers: action, aggression, assertiveness, battle/war, challenges, courage, discipline, energy, healing, honor, integrity, justice, passion, purification, strength, truth

Wednesday

Zodiac: Gemini
Solar System: Mercury
Rune: Odal
Number: 3
Colors: Orange, Purple, Silver, Violet, Yellow
Tarot: The Magician, Wheel of Fortune, Pentacles (8)
Trees: Aspen, Hazel, Rowan
Misc. Plant: Fern
Herb and Garden: Dill, Jasmine, Lavender, Lily of the Valley
Gemstones and Minerals: Agate, Amethyst, Aventurine, Lodestone, Opal, Ruby (star), Turquoise
Metal: Mercury
From the Sea:
Goddess: Athena
Gods: Hermes, Mercury, Odin
Angel or Magical Beings: Raphael
Issues, Intentions, and Powers: business, cleverness, communication, creativity, crossroads, divination, fear, improvement (self), insight, intelligence, introspection, knowledge, loss, money, problems, skills, travel, wisdom

Thursday

Zodiac: Capricorn, Pisces
Solar System: Jupiter
Rune: Thorn
Numbers: 4, 8
Colors: Blue (royal), Green, Indigo, Purple
Tarot: Pentacles (ace, 9, 10)
Trees: Laurel, Maple, Oak, Pine
Misc. Plants: Cinnamon, Cinquefoil, Grain (wheat), Nutmeg
Herb and Garden: Honeysuckle, Sage
Gems and Minerals: Amethyst, Carnelian, Cat's Eye, Chrysoberyl, Sapphire, Turquoise
Metal: Tin
From the Sea:
Goddess: Juno
Gods: Jupiter, Thor, Zeus
Angel or Magical Beings:
Issues, Intentions, and Powers: abundance, business, desire, endurance, fidelity, honor, justice (legal matters), leadership, loyalty, luck, money, prosperity, relationships, success, well-being

Friday

Zodiac: Taurus
Solar System: Venus
Rune: Peorth
Numbers: 6, 9
Colors: Aqua, Blue, Green, Indigo, Pink
Tarot: Empress, Lovers, Cups (2)
Trees: Apple, Birch, Myrtle
Misc. Plants: Saffron, Sandalwood
Herb and Garden: Feverfew, Raspberry, Rose, Strawberry, Thyme, Violet
Gemstones and Minerals: Alexandrite, Amber, Cat's Eye, Chrysoberyl, Emerald, Rose Quartz, Ruby
Metal: Copper
From the Sea:
Goddesses: Aphrodite, Freya, Frigg, Lakshmi, Venus
God: Eros
Angel or Magical Beings: Auriel
Issues, Intentions, and Powers: beauty, emotions, fertility, friend/ ship, happiness, love, magic, passion, pleasure, romance, sex/uality, wisdom

Saturday

Zodiac: Aquarius
Solar System: Saturn
Rune: Dag
Number: 7
Colors: Black, Gray (dark), Indigo, Purple (dark)
Tarot: Temperance, Swords (knight, 2)
Trees: Alder, Cypress, Hawthorn, Pomegranate
Misc. Plants: Mullein, Myrrh
Herb and Garden: Morning Glory, Thyme
Gems and Minerals: Amethyst, Apache Tears, Diamond, Hematite, Jet, Labradorite, Turquoise
From the Sea:
Goddess: Hecate
God: Saturn
Angel or Magical Beings: Fairies
Issues, Intentions, and Powers: banish, bind, business, death, discipline (self), freedom, justice, karma, life, limitations/ boundaries, money, motivation, negativity, obstacles, peace, problems, protection, willpower, wisdom

Time of the Day for Spells and Rituals

Dawn

At dawn, the sun's fragile rays spread like a blanket of hope over an awakening world. Now, choices are made, and paths unfold, full of life-giving potentiality.

Midday/Noon

Midday is when sunlight shines the strongest - a reminder of our strength and courage to tackle whatever lies ahead. It provides the motivation we need to persevere, no matter what obstacle stands in our way.

Dusk/Twilight

As dusk approaches, the sun bids a wistful farewell to the sky. Its goodbye is made of change and final goodbyes, an invitation to new beginnings if we're brave enough to open our hearts.

Midnight

At midnight, we come to the precipice of a journey into uncertainty. Here, paths diverge, and endings have no choice but to be accepted. It's an inevitable transition from one day to another, filled with promise yet cloaked in sadness.

Do what makes you feel comfortable. There's no need to wait for the "right" time to perform rituals or divination. You do you, Boo!

Dawn

Zodiac:
Solar System: Venus
Runes: Beorc, Hagal, Thorn
Number:
Color:
Tarot: Swords
Trees:
Misc. Plants:
Herb and Garden:
Gemstones and Minerals:
Metal:
From the Sea:
Goddess: Brigid
Gods: Byelobog, Janus, Njord, Surya
Angel or Magical Beings: Raphael
Issues, Intentions, and Powers: activate/awaken, beginnings, crossroads, fertility, hope, life (vitality), light, nurture, purpose, romance, youth

Midday/Noon

Zodiac: Leo
Solar System: Sun
Runes: Dag, Rad, Sigel
Number:
Color:
Tarot: Wands
Trees:
Misc. Plants:
Herb and Garden:
Gemstones and Minerals:
Metal:
From the Sea:
Goddess:
God: Byelobog
Angel or Magical Beings: Michael
Issues, Intentions, and Powers: determination, obstacles, strength, willpower

Gratitude Spell

Ingredients:
A white candle dressed with olive oil and rosemary
A few items to represent the things for which you are grateful
Optional: a sigil (mine is for "I am grateful for all that I receive")

Directions:
Light the candle and take a few moments to reflect upon your items and what they represent
Say aloud what you are thankful for. You can write it into a poem, a list that you seal by burning.

Gratitude Happiness Spell

Ingredients
small candle (yellow or orange)
a piece of paper, and a pen.

Directions
Find a quiet and comfortable space where you can focus without distractions.
Light the candle and sit in front of it.
Take a few deep breaths to center yourself and clear your mind.
On the piece of paper, write down three things you are grateful for in your life. These can be big or small, specific or general.
Hold the paper in your hands and close your eyes. Visualize each item on your list and feel the gratitude welling up inside you.
As you hold onto this feeling of gratitude, say aloud or silently:
"By the light of this flame, I call upon the power of gratitude. May it fill my heart with happiness and joy."
Place the paper near the candle so that it catches the light.
Sit quietly for a few moments, basking in the warmth of the candle and the feelings of gratitude and happiness.
When you feel ready, blow out or snuff out the candle and give thanks for the blessings in your life.
Keep the paper in a safe place as a reminder of the abundance and happiness that surrounds you.
Repeat this spell whenever you feel the need to cultivate gratitude and happiness in your life.

CHAPTER 8

The Moon

The Phases of the Moon

New

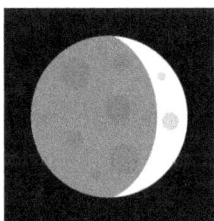

Sometimes called the Crescent Moon, when you can see the very first sliver of light in the sky. This phase promotes new beginnings, new endeavors, and new relationships. It is the time to make positive changes and plant seeds of ideas that will be harvested later.

Waxing

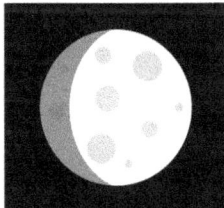

In this phase, the Moon appears to be growing in size, shifting from new to full as though it's gaining strength. It makes sense, then, that this is an excellent time to focus on increasing your knowledge, bank accounts, and relationships. This phase promotes healing.

Full

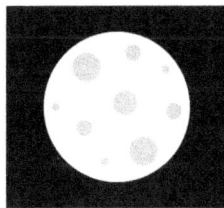

The Moon's most potent phase is when we see her entire illuminated face. This is a time of fulfillment, activity, and increased psychic ability for perfecting ideas, in other words, "getting your act together," celebrations, or renewing commitments to people or projects—the best time for spells of any kind.

Waning

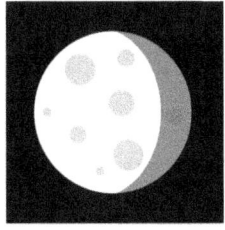

The Moon is decreasing in size as it journeys from full to dark. The waning Moon is a time of decrease, release, letting go, and completion. It is an excellent time to begin dieting, breaking bad habits, breaking off relationships, or dealing with legal matters.

Moons of the Year

A rare second Full Moon in a single month is called a "Blue Moon." A rare second New Moon in a month is called a "Black Moon."

Different cultures gave the Moon different titles to express what the Moon means to them in a given month. As a result, some of the moon names make sense, while others may not make any sense.

Full Moon – January
Native American Tribes: Old Moon, Wolf Moon, Ice Moon, Moon after Yule, and Winter Moon
Siouan (Assiniboines) Tribe: Hard Time Moon
Inuit People of Northern Canada: Dwarf Seal Moon
Celtic: Wolf Moon, Stay Home Moon, Moon after Yule
Chinese: Holiday Moon
Fairy: Icicle Moon

Full Moon – February
Native American Tribes: Hunger or Starvation Moon, Storm Moon, Trapper's Moon, Moon of Ice, and Tree Moon
Siouan (Assiniboines) Tribe: Long Day Moon
Inuit People of Northern Canada: Seal Pup Moon
Celtic: Storm Moon, Ice Moon, and Snow moon
Chinese: Budding Moon
Fairy: Snowdrop Moon

Full Moon – March
Native American Tribes: Worm Moon, Crow Moon, Moon of Winds, Sap Moon, Fish Moon, Chaste Moon, and Death Moon
Siouan (Assiniboines) Tribe: Sore Eye Moon
Inuit People of Northern Canada: Snow Bird Moon
Celtic: Plough Moon, Wind Moon, Lenten (lengthening) Moon
Chinese: Sleeping Moon
Fairy: Waking Wood Moon

Moons of the Year

Full Moon – April
Native American Tribes: Pink Moon, Seed Moon, Frog Moon, Egg Moon, and Awakening Moon
Siouan (Assiniboines) Tribe: Frog's Moon
Inuit People of Northern Canada: Snow Melt Moon
Celtic: Budding Moon, New Shoots Moon, and Seed Moon
Chinese: Peony Moon
Fairy: Birthing Moon

Full Moon – May
Native American Tribes: Flower Moon, Hare Moon, Milk Moon, and Grass Moon
Siouan (Assiniboines) Tribe: Idle Moon
Inuit People of Northern Canada: Goose Moon
Celtic: Mother's Moon and Bright Moon
Chinese: Dragon Moon
Fairy: Moon of White Petals

Full Moon – June
Native American Tribes: Strawberry Moon, Planting Moon, and Green Corn Moon
Siouan (Assiniboines) Tribe: Full Leaf Moon
Inuit People of Northern Canada: Hunting Moon
Celtic: Mead Moon, Horse Moon, Dyan Moon, and Rose Moon
Chinese: Lotus Moon
Fairy: Wild Cherry Moon

Full Moon – July
Native American Tribes: Hay Moon, Summer Moon, Thunder Moon, and Buck Moon
Siouan (Assiniboines) Tribe: Red Berries Moon
Inuit People of Northern Canada: Dry Moon
Celtic: Claiming Moon, Wyrt or Herb Moon, and Mead Moon
Chinese: Hungry Ghost Moon
Fairy: Dancing Delight Moon

Full Moon – August
Native American Tribes: Sturgeon Moon, Corn Moon, Green Corn Moon, Dog Days Moon, and Lightening Moon
Siouan (Assiniboines) Tribe: Black Cherries Moon
Inuit People of Northern Canada: Swan Flight Moon
Celtic: Dispute Moon, Lynx Moon, and Grain Moon
Chinese: Harvest Moon
Fairy: Blackberry Harvest Moon

Moons of the Year

Full Moon – September
Native American Tribes: Singing Moon and Barley Moon
Siouan (Assiniboines) Tribe: Yellow Leaf Moon
Inuit People of Northern Canada: Harpoon Moon
Celtic: Wine Moon, Song Moon, Harvest Moon, and Barley Moon
Chinese: Chrysanthemum Moon
Fairy: Chestnut Moon

Full Moon – October
Native American Tribes: Traveller's Moon and Blackberry Moon
Siouan (Assiniboines) Tribe: Gophur Looks Back Moon
Inuit People of Northern Canada: Ice Moon
Celtic: Hunter's Moon, Blood Moon, and Seed Fall Moon
Chinese: Kindly Moon
Fairy: Moon of the Wild Hunt

Full Moon - November
Native American Tribes: Frosty Moon, Beaver Moon, Dark Moon, Tree Moon, Snow Moon, Freezing Moon, Ice Moon, and Migrating Moon
Siouan (Assiniboines) Tribe: Frost Moon
Inuit People of Northern Canada: Freezing Mist Moon
Celtic: Mourning Moon and Darkest Depths Moon
Chinese: White Moon
Fairy: Moon of the Wild Hunt

Full Moon – December
Native American Tribes: Cold Moon, Long Night Moon,
Siouan (Assiniboines) Tribe: Younger Hard Time Moon
Inuit People of Northern Canada: Dark Night Moon
Celtic: Oak Moon, Full Cold Moon
Chinese: Bitter Moon
Fairy: Mistletoe Moon

Full Moon Spell

Release and Gratitude
The Full Moon is a powerful time for releasing what no longer serves you and expressing gratitude for what you have.

Ingredients
White sage or palo santo for cleansing
A small bowl of water
Black candle
Rose quartz crystal

Instructions
Begin by smudging your space with white sage or palo santo to cleanse the energy.
Fill the small bowl with water and place it in front of you.
Light the black candle and sit quietly, reflecting on what you wish to release.
Write down anything you want to let go of on a piece of paper.
Hold the paper over the flame of the candle and say aloud what you are releasing.
Drop the paper into the bowl of water to extinguish the flame, symbolizing the release of those energies.
Hold the rose quartz crystal in your hand and express gratitude for the blessings in your life.
Place the crystal next to the candle and let it burn down completely, absorbing and transmuting any remaining negative energy.

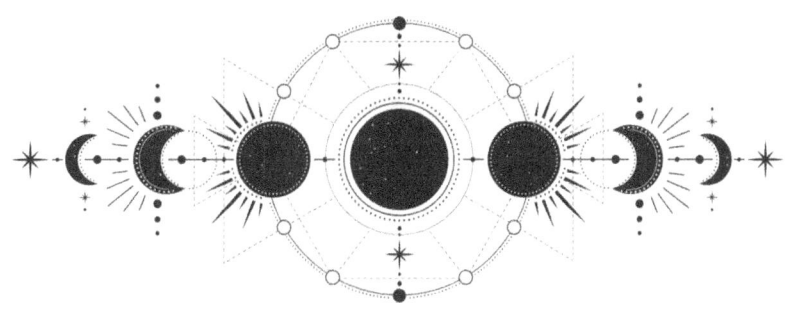

Waning Moon Spell

Banishing Negativity
The Waning Moon phase is ideal for banishing negativity and obstacles from your life.

Ingredients
Black candle
Smoky quartz crystal
Patchouli or cedarwood essential oil

Instructions
Anoint the black candle with patchouli or cedarwood oil while focusing on banishing negativity.
Light the candle and place it in front of you.
Hold the smoky quartz crystal in your hand and visualize any negative energies leaving your body.
Repeat a banishing incantation or affirmation, such as "I release all that does not serve me" or "I banish negativity from my life."
Allow the candle to burn down completely, visualizing the negativity being consumed by the flame.
Once the candle has burned out, bury the leftover wax away from your home to symbolize the permanent removal of negativity from your life.

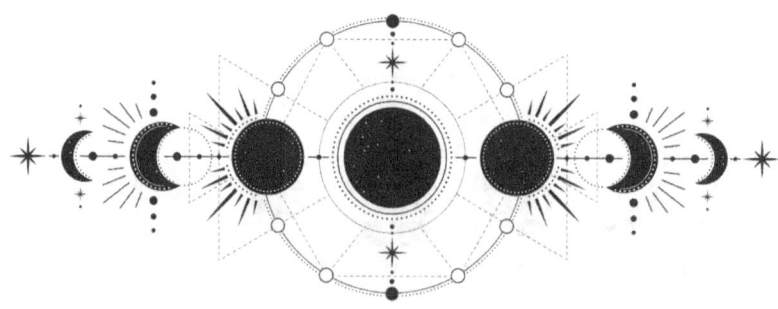

Waxing Moon Spell

Growth and Manifestation
The Waxing Moon phase is a time of growth and expansion. Use this spell to amplify your intentions and manifest your desires.

Ingredients
Green candle
Bay leaves
Pen and paper
Patchouli essential oil

Instructions
Anoint the green candle with patchouli oil while visualizing your goals of growing and expanding.
Write your intentions or desires on the bay leaves using the pen and paper.
Light the candle and place it in front of you.
Hold each bay leaf over the flame, allowing it to catch fire briefly, and then drop it into a fireproof container.
As the leaves burn, visualize your intentions manifesting with each flame.
Once all the bay leaves have burned, extinguish the candle and give thanks for the abundance that is coming your way.

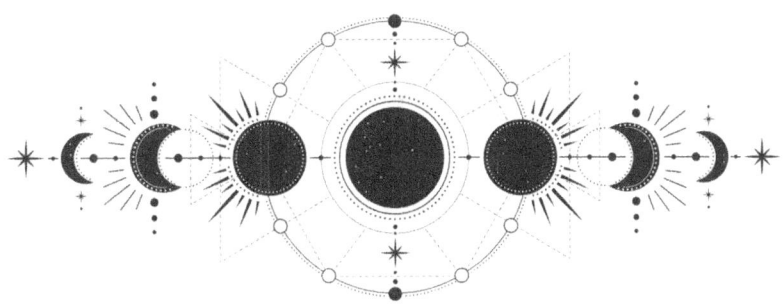

New Moon Spell

Setting Intentions
During the New Moon, the sky is dark, representing new beginnings and potential. This is an ideal time for setting intentions for the upcoming lunar cycle.

Ingredients
White candle
Pen and paper
Essential oil (such as lavender or sandalwood)
Clear quartz crystal

Instructions
Begin by cleansing your space with the essential oil and lighting the white candle. Sit in a comfortable position and take several deep breaths to center yourself.
Write down your intentions or goals on the paper, focusing on what you wish to manifest during this lunar cycle.
Hold the clear quartz crystal in your hand and visualize your intentions coming to fruition.
Place the paper under the candle and let it burn while you continue to meditate on your intentions.
Once the candle has burned down, bury the ashes outside or keep them in a special place as a reminder of your goals.

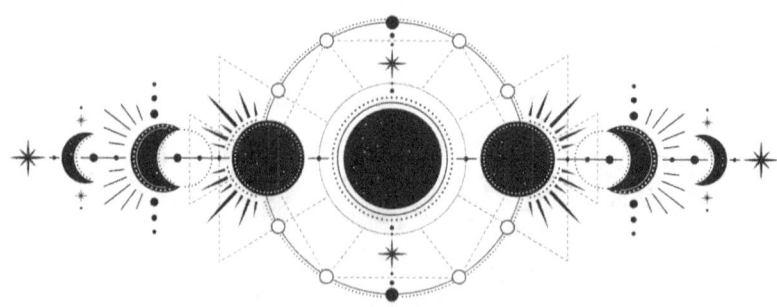

CHAPTER 9

Solar
System

Solar System

The boundless expanse of the universe holds a captivating realm known as the solar system, a complex web of celestial bodies that has fascinated humanity for generations. At the heart of this cosmic spectacle is the radiant and mighty Sun, a colossal star that provides the life-giving energy that fuels our world. Our loyal companion, the Moon, orbiting Earth, enchants us with its shimmering phases and mysterious allure. Together, these elements paint a mesmerizing portrait of the grandeur and diversity present in our cosmic neighborhood. In this journey of exploration, we'll delve into the wondrous dynamics that define the solar system, bask in the brilliance of the Sun, and unravel the enigma of the Moon's influence on our planet.

Earth

Solar System: Earth
Zodiac: Capricorn, Taurus, and Virgo
Chakra: Root
Celebrations: Earth Day and Walpurgis
Season: Winter
Day:
Time of Day: Midnight
Rune:
Number: 4
Colors: Black, Brown, Green, and White
Tarot:
Trees: Acacia and Oak
Misc. Plant: Grain
Herb and Garden:
Gemstones and Minerals: Agate (brown), Ametrine, Andalusite, Bloodstone, Carnelian, Chrysoprase, Citrine, Diopside, and Moss Agate
Metal:
From the Sea:
Goddesses: Anat, Ceres, Coatlicue, Cybele, Demeter, Gaia, Inanna, Isis, Maia, and Nanna
Gods: Adonis, Attis, Dionysus, Dumuzi, Ea, Enki, Faunus, Geb, and Vertimnus
Angel: Auriel
Issues, Intentions, and Powers: agriculture, creativity, grounding, healing, the home, magic (animal), nurture, peace, protection, purpose, revenge, and spirits

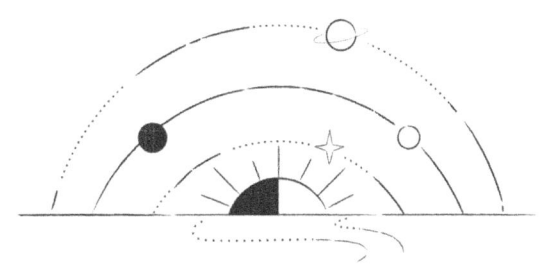

Jupiter

2_|

Solar System: Jupiter
Zodiac: Pisces and Sagittarius
Chakras: 3rd Eye, Heart, and Solar Plexus
Celebrations:
Season:
Day: Thursday
Time of Day:
Rune: Man
Numbers: 3, 4, and 5
Colors: Blue, Green (light, sea), Indigo, Purple, Turquoise, and Violet
Tarot: Wheel of Fortune
Trees: Birch, Cedar, Chestnut, Fir, Horse Chestnut, Linden, Magnolia, Maple, Oak, Olive, Palm (coconut), Pine, Sycamore, Walnut, and Yew
Misc. Plant: Aloe, Anise, Betony, Cinquefoil, Meadowsweet, Myrrh, Nutmeg, and Star Anise
Herb and Garden: Agrimony, Borage, Clove, Dandelion, Honeysuckle, Lemon Balm, and Sage
Gemstones and Minerals: Amethyst, Ametrine, Diopside, Emerald, Lepidolite, Sapphire,
Sugilite, Turquoise, and Zircon (red)
Metal: Tin
From the Sea:
Goddesses: Devi, Hera, Justitia, and Nut
Gods: Baal, Indra, Jupiter, Marduk, and Zeus
Mythical Being: Unicorn
Issues, Intentions, and Powers: abundance, astral realm, authority, business, control, dignity, discipline, favors, generosity, honor, influence, intuition, justice, kindness, leadership, luck, the mind, money, opportunities, optimism, power, pride, problems, prosperity, responsibility, spirituality, success, wealth, well-being, and wisdom

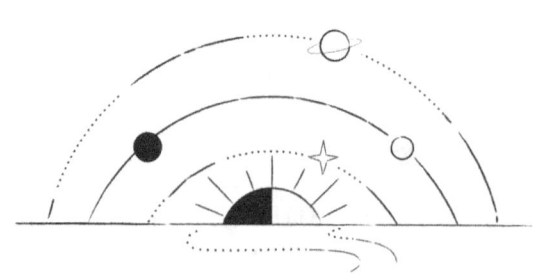

Mars

Solar System: Mars
Zodiac: Aries and Scorpio
Chakras: Root, Sacral, Solar Plexus, and Throat
Celebrations:
Season:
Day: Tuesday
Time of Day:
Rune: Man
Numbers: 2, 3, 5, and 9
Colors: Crimson, Maroon, Orange, Pink, and Red
Tarot: Devil, Emperor, and Tower
Trees: Alder, Blackthorn, Fir, Hawthorn, Holly, Juniper, Palm (dragon's blood), Pine, and Yew
Misc. Plant: Allspice, Anise, Asafoetida, Black Cohosh, Blessed Thistle, Bloodroot, Coriander, Cumin, Deer's Tongue, Galangal, Ginger, High John, Mustard, Nettle, Pepper, Reed, Thistle, and Wormwood
Herb and Garden: Anemone, Basil, Broom, Garlic, Gorse, Honeysuckle, Pennyroyal, Rue, Snapdragon, and Sweet Woodruff
Gemstones and Minerals: Beryl, Bloodstone, Citrine, Diamond, Garnet, Hematite, Jasper (red), Onyx, Pyrite, Rhodochrosite, Rhodonite, Ruby, Sard, Sardonyx, Tourmaline (red, watermelon), Tsavorite, and Zircon (red)
Metals: Iron and Steel
From the Sea: Coral (red)
Goddesses: Anat, Astarte, Badb, Durga, Macha, Maeve, Minerva, and Nanna
Gods: Ares, Indra, Mars, Nergal, Odin, Set, and Thor
Mythical Being: Unicorn
Issues, Intentions, and Powers: action, aggression, anger, assertiveness, battle/war, beginnings, courage, death, defense, desire, determination, emotions, endurance, energy (sexual), enmity, growth, justice, life, lust, magic (general, defensive, dragon, sex), passion, power, sexuality (male), skills, strength, and willpower

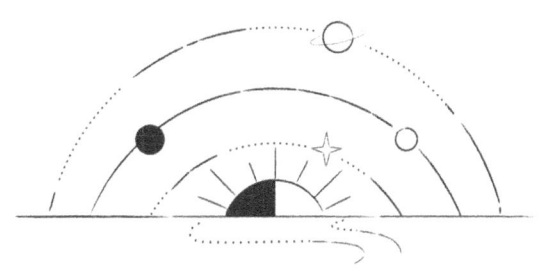

Mercury

Solar System: Mercury
Zodiac: Gemini and Virgo
Chakras: 3rd Eye, Root, Sacral, Solar Plexus, and Throat
Celebrations:
Season:
Day: Wednesday
Time of Day:
Rune:
Numbers: 1, 4, 5, and 8
Colors: Blue (navy), Gray, Green, Orange, Purple, Silver, Violet, and Yellow
Tarot: Hermit, Lovers, and Magician
Trees: Ash, Aspen, Cedar, Cherry, Elder, Hazel, Juniper, Linden, Olive, Pomegranate, and Acacia
Misc. Plants: Anise, Betony, Bittersweet, Cinquefoil, Flax, Horehound, Mandrake, Mistletoe, and Sandalwood
Herb and Garden: Agrimony, Bergamot, Clover, Dandelion, Dill, Fennel, Fern, Honeysuckle, Jasmine, Lavender, Lilac, Lily of the Valley, Marjoram, Peppermint, Periwinkle, Rosemary, Sage, and Valerian
Gemstones and Minerals: Agate (fire, green, red, snakeskin, tree), Amber, Aventurine, Blue Lace Agate, Carnelian, Cat's Eye, Citrine, Fluorite, Hematite, Jasper, Moss Agate, Onyx, Opal, Peridot, Rhodochrosite, Sardonyx, Sodalite, Sphene, and Topaz
Metals: Aluminum and Mercury
From the Sea: Coral (red)
Goddesses: Athena, Maat, Maia, Minerva, and Seshat
Gods: Anubis, Arawn, Coyote, Hermes, Loki, Lugh, Mercury, Odin, Ogma, Thor, and Thoth
Angels: Michael and Raphael
Issues, Intentions, and Powers: adaptability, balance, business, change(s), cleverness, communication, creativity, crossroads, deceit, divination, fear, improvement, inspiration, intelligence, justice, learning, love, magic, memory/memories, messages/ omens, the mind, money, moods, power, rebirth, renewal, skills, travel, wealth, and wisdom

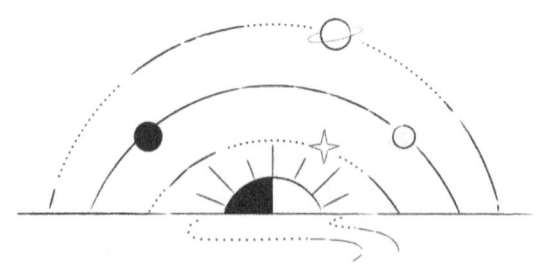

Moon

Solar System: Moon
Zodiac: Cancer
Chakra: Sacral
Celebrations: Beltane, Imbolc, Lughnasadh, and Samhain
Season:
Day: Monday
Time of Day:
Runes: Is and Lagu
Numbers: 2, 3, 0, and 13
Colors: Blue, Gray Green (sea), Orange, Silver, and White
Tarot: Chariot, High Priestess, and Moon
Trees: Birch, Mesquite, Olive, Palm, Rowan, and Willow
Misc. Plants: Aloe, Lotus, Moonwort, Myrrh, Nutmeg, Saffron, and Sandalwood
Herb and Garden: Bergamot, Blackberry/Bramble, Gardenia, Grape, Iris, Jasmine, Lemon Balm Lily, Poppy, and Rosemary
Gemstones and Minerals: Agate, Angelite, Aquamarine, Beryl, Calcite (clear), Herkimer Diamond, Moonstone, Morganite, Opal, Quartz, Sapphire, Selenite, and Turquoise
Metal: Silver
From the Sea: Coral (white), Moon Snail, Mother-of-Pearl, Mussel, and Pearl
Goddesses: Aine, Aphrodite, Ariadne, Arianrhod, Artemis, Cerridwen, Diana, Freya, Hecate, Ishtar, Isis, Juno, Luna, Nanna, Persephone, Rhiannon, Sedna, Selene, and Spiderwoman
Gods: Aegir, Hermes, Horus, Janus, Jupiter, Khensu, Shiva, and Thoth
Angel: Gabriel
Magical Beings: Fairies, Mermaids and Dragons
Issues, Intentions, and Powers: action, agriculture, animals, balance (inner), beginnings, change(s), consciousness (and subconscious), creativity, cycles, darkness, death, divination, dream work, emotions, enchantment, endings, energy (general, receptive), family, fertility, growth, guidance, healing, hexes, the home, illumination, imagination, inspiration, intuition, jealousy, life (rhythms), light, loneliness, love, magic (general, crone, moon, night), manifestation, moods, negativity, night-mares, obstacles, peace, power, pregnancy/childbirth, protection, psychic ability, rebirth/renewal, secrets, self-work, sensitivity, sorrow, spirits, transformation, wisdom, and witches/ witchcraft

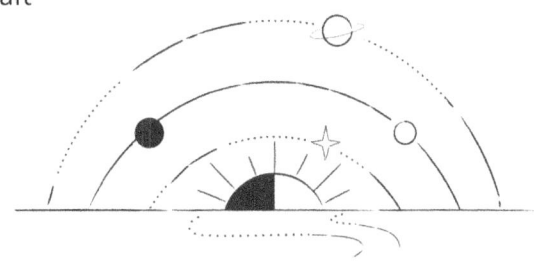

Neptune

Solar System: Neptune
Zodiac: Aquarius and Pisces
Chakras: 3rd Eye and Crown
Celebrations:
Season:
Day:
Time of Day:
Rune:
Number: 7
Colors: Blue, Green (light, sea), Indigo, Lavender, Purple, and Turquoise
Tarot: Hanged Man
Trees: Ash
Misc. Plants:
Herb and Garden:
Gemstones and Minerals: Amethyst, Angelite, Aquamarine, Beryl, Celestite, Fluorite, Jade, Labradorite, Lapis Lazuli, Lepidolite, Sapphire, and Turquoise
Metal:
From the Sea: Coral and Mother-of-Pearl
Goddesses: Amphitrite, Brigid, Ran, Sedna and Tiamat
Gods: Aegir, Manannan, Neptune, and Poseidon
Angel:
Magical Beings: Fairies and Mermaids
Issues, Intentions, and Powers: awareness (expand), clairvoyance, community, consciousness (subconscious), creativity, dream work, enchantment, energy (psychic), guardian, guidance, inspiration, intuition, life, the otherworld/ underworld, power, protection, psychic ability, sensitivity, visions

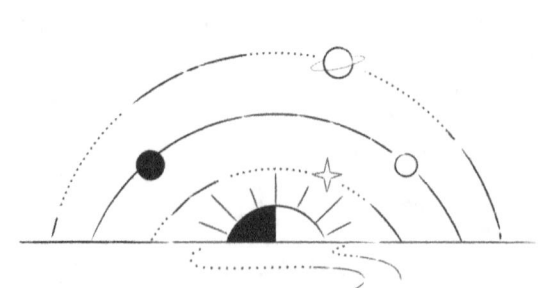

Pluto

Solar System: Pluto
Zodiac: Cancer and Scorpio
Chakra: Sacral
Celebrations:
Season:
Day:
Time of Day:
Rune:
Number:
Colors: Blue, Green (light, sea), Indigo, Lavender, Purple, and Turquoise
Tarot: Hanged Man
Tree: Cypress
Misc. Plants: Belladonna, Bittersweet, Nettle, and Reed
Herb and Garden: Basil and Fern (bear paw)
Gemstones and Minerals: Amethyst, Garnet, Jet, Kunzite, Labradorite, Obsidian, Quartz (tourmalated), Spinel, Tourmaline, and Tsavorite
Metal:
From the Sea:
Goddesses: Ereshkigal, Hathor, Hecate, Hel, Hera, Kali, the Morrigan, and Persephone
Gods: Pluto and Osiris
Angel:
Magical Beings:
Issues, Intentions, and Powers: the afterlife, changes, danger, darkness (inner), death, dream work, justice, karma, memory/memories, the otherworld/underworld, rebirth/renewal, secrets, sexuality, spirituality, transformation, and wealth

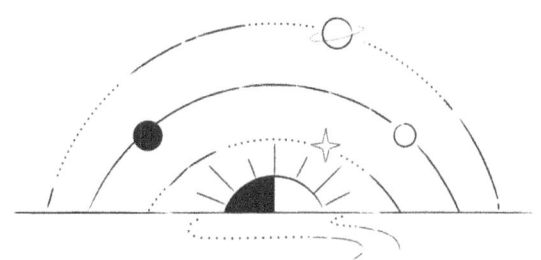

Saturn

Solar System: Saturn
Zodiac: Aquarius, Capricorn, and Libra
Chakra: Crown, Heart, Root, and Throat
Celebrations:
Season:
Day: Saturday
Time of Day:
Rune: Peorth
Numbers: 3, 7, and 8
Colors: Black, Blue (navy), Brown, Gray (dark), Green (dark), Indigo, and Yellow (light)
Tarot: Death, Hanged Man, and World
Tree: Aspen, Beech, Blackthorn, Cypress, Elm, Fir, Holly, Magnolia, Mesquite, Mimosa, Pine, Poplar, Rowan, Witch Hazel, and Yew
Misc. Plants: Cinnamon, Clove, Bamboo, Eyebright, Frankincense, Galangal, Ginseng, Grain
Herb and Garden: Amaranth, Carnation, Comfrey, Ivy, Monkshood, Morning Glory, Rue, and Solomon's Seal
Gemstones and Minerals: Apache Tears, Azurite, Carnelian, Hematite, Jasper (brown), Jet, Obsidian, Onyx, Sapphire, Sardonyx, Serpentine, and Tourmaline (black)
Metal: Lead
From the Sea: Coral (black)
Goddesses: Ariadne, Ceres, Demeter, Dôn, Durga, Hecate, Hera, Juno, Kali, and Rhea
Gods: Amun, Khensu Saturn
Angel:
Magical Beings:
Issues, Intentions, and Powers: agriculture, ambition, astral realm, authority, banish, bind, business, concentration/ focus, darkness, death, discipline, endings, endurance, freedom, goals, grounding, justice, karma, knowledge, limitations/ boundaries, longevity, loyalty, lust, the mind, obstacles, peace, purification, relationships, stability, strength.

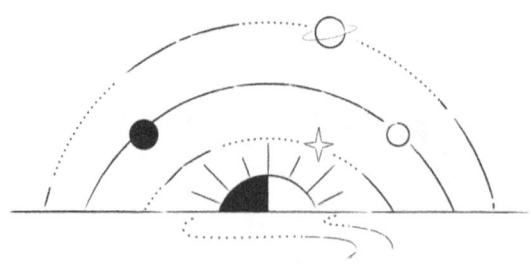

Sun

Solar System: Sun
Zodiac: Aries, Cancer, and Leo
Chakra: Solar Plexus
Celebrations: Litha, Mabon, Ostara, Walpurgis, and Yule
Season:
Day: Sunday
Time of Day: Noon
Rune: Jera and Sigel
Numbers: 1 and 6
Colors: Gold, Orange, and Yellow
Tarot: Death, Hanged Man, and World
Tree: Acacia, Ash, Birch, Cedar, Chestnut, Hazel, Horse Chestnut, Juniper, Laurel, Linden, Oak, Olive, Palm, Rowan, Walnut, and Witch Hazel
Misc. Plants: Belladonna, Bittersweet, Henbane, Lady's Slipper, Mandrake, Mullein, Patchouli, Skullcap, and Thornapple
Herb and Garden: Angelica, Broom, Carnation, Chamomile, Chrysanthemum, Daffodil, Daisy, Goldenseal, Gorse, Heliotrope, Lovage, Marigold, Peony, Rosemary, St. John's Wort, and Sunflower (com), Lotus, Mistletoe, and Saffron
Gemstones and Minerals: Amber, Ametrine, Beryl (golden), Calcite (orange, red), Carnelian, Chrysoberyl, Citrine, Diamond, Herkimer Diamond, Peridot, Quartz, Ruby, Sunstone, Tiger's Eye, Topaz, Tourmaline (black), and Zircon
From the Sea: Coral (black)
Goddesses: Aine, Amaterasu, Bast, Brigid, Hathor, Phoebe, Sekhmet, and Spider-Woman
Gods: Adonis, Agni, Amun, Apollo, Baal, Belenus, Helios, Horus, Jupiter, Lugh, Marduk, Mithras, Ogma, Osiris, Pushan, Ra, Shiva, Surya, and Vishnu
Angel: Raphael
Magical Beings: Dragon, Griffin, Phoenix, Sphinx, Unicorn, Dragon, Griffin, Phoenix, Sphinx, and Unicorn
Issues, Intentions, and Powers:

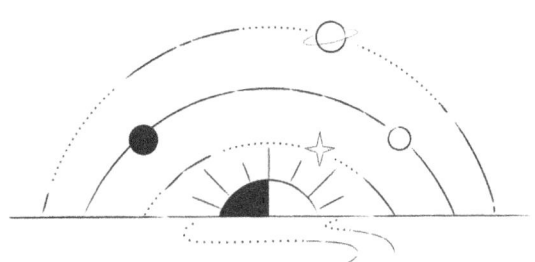

Uranus

Solar System: Uranus
Zodiac: Aquarius and Gemini
Chakras: Brow, Crown, and Throat
Celebrations:
Season:
Day: Sunday
Time of Day:
Rune:
Number: 4
Colors: Indigo and Yellow (light)
Tarot: Fool, Star, and Tower
Tree: Ash and Rowan
Misc. Plants: Belladonna, Bittersweet, Henbane, Lady's Slipper, Mandrake, Mullein, Patchouli, Skullcap, and Thornapple
Herb and Garden: Angelica, Broom, Carnation, Chamomile, Chrysanthemum, Daffodil, Daisy, Goldenseal, Gorse, Heliotrope, Lovage, Marigold, Peony, Rosemary, St. John's Wort, and Sunflower (com), Lotus, Mistletoe, and Saffron
Gemstones and Minerals: Amazonite, Aventurine, Herkimer Diamond, Labradorite, and Quartz
From the Sea: Coral (black)
Goddesses: Anat, Aphrodite, Danu, Inanna, Ishtar, and Isis
Gods:
Angel:
Magical Beings:
Issues, Intentions, and Powers: ambition, anger, change(s), community, cooperation, freedom, goals, hope, illumination, improvement, intuition, motivation, power, and relationships

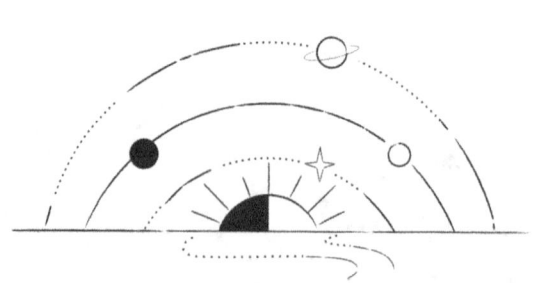

Venus

Solar System: Venus, Also known as the Morning and Evening Star
Zodiac: 3rd Eye, Heart, Sacral, and Throat
Chakras: Brow, Crown, and Throat
Celebrations:
Season:
Day: Friday
Time of Day: Dawn, Dusk, and Midnight
Rune: As and Ken
Numbers: 5, 6, and 7
Colors: Aqua, Blue (light), Green, Indigo, Lavender, Mauve, Pink, Rose, White, and Yellow (light)
Tarot: Empress, Justice, and Star
Tree: Alder, Apple, Aspen, Birch, Cherry, Elder, Magnolia, Myrtle, Sycamore, and Willow
Misc. Plants: loe, Burdock, Cardamom, Coltsfoot, Cowslip, Dittany, Orris Root, and Sandalwood
Gemstones and Minerals: Alexandrite, Aventurine, Azurite, Calcite, Carnelian, Cat's Eye, Celeste Chrysoberyl, Chrysocolla, Chrysoprase, Desert Rose, Diamond, Dioptase, Emerald, Jade, Jasper (green), Kunzite, Lapis Lazuli, Lodestone, Malachite, Peridot, Rhodochrosite, Rose Quart, Sapphire, Sodalite, Tourmaline (blue, green, pink, watermelon), Tsavorite, Turquoise
Metal: Copper
From the Sea:
Goddesses: Astarte, Ishtar, and Venus
Gods: Quetzalcoatl
Angel:
Magical Beings:
Issues, Intentions, and Powers: affection, agriculture, astral realm, attraction, beauty, beginnings, connections, creativity, desire, emotions, energy (receptive, sexual), fertility, friendship, gentleness, happiness, harmony: kindness, love, lust, magic (sex), needs, passion, pleasure rebirth/renewal, relationships, reversal, romance, sensuality, sexuality, stress, and unity

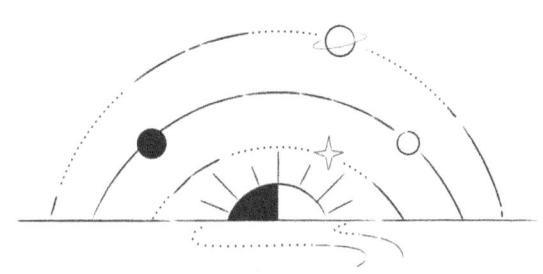

Retrogrades

What is retrograde?

A planet could be retrograde—meaning that it appears to be spinning backward from the vantage point of Earth. What's happening? The Earth is completing its orbit around the Sun faster than other planets outside its orbit. Periodically, it will outpace them— that's when retrograde mayhem breaks loose!

Much like a speeding car or train passing a slower one, the planet being passed will appear to stop and move backward—the apparent retrograde period.

Then, once the Earth completely passes this planet in its orbit, the motion appears normal again, and the planet is said to be "direct" or "prograde" (to use the short scientific term). Chances are, you've been in a vehicle before that felt like it was moving in reverse when it was passed; this is just like that!

What about the "shadow" period?

It isn't over 'til it's over! Each retrograde cycle has a "shadow period" — the awkward adjustment of the retrograde planet from apparent backward to forward motion...and vice-versa. For that reason, you may feel the stirrings of a retrograde cycle for several days, even weeks, before it officially begins.

Pluto
Saturn
Neptune
Chiron
Jupiter
Uranus
Mars
Venus

Planetary Retrogrades

Planetary retrograde is an astrological occurrence that occurs when a planet seems to move backward in its orbit from Earth's perspective. This happens due to differences in the planets' orbital speeds relative to Earth's position. It's important to note that planets don't change their direction, but the apparent retrograde motion occurs due to how the Earth orbits around the Sun.

Astrologers believe that planetary retrogrades can influence the energy and vibration of the planet in question, which can affect us. During a retrograde, the planetary energy is said to turn inward, and its impact can be felt more strongly in our lives. Different planets are believed to affect us differently, and their retrogrades may also have other effects.

Mercury Retrograde occurs three to four times a year for around three weeks. It is known for causing communication issues, technology malfunctions, and travel delays. Therefore, it's essential to take extra care when making important decisions or signing contracts during this time.

Venus Retrograde: This happens every eighteen months for about 40-43 days. It's a time for re-evaluating relationships, romantic connections, and money matters. It's a good time for reflection and introspection on handling these areas.

Mars Retrograde: This happens every two years for two months
It brings up feelings of frustration, anger, and aggression. It is important to be patient and avoid impulsive actions during this time.

Jupiter Retrograde: This happens every thirteen months for around four months. It can be a time for introspection and personal growth, but it can also cause setbacks in areas of expansion and growth.

Saturn Retrograde: This occurs every year for around four months. It is time to take stock of responsibilities and make necessary changes. Obstacles and lead to personal growth and development.ItCanBringChallengesAnd

Uranus Retrograde: This happens every year for around five months. It can bring unexpected changes and upheavals, but it can also bring innovation and new ideas.

Neptune Retrograde: This occurs every year for around five months. It's a time for spiritual growth and reflection, but it can also cause confusion and delusion.

Pluto Retrograde: This happens every year for around six months. It's a time for transformation and personal growth, but it can also bring power struggles and intense emotional experiences.

Retrogrades

Mercury Retrograde:

Mercury takes 88 days to make one complete revolution around the Sun. Mercury moves into retrograde three times per year for anywhere between 19 to 24 days. When Mercury retrogrades, mistakes, misunderstandings, and problems in communication and transportation are likely. Do not sign contracts, buy new items, or begin new projects. It is an excellent time to plan, research, and prepare for something that will happen later. Try to evaluate how you communicate and actively remain present.

Venus Retrograde:

Venus takes 225 days to make a complete revolution around the Sun and is stationary for between a few hours or 3 or 4 days. Venus moves into retrograde every 18 months and then stays that way for about six weeks. When Venus goes retrograde, money and love areas are reviewed, and old relations could return to resume or be completed. New love relationships may produce a change of heart when Venus goes direct. Investments done during the retrograde phase of Venus could lose value. Old relationship issues you thought were settled rear their ugly heads. Heal those issues.

Mars Retrograde:

Mars takes approximately 2 years or 687 days to complete a revolution around the Sun. Mars moves into retrograde every 2 years and 2 months and then stays that way for about 55 to 80 days. When Mars goes retrograde, any direct action becomes difficult. Traveling within, finishing incomplete tasks, redoing, renovating, and repairing will work better than pushing forward with any new direct ventures. Look your issues in the eye and tackle them once and for all. Self-care is your best friend during these times.

Jupiter Retrograde:

Jupiter takes around 12 years to make a complete revolution around the Sun. After that, Jupiter goes retrograde every year for about 120 days. When Jupiter goes retrograde, reviewing our visions, ideals, and belief systems in life is good. This reminds us that we must work to achieve our dreams and re-align with our authentic selves.

Saturn Retrograde:

Saturn takes around 29.5 years to make a complete revolution around the Sun. Saturn goes retrograde every year for about 140 days. When Saturn goes retrograde, it is an excellent time to revisit our relationship and work on long-term goals, responsibilities, and duties. It is a time to restructure how we manifest our reality and find a new attitude towards obstacles—a chance to revisit karmic lessons, which are gentler and more familiar than new ones. Focus on self-discipline.

Retrogrades

Uranus Retrograde:
Uranus takes about 84 years to make a complete revolution around the Sun, thus spending almost 7 years in each sign of the Zodiac. Uranus moves into retrograde approximately every year for around 148 days. When Uranus goes retrograde, our inner freedom is the focus. It is an excellent time to look for new paths toward accomplishing older intentions, using its energy to help us think creatively.

Neptune Retrograde:
Neptune takes about 164 years to make a complete revolution around the Sun, thus spending almost 14 years in each sign of the Zodiac. Neptune moves into retrograde approximately every year for around 150 days. When Neptune retrogrades, our spirituality, inner tranquility, and vision become the focus. Smashes illusion, giving us the sometimes-surprising opportunity to see ourselves more clearly, unlike the other retrogrades. It forces you out of your comfort zone.

Chiron Retrograde:
 It is a comet between Saturn and Uranus; Chiron takes about four years to move from sign to sign, although it spends 7 to 8 years in Aries and Pisces and only one to two years in Virgo and Libra. It entered Aries on April 17, 2018, retrograded back into Pisces on September 25, 2018, and finally moved back into the cardinal fire sign on February 18, 2019, which will remain until June 19, 2026. Chiron retrograde can be valuable for paying attention to your dreams, journaling, or addressing past trauma alongside a therapist.

Pluto Retrograde:
Pluto takes 248 years to make a complete revolution around the Sun, thus spending, on average, about 21 years in each sign of the Zodiac. Pluto moves into retrograde approximately every year for around 5 or 6 months. When Pluto goes retrograde, reflecting on how we are doing with change and transformation is good. It urges us to evaluate our relationship with power. Embrace your inner strength and use it to empower others.

Mercury in Retrograde
Altar Set Up

Many people feel wary when they hear we are entering Mercury Retrograde season.

While they are common and manageable, this is a suggested list of things you can arrange on your altar to ensure a smooth and easy-flowing Mercury Retrograde.

Magician tarot card:
The Magician is connected to Mercury energy, representing communication, learning, and action. The Magician can assist you with keeping your thoughts, words, and actions clear through Mercury Retro-grade.

A living plant associated with Mercury: Allow the energy of Mercury to thrive and grow on your altar with plants such as lavender, rosemary, peppermint, or thyme.

Incense associated with Mercury:
Burn incense with benzoin, gum mastic, frankincense, and rosemary to help purify your sacred space, stimulate mental agility, support concentration, and awaken spiritual awareness.

An image or statue of the god Mercury: If you feel like it, leave petitions for clarity, safe travels, speedy delivery, and smooth transactions with Mercury. Leave him offerings of almonds, hazelnuts, star anise, drawings of the Mercury glyph, lit yellow candles, images of the caduceus, or amulets shaped like wings.

Mercury-corresponding crystals: Dress your altar with crystals associated with the planet Mercury, such as hematite, mica, or muscovite. While the element known as Mercury is poisonous and should never be used, you can still represent it with a jar of water mixed with silver glitter, ink, and dye.

CHAPTER 10

Birth Chart Meanings

Your **Sun** is about yourself.

Your **Moon** is your heart.

Your **Rising** is how you look.

Your **Mercury** is the way you think.

Your **Venus** is how you love.

Your **Mars** is how you deal with life.

Your **Jupiter** is your luck.

Your **Saturn** is how you discipline yourself and your responsibilities.

Your **Uranus** is how unique you are.

Your **Neptune** is your imagination.

Your **Pluto** is your transformation.

Your **Chiron** is how you heal.

Your **Ceres** is how you take care of yourself.

Your **Pallas** is your relationship.

Your **Juno** is beauty and influence.

Your **Vesta** is your potential and your organization.

Your **North Node** is how you develop in your current life.

Your **South Node** is how you developed in your past life.

Your **Midheaven** is your career; how others view you.

Your **Lilith** is your hidden emotions.

For help with your birth chart try:
https://astro.cafeastrology.com/natal.php

Rising Sun and Moon

Rising: The awareness of the self, incarnate. How we distinguish ourselves as an individual. How we navigate the world around us. How we project ourselves into the world.

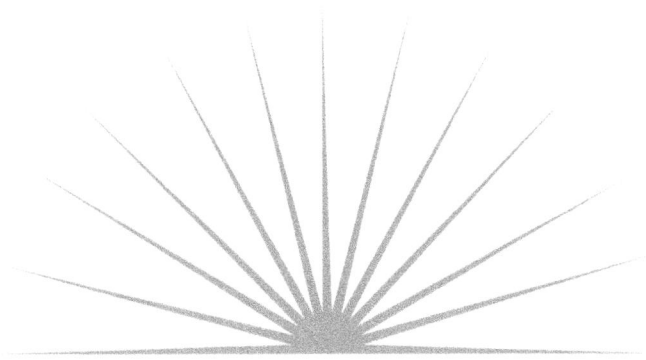

Sun: The qualities in which we focus our self-identity and individual radiance. Our personal magnetism, and how we express ourselves.

Moon: Foundations of our needs and our emotive drive. Our style of connecting to others and the environment. Our instinctual nature. How we nourish our inner world.

Astrological Signs

Aries
March 21 - April 19
for those born under the sign of
The Ram

Taurus
April 20 - May 20
for those born under the sign of
The Bull

Gemini
May 21 - June 20
for those born under the sign of
The Twins

Cancer
June 21 - July 22
for those born under the sign of
The Crab

Leo
July 23 - August 22
for those born under the sign of
The Lion

Virgo
August 23 - September 22
for those born under the sign of
The Virgin

Libra
September 23 - October 22
for those born under the sign of
The Scales

Scorpio
October 23 - November 21
for those born under the sign of
The Scorpion

Sagittarius
November 22 - December 21
for those born under the sign of
The Archer

Capricorn
December 22 - January 19
for those born under the sign of
The Goat

Aquarius
January 20 - February 18
for those born under the sign of
The Water Bearer

Pisces
February 19 - March 20
for those born under the sign of
The Fishes

Asteroid Astrology

Asteroid astrology, also known as asteroid interpretation or asteroid astrology analysis, is a field within astrology that involves examining and interpreting asteroids during astrological readings. While traditional astrology focuses on the Sun, Moon, planets, and lunar nodes, the discovery of numerous asteroids orbiting the Sun prompted astrologers to explore their potential significance in astrological charts.

In asteroid astrology, these celestial bodies are believed to influence human life and personality traits despite their smaller size and lesser-known status compared to planets. Each asteroid is named after a mythological figure, concept, or astronomical phenomenon. Astrologers assign symbolic meanings to these names based on their mythological associations and orbital paths.

 **Chiron**, often called the "Wounded Healer," is associated with themes of healing, transformation, and integrating personal wounds. Its placement in the natal chart indicates areas of deep emotional or spiritual growth and the potential for healing and transcendence.

 **Ceres**, named after the Roman goddess of agriculture, is associated with nurturing, nourishment, and the maternal instinct. Its placement in the chart can reveal patterns related to family dynamics, caretaking tendencies, and issues surrounding food and sustenance.

 **Pallas,** named after the goddess of wisdom and strategic warfare, is associated with intellect, strategy, and problem-solving abilities. Its placement in the chart can indicate areas of strength and skill and potential challenges that require analytical thinking and strategic planning.

 **Juno**, named after the queen of the gods in Roman mythology, is associated with themes of partnership, commitment, and marital harmony. Its placement in the chart can reveal patterns related to relationships, marriage, and partnership dynamics.

 Vesta, named after the Roman goddess of the hearth and home, is associated with devotion, purity, and focus. Its placement in the chart can indicate areas where we feel a strong sense of dedication and where we may need to prioritize our energy and attention.

CHAPTER 11

Elemental
Magic

Elemental Magic

The elements are another essential aspect of Witchcraft; we often call on them during spells and rituals. There are four primary elements, each of which has particular associations. Each element represents a different type of energy that you can harness.

Earth Magic - The element of Earth is the foundation of all life. The color green and the northern quarter align with the element of Earth. It is potent in spells that require wisdom and spells for fertility, prosperity, strength, and wealth.

Air Magic - The element of air is light fuel for all living things. It is represented by the color yellow and the eastern quarter when casting a circle. Spells for renewal, change, intuition, and knowledge call upon the air.

Fire Magic - The element of fire is a source of creation and destruction of life. It is represented by the color red and the southern quarter when casting a circle. Spells for passion, inspiration, intuition, creativity, and protection use fire.

Water Magic - Water represents the flow of life. It is represented by the color blue and the western quarter when casting a circle. It is powerful in spells for healing, peace, and compassion.

Element Spell Jars

Air
Star Anise
Mint
Lavender
Lemongrass
Salt
Flourite
Amethyst

Earth
Mugwort
Patchouli
Corn Kernels
Primrose
Some dirt
Unakite
Tiger's Eye

Fire
Cloves
Rosemary
Pepper Flakes
Calendula
Red Salt
Garnet
Carnelian

Water
Chamomile
Roses
Eucalyptus
Sea Salt
Aquamarine
Lapis Lazuli

How to personalize your spell jar
Include handwritten intentions, sigils, or doodles.
Add an inspiring quote or poetry.
Use several items that resonate with you.
Use locally grown herbs and flowers that you have foraged.
Personal things related to your desired outcome.

Air

Symbol: △
Number: 5
Solar System: Jupiter, Mercury, and Uranus
Zodiac: Aquarius, Gemini, and Libra
Celebration: Ostara
Season: Spring
Time of Day: Dawn
Runes: Beorc, Hagal, and Thorn
Ogham: Onn
Tarot: Fool, Swords, and Wands
Direction: East
Sense: Smell
Energy: Yang
Chakras: Crown, Heart, and Throat
Colors: Blue (light), Gray, Lavender, Pink, Red, Silver, White, and Yellow (bright, light)
Trees: Acacia, Alder, Apple, Ash, Aspen, Cedar, Chestnut, Elder, Elm Fir, Hawthorn, Hazel, Holly, Horse Chestnut, Laurel, Linden, Maple, Mesquite, Oak, Olive, Palm, Pine, Sycamore, Walnut, and Yew
Herbs and Flowers: Agrimony, Anemone, Bergamot, Borage, Broom, Clover, Comfrey, Dandelion, Fern, Ivy, Lavender, Lily of the Valley, Marjoram, Marigold, Mugwort, Peppermint, Primrose, Sage, Spearmint, Thyme, Vervain, Violet, and Yarrow
Misc. Plants: Anise, Bamboo, Bittersweet, Eyebright, Frankincense, Goldenrod, Horehound, Meadowsweet, Mistletoe, Myrrh, Nutmeg, Reed, Sandalwood, Star Anise, and Wormwood
Gemstones and Minerals: Agate (tree), Ametrine, Angelite, Aragonite, Aventurine, Blue Lace Agate, Celestite, Chrysoberyl, Desert Rose, Moldavite, Opal, Quartz (clear), Sodalite, Sphene, Staurolite, Topaz (blue), and Tourmaline (blue)
Metals: Aluminum, Mercury, and Tin
From the Sea: Angel Wing and Jingle

Air

Angels: Michael and Raphael
Goddesses: Amaterasu, Athena, Arianrhod, Hera, Nut, and Phoebe
Gods: Hermes, Khnum, Mimir, Mercury, Quetzalcoatl, Thoth, and Zeus
Magical Beings: Elves, Fairies, Pixies
Animal: Gazelle
Birds: Albatross, Condor, Eagle, Falcon, Hawk, and Seagull
Reptile:
Insect/Misc.: Firefly
Mythical: Dragon, Sphinx, and Thunderbird
Ritual Tools: Athame, Incense, and Sword
Principle: To Know
Issues, Intentions, and Powers: acceptance, action, Astral Realm, beginnings, business, clairvoyance, clarity, communication, concentration/ focus, consecrate/bless, creativity, divination, enchantment, energy, enlightenment, fairness, freedom, harmony, healing, imagination, inspiration, intelligence, intuition, justice, knowledge, learning, life, light, loss, magic (animal, dragon), memory/memories, the mind, money, motivation, order/ organize, power, protection, psychic ability, purification, relationships, release, the senses (hearing, smell, touch), shamanic work, spirits, spirituality, travel, visions, weather (general, lightning, storms), willpower, and wisdom

Earth

Symbol: ▽
Numbers: 4, 6, 8
Solar System: Earth, Saturn, and Venus
Zodiac: Capricorn, Taurus, and Virgo
Celebrations: Earth Day, Hunting of the Wren, and Yule
Season: Winter
Time of Day: Midnight
Runes: Is, Tyr, and Ur
Ogham: Ioho
Tarot: Pentacles
Direction: North
Sense: Touch
Energy: Yin
Chakra: Root
Colors: Black, Brown, Green, and White
Trees: Ash, Blackthorn, Cedar, Cypress, Elder, Elm, Holly, Juniper, Locust, Magnolia, Maple, Oak, Olive, Pine, Pomegranate, Rowan, Spruce, and Witch Hazel
Herbs and Flowers: Comfrey, Fern, Honeysuckle, Ivy, Jasmine, Mugwort, Primrose, Sage, and Vervain
Misc. Plants: Cinquefoil, Clove, Grains, Henbane, High John, Horehound, Mandrake, Patchouli, and Reed
Gemstones and Minerals: Agate, Alexandrite, Amazonite, Amber, Andalusite, Apophyllite, Calcite (green), Cat's Eye, Cerussite, Chrysocolla, Chrysoprase, Diopside, Emerald, Fluorite, Hematite, Jade, Jasper, Jet, Kunzite, Malachite, Moss Agate, Peridot, Petrified Wood, Quartz (rutilated), Salt, Smoky Quartz, Staurolite, Sugilite, Tourmaline (black, brown, green, watermelon), Turquoise, and Unakite
Metals: Lead and Mercury
From the Sea: Coral (black)

Earth

Angels: Gabriel and Auriel

Goddesses: Anat, Ariadne, Artemis, Asherah, Bertha, Ceres, Demeter, Gaia, Kore, Nephthys, Persephone, Rhea, and Rhiannon

Gods: Adonis, Arawn, Cernunnos, Dionysus, Geb, the Green Man, Khnum, Marduk, Mimir, Pan, Prometheus and Vishnu

Magical Beings: Brownies, Dryads, Elves, Fairies, Gnomes, Pixies

Animals: Antelope, Armadillo, Badger, Bear, Boar, Buffalo / Bison, Cattle, Deer (stag), Dog, Elephant, Goat, Groundhog, Hippopotamus, Jaguar, Mole, Otter, Pig, Prairie Dog, and Wolverine.

Birds: Blue Jay, Chicken, Crow, Goose, Sparrow, Swan, Turkey, and Woodpecker

Reptiles: Crocodile, Snake, Toad, Tortoise, and Turtle

Insect/Misc: Dragonfly

Mythical: Dragon and Selkies

Ritual Tool: Pentacle

Principle: To Be Silent

Issues, Intentions, and Powers: abundance, acceptance, agriculture, anxiety, balance, beginnings, business, comfort, communication, consecrate/bless, consciousness, creativity, cycles, death, endurance, energy (general, receptive), family, fertility, gentleness, grounding, growth, healing, hexes, the home, justice, life, magic (dragon), manifestation, money, nurture, the otherworld/underworld, patience, peace, pregnancy/childbirth, prosperity, protection, purpose, rebirth/renewal, relationships, the senses (smell, touch), sensuality, sexuality, spirits (nature spirits), stability, strength, success, support, travel, warmth, wealth, weather, well-being, willpower, and wisdom

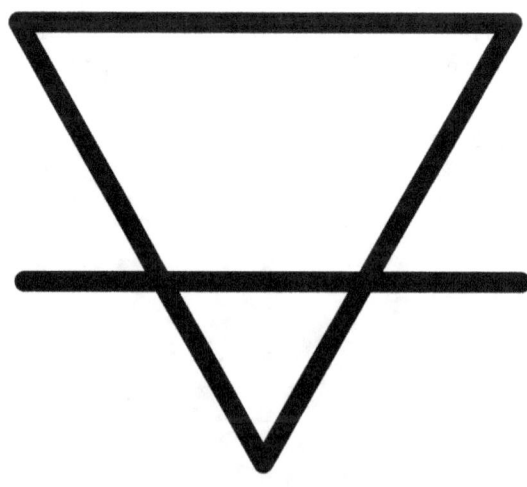

Fire

Symbol:
Numbers: 1, 3, 9
Solar System: Jupiter, Mars, and Sun
Zodiac: Aries, Leo, and Sagittarius
Celebrations: Beltane, Imbolc, and Litha
Season: Summer
Time of Day: Midday
Runes: Dag, Ken, Rad, and Sigel
Ogham: Ur
Tarot: Judgement, Swords, and Wands
Direction: South
Sense: Sight
Energy: Yang
Chakra: Solar Plexus
Colors: Crimson, Gold, Orange, Pink, Red, White, and Yellow
Trees: Alder, Ash, Beech, Blackthorn, Cedar, Cherry, Chestnut, Elder, Hawthorn, Holly, Horse Chestnut, Juniper, Laurel, Mesquite, Oak, Olive, Palm (dragon's blood), Pine, Pomegranate, Rowan, Walnut, Willow, Witch Hazel, and Yew
Herbs & Flowers: Amaranth, Anemone, Angelica, Basil, Carnation, Chrysanthemum, Dill, Fennel, Garlic, Goldenseal, Gorse, Heliotrope, Hibiscus, Holy Basil, Lovage, Marigold, Pennyroyal, Peony, Peppermint, Poppy, Primrose, Rosemary, Rue, St. John's Wort, Snapdragon, Sunflower, Sweet Woodruff, and Vervain
Misc. Plants: Allspice, Asafetida, Betony, Black Cohosh, Blessed Thistle, Bloodroot, Cinnamon, Cinquefoil, Clove, Coriander, Cumin, Deer's Tongue, Flax, Frankincense, Galangal, Ginger, Ginseng, High John, Mandrake, Mullein, Mustard, Nettle, Nutmeg, Pepper, Thistle, and Wormwood
Gemstones & Minerals: Agate (banded, black, brown, fire, red, red-banded, snakeskin), Amber, Amet-rine, Apache Tears, Beryl (golden), Bloodstone, Calcite (orange, red), Carnelian, Citrine, Diamond, Garnet, Hematite, Herkimer Diamond, Jasper (red), Obsidian, Onyx, Opal (fire), Peridot, Pyrite, Quartz, Rhodochrosite, Rhodonite, Ruby, Sard, Sardonyx, Serpentine, Smoky Quartz, Spinel, Staurolite, Sunstone, Tiger's Eye, Topaz, Tourmaline (red), Tsavorite, and Zircon (red)
Metals: Antimony, Brass, Gold, Iron, and Steel
From the Sea: Coral (red)

Fire

Angel: Michael

Goddesses: Aine, Amaterasu, Bertha, Brigid, Danu, Durga, Freya, Hestia, Kupala, Pele, Phoebe, Sekhmet, Spider-Woman, and Vesta

Gods: Agni, Belenus, Brahma, Dionysus, Hephaestus, Horus, Inari, Indra, Khnum, Mimir, Nergal, Nord, Perun, Prometheus, and Vulcan

Magical Beings: Mermaids and Salamanders

Animals: Goat, Hedgehog, Horse, Lion, Porcupine, Sheep (ram), and Tiger

Birds: Crane, Eagle, Falcon, Heron, Macaw, Peacock, Quail, Robin, Swallow, Woodpecker, and Wren

Reptiles: Lizard, Salamander, and Snake

Insects/Misc.: Bee, Cicada, Firefly, Ladybug, Praying Mantis, and Scorpion

Mythical: Dragon and Phoenix

Ritual Tools: Censer and Wand

Principle: To Will

Issues, Intentions, and Powers: action, activate/awaken, ambition, anger, authority, battle/war, cheerfulness, communication, concentration/ focus, confidence, consecrate/bless, courage, creativity, defense, desire, destruction, divination, energy, faith, freedom, healing, honor, illumination, influence, inspiration, intelligence, intuition, justice, leadership, life, light, love, lust, magic (general, defensive, dragon, sex), the mind, motivation, passion, power, protection, psychic ability, purification, purity, purpose, release, revenge, sexuality, stimulation, transformation, truth, warmth, weather (general, lightning), and willpower

Water

Symbol:
Numbers: 2, 7
Solar System: Mercury, Moon, Neptune, Pluto, and Saturn
Zodiac: Cancer, Pisces, and Scorpio
Celebrations: Mabon and Neptunalia
Season: Autumn
Time of Day: Dusk
Runes: Feoh, Jera, Lagu, and Peorth
Ogham: Eadha, and Eamhancholl
Tarot: Cups, Hanged Man, and Moon
Direction: West
Sense: Taste
Energy: Yin
Chakra: Sacral
Colors: Aqua, Black, Blue, Gray, Green (blue, sea), Indigo, Lilac, Purple, Silver, Turquoise, Violet, and White
Trees: Alder, Apple, Ash, Aspen, Beech, Birch, Cedar, Cherry, Chestnut, Cypress, Elder, Elm, Hazel, Horse Chestnut, Locust, Magnolia, Mesquite, Mimosa, Myrtle, Olive, Poplar, Spindle-tree, Spruce, Sycamore, Willow, Witch Hazel, and Yew
Herbs & Flowers: Aster, Blackberry / Bramble, Catnip, Chamomile, Columbine, Comfrey, Daffodil, Daisy, Feverfew, Foxglove, Gardenia, Geranium, Grape, Heather, Hibiscus, Hyacinth, Iris, Ivy, Jasmine, Lady's Mantle, Lemon Balm, Lilac, Lily, Monkshood, Morning Glory, Passionflower, Periwinkle, Poppy, Raspberry, Rose, Solomon's Seal, Spearmint, Strawberry, Thyme, Valerian, Violet, and Yarrow
Misc. Plants: Aloe, Belladonna, Burdock, Cardamom, Coltsfoot, Cowslip, Dittany, Henbane, Lady's Slipper, Lotus, Meadowsweet, Moonwort, Myrrh, Orris Root, Reed, Sandalwood, Skullcap, Spikenard, Star Anise, Thornapple, Vanilla, and Water Lily
Gemstones & Minerals: Alexandrite, Amethyst, Ametrine, Angelite, Aquamarine, Aragonite, Azurite, Beryl, Blue Lace Agate, Calcite, Charoite, Chrysocolla, Dioptase, Fluorite, Jade, Jasper (ocean), Jet, Kyanite, Labradorite, Lapis Lazuli, Larimar, Lepidolite, Lodestone, Moonstone, Morganite, Obsidian (gold sheen), Opal, Quartz, Rose Quartz, Sapphire, Selenite, Sodalite, Staurolite, Sugilite Topaz (blue), Tourmaline (black, blue, pink, watermelon), Tsavorite, Turquoise, and Zircon (blue)
Metals: Copper, Mercury, and Silver
From the Sea: Coral, Mother-of-Pearl, and Pearl

Water

Angels: Raphael

Goddesses: Amphitrite, Aphrodite, Bad, Boann, Brigantia, Chalchiuhtlicue, Coventina, Isis, Kupala, Ran, Sarasvati, Sedna, and Tiamat

Gods: Aegir, Belenus, Ea, Khnum, Mabon, Manannan, Mimir, Neptune, Njord, Osiris, Poseidon, and Prometheus

Magical Beings: Mermaids, Norns, and Undines

Animals: Bat, Beaver, Cattle (cow), Dog, Hare, Hippopotamus, Horse, Moose, Otter, Polar Bear, and Raccoon

Birds: Albatross, Blackbird, Cormorant, Crane, Dove, Duck, Heron, Kingfisher, Seagull, Stork, Swan, Swift, and Vulture

Reptiles: Crocodile, Frog, Salamander, Snake, and Toad

Insect/Misc.: Dragonfly

Mythical: Dragon and Selkies

Ritual Tools: Cauldron, Chalice, and Cup

Principle: To Dare

Issues, Intentions and Powers: adaptability, agriculture, balance, beginnings, change/s, clairvoyance, compassion, consecrate/bless, consciousness (subconscious), creativity, desire, divination, dream work, emotions, empathy, energy (general, psychic, receptive), fertility, friendship, grace, growth, healing, heartbreak, influence, introspection, intuition, life, magic (animal, dragon, moon), memory /memories, nurture, patience, power, pregnancy/childbirth, protection, psychic ability, purification, purity, rebirth/ renewal, reconciliation, reversal, secrets, sensitivity, sensuality, shamanic work, sleep, sorrow, spirituality, strength (inner), stress, transformation, weather (general, storms), well-being, and wisdom

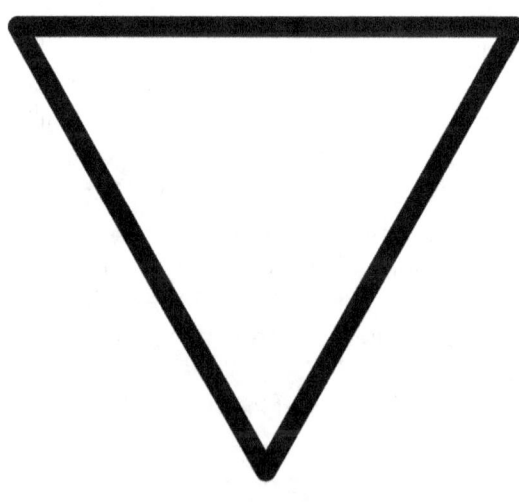

CHAPTER 12

Leaf Divination

Take a walk outdoors and collect a variety of colorful autumn leaves. Choose leaves that resonate with you or speak to you intuitively.

Once you have collected the leaves, find a quiet space where you can sit and focus on your questions or concerns.

Using a pen or marker, write a different question or topic on each leaf. These questions can be related to any aspect of your life that you seek guidance or clarity on.

Holding the leaves in your hands, close your eyes and take a few deep breaths to center yourself. When you feel ready, you can throw the leaves into the air.

Observe how the leaves land and the patterns they form on the ground. Trust your intuition to interpret the messages conveyed by the placement of the leaves and their orientation.

Take note of any insights or revelations that arise from this divination practice and use them to guide your actions and decisions in the coming days and weeks.

Balancing Act Ritual

Choose an apple or a small pumpkin to represent the balance of light and darkness during the equinox. You can also decorate the apple or pumpkin with symbols or sigils that resonate with you.

Find a sturdy stick or dowel and carefully pierce it through the center of the apple or pumpkin, ensuring it remains balanced.

Place the apple on a flat surface or the pumpkin on a plate or pedestal. As you do so, visualize the energies of light and darkness coming into perfect harmony and balance. Sit quietly with the apple or pumpkin in front of you and meditate on the areas of your life where you seek balance and equilibrium. Reflect on how you can bring greater harmony to these aspects of your life.

Once you feel ready, offer words of gratitude to the energies of the equinox and the natural world for their guidance and support.

Leave the apple or pumpkin on your altar or in a sacred space as a reminder of the importance of balance in your life, and return to it whenever you need to realign your energies.

Equinox Cleansing Bath

Prepare a soothing bath by filling your tub with warm water and adding a handful of dried herbs such as chamomile, lavender, and rosemary. These herbs are known for their cleansing and purifying properties.

Light candles around the tub's edge and dim the lights to create a relaxing atmosphere. You may also play soft music or use essential oils to enhance the sensory experience.

As you soak in the bath, close your eyes and take several deep breaths, allowing the warm water and herbal scents to envelop you. Visualize any tension, stress, or negative energy melting away and being replaced by pure, healing light.

Focus on your intention to cleanse and purify your energy field, releasing anything that no longer serves your highest good. Surrender to the healing power of the water and herbs, allowing them to wash away any energetic debris.

Take your time to immerse yourself in fully the experience, allowing your body, mind, and spirit to be rejuvenated and refreshed. You may wish to stay in the bath for as long as feels comfortable, savoring the sense of renewal, and vitality that it brings.

When you are ready to exit the bath, take a moment to express gratitude for the cleansing and healing that you have received. Pat yourself dry with a soft towel and take a few moments to ground yourself before returning to your daily activities.

Root Vegetable Spell Bags

Gather a selection of root vegetables such as carrots, potatoes, onions, and turnips. Choose vegetables that resonate with you and that you associate with grounding, nourishment, and stability.

Cleanse the vegetables under cold running water, visualizing any impurities or negative energies being washed away.

As you handle each vegetable, focus on your intention to bring more significant grounding and stability into your life. Visualize yourself rooted firmly to the Earth, drawing strength and support from the soil beneath you.

Once the vegetables are clean, set them aside to dry completely. While drying, prepare small pouches or sachets using fabric or muslin bags.

Assemble the root vegetables in the pouches, adding a mixture of herbs or crystals for added potency if you'd like. You may also include a written intention or sigil to reinforce your goals for grounding and stability.

Once the bags are filled, tie them securely with a ribbon or string, infusing each knot with your intentions and blessings. Place the bags in your kitchen or pantry, or hang them in areas of your home where you spend the most time.

Whenever you need to feel more grounded or centered, hold the spell bags in your hands and visualize yourself connecting deeply with the Earth's energy. Feel the roots of your being sinking into the soil, anchoring you firmly in place and providing a sense of stability and security.

Mabon Gratitude Ritual

This short gratitude ritual incorporates elements you and your group can use to express your gratitude for everything you have. You can also perform it yourself, although it holds even more power if a tight-knit pagan community performs it during Mabon night. It can be incorporated into other traditions or beliefs or, kept as it is, a short pagan rite for giving thanks. It includes symbols of your life that you are grateful to have.

Ingredients:
Gold or green candles represent abundance
Basket of apples or grapes
1/8 cup of neutral oil of your choice
5 drops of rose oil
2 drops of vetiver oil
1 drop of agrimony oil
A pinch of ground cinnamon
Cornucopias as the symbol of bounty
An abundance symbol (preferably handcrafted)
Representations of things you are grateful for (health, career, and family.)
Pieces of cloth or craft material in colors associated with abundance

Directions:
If you have not prepared it, make your oil blend by mixing all the oils with the cinnamon.

To make your altar, you can begin by placing a fruit basket in the center and arranging symbols in front of it. Place two candles on either side of the basket. Then, scatter other items and colorful pieces of material around the centerpiece. Remember, your altar is your own private space to decorate.

Take a moment to reflect on all the things you have in abundance. Remember, it's not just about material possessions or a high income. Consider your relationships with friends and family, even those who have passed away. Be grateful for the wisdom your ancestors have passed down to you. If you have a trusted spiritual guide, you can also include them in your expression of gratitude.

To perform this gratitude ritual, anoint a candle with an oil mixture and light it. After expressing your gratitude, take five minutes to meditate.

Mabon Difuser Blend

6 Drops of Clove   ◊ ◊ ◊ ◊ ◊ ◊
4 Drops of Frankincense   ◊ ◊ ◊ ◊
3 Drops of Cedarwood   ◊ ◊ ◊

3 Drops of Vetiver   ◊ ◊ ◊
3 Drops of Orange   ◊ ◊ ◊
2 Drops of Pine   ◊ ◊
1 Drop of Cinnamon Bark   ◊
1 Drop of Clove   ◊
1 Drop of Cypress   ◊

Mabon Oils

Mabon Love Oil
1 oz. base of Grapeseed EO
5 drops of Pine EO
6 drops of Lavender EO
2 drops of Patchouli EO
1 golden Crystal or yellow Agate

Mabon Offering Oil
1 oz. base of Grapeseed oil
4 drops of Frankincense EO
4 drops of Myrrh EO
2 drops of Orange EO
2 drops Ginger EO
3 drops of Rosemary EO
½ tsp. Chamomile dried herb

Mabon Temple Oil
1 oz. base of Grapeseed oil
3 drops of Rose Geranium EO
4 drops of Rosemary EO
3 drops of Chamomile EO
5 drops of Cedar EO
1 drop of Cinnamon EO

Mabon Ritual Oil
1 oz. base of Grapeseed oil
5 drops of Cedar EO
6 drops Rosemary EO
1/2 tsp Marigold dried herb
1 Apple Seed

Mabon God Oil
1 oz. base of Grapeseed oil
I drop of Cinnamon EO
8 drops of Frankincense EO
3 drops of Orange EO

Mabon Spirit Oil
1oz. base of Grapeseed oil
3 drops of Frankincense EO
2 drops of Pine EO
2 drops of Juniper EO
1 drop of Sandalwood EO

Mabon Physic Oil
1 oz. base of Grapeseed oil
3 drops of Ylang Ylang EO
4 drops of Jasmine EO
2 drops of Lemon EO
5 drops of Chamomile EO
1 tiny Sea Shell crushed

Autumn Equinox Offering Oil

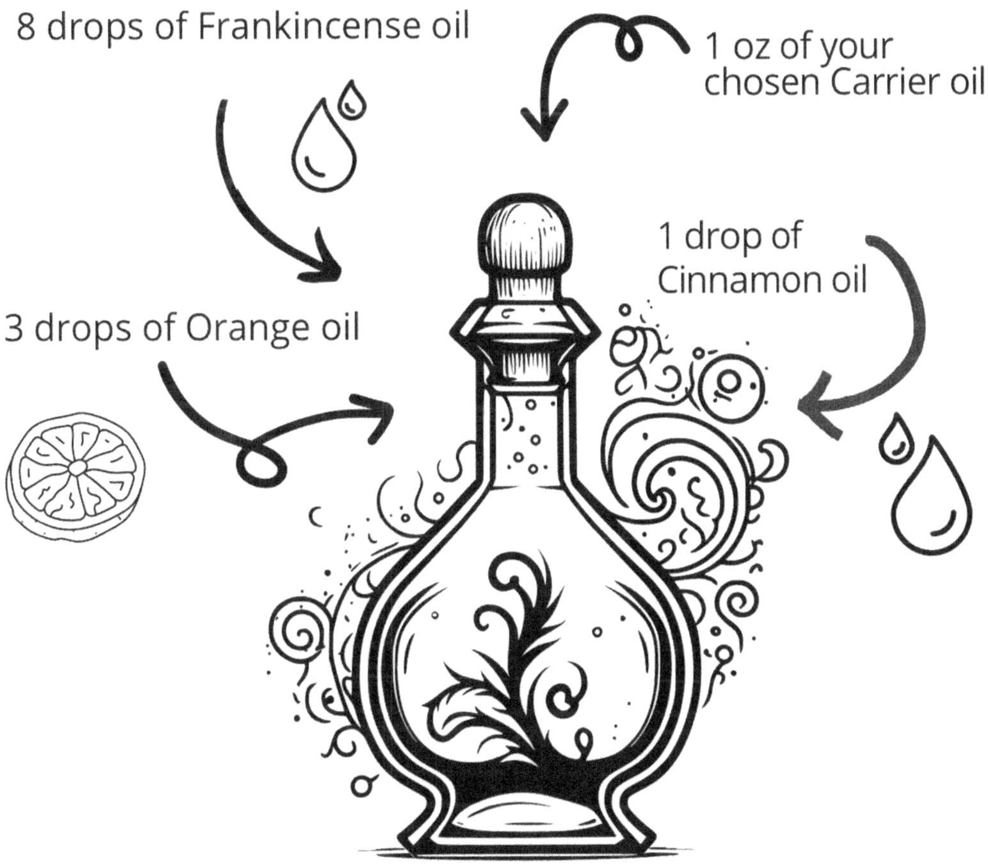

8 drops of Frankincense oil

1 oz of your chosen Carrier oil

1 drop of Cinnamon oil

3 drops of Orange oil

Autumn Equinox Spirit Oil

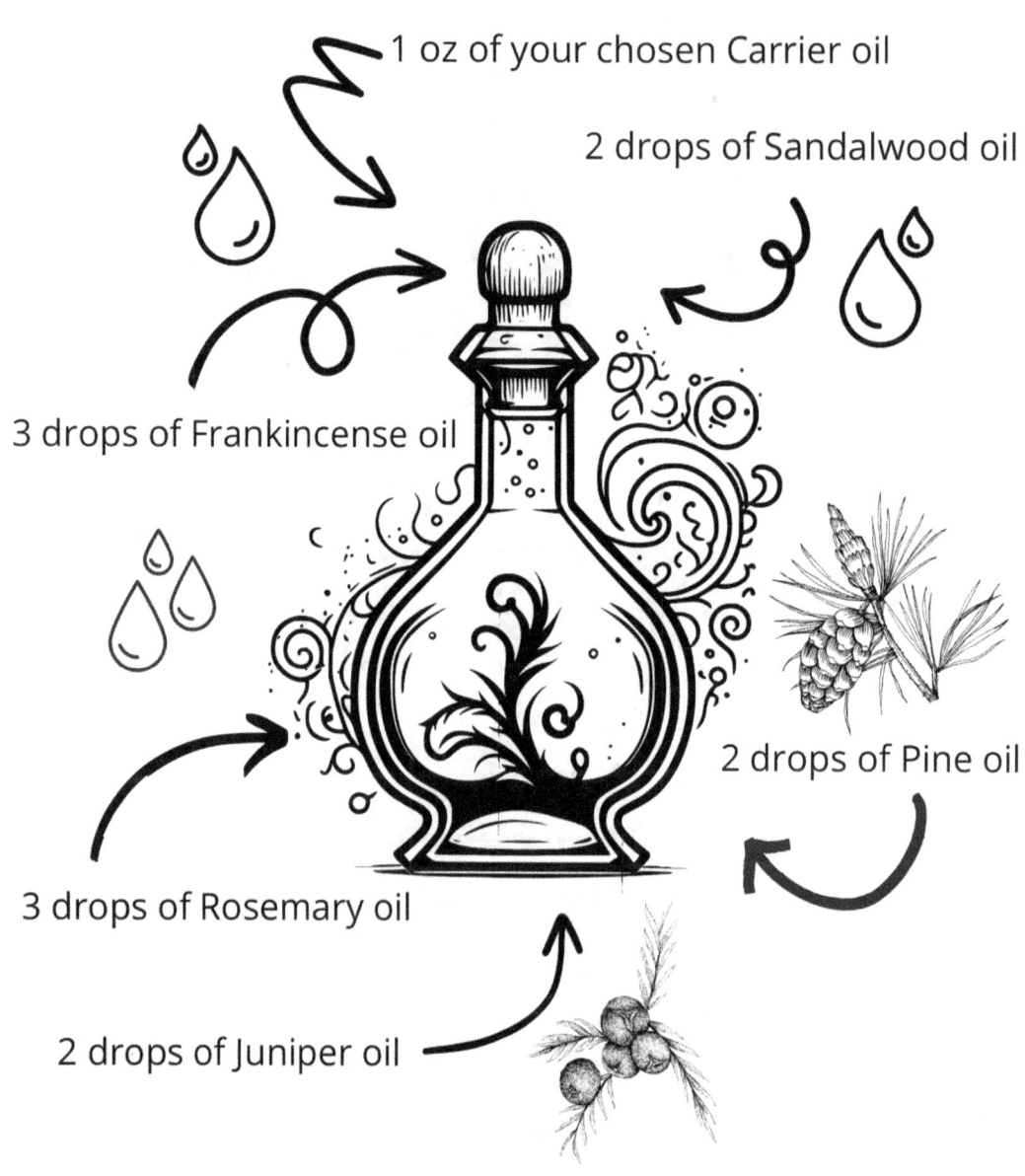

1 oz of your chosen Carrier oil

2 drops of Sandalwood oil

3 drops of Frankincense oil

2 drops of Pine oil

3 drops of Rosemary oil

2 drops of Juniper oil

Autumn Equinox Psychic Oil

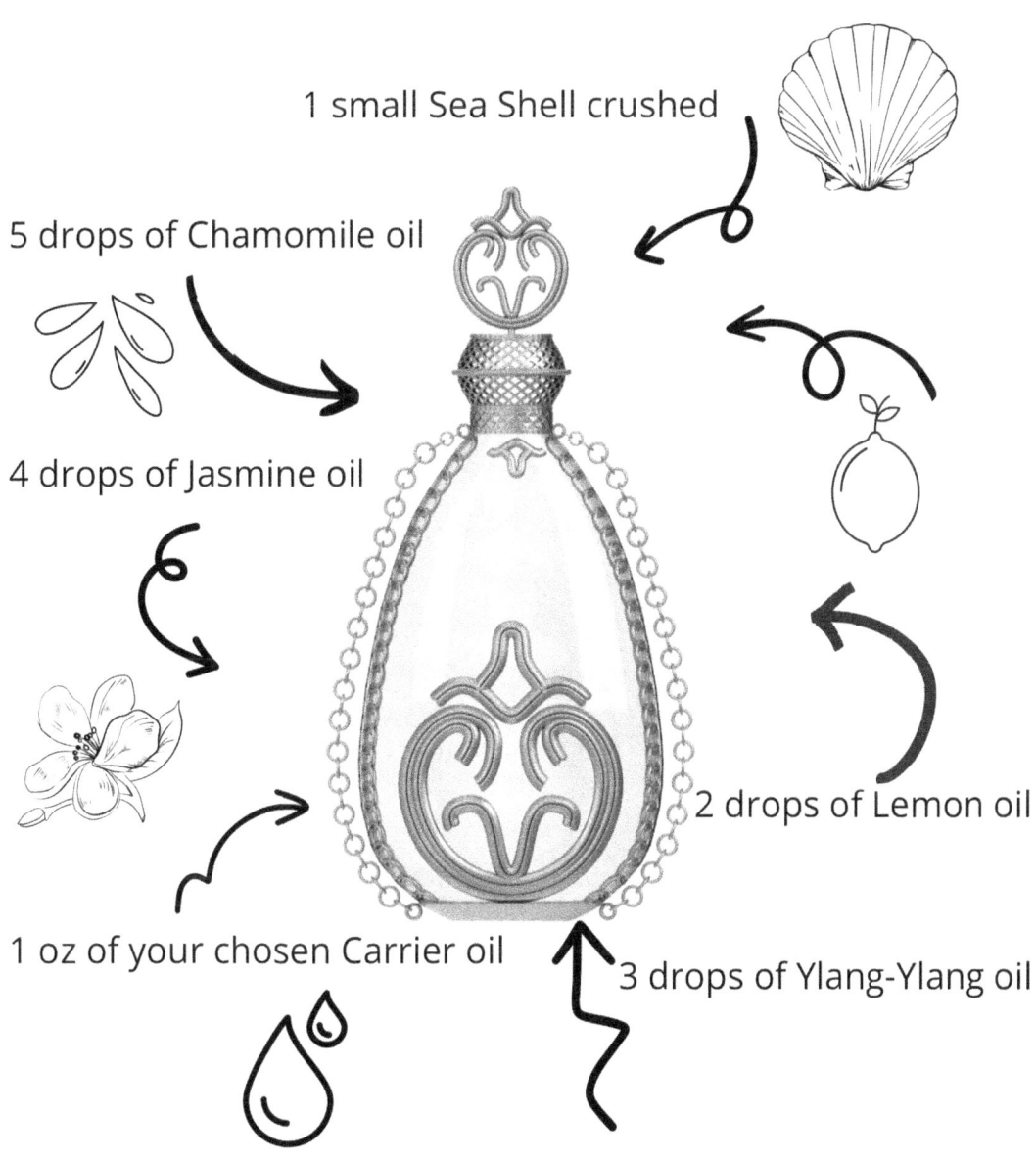

1 small Sea Shell crushed

5 drops of Chamomile oil

4 drops of Jasmine oil

2 drops of Lemon oil

1 oz of your chosen Carrier oil

3 drops of Ylang-Ylang oil

Gratitude Jar

Materials:
Jar or Container
Decorative elements (Optional): You got the paint out, so why not use it or add ribbons, twine, or other decorative elements to embellish the jar?
Gratitude Notes
Pen or Markers

Directions:
Select your jar and decorate it to add a personal touch. You can tie a ribbon around the lid, attach a tag, or paint the jar with colors and symbols representing gratitude.
Cut into small pieces of paper or use pre-cut cards. These will serve as the space for your gratitude entries.
Write your first note by starting the gratitude jar by writing down something you are thankful for on one of the notes. It could be a specific moment, a person, or even a simple pleasure.
Set a routine for adding gratitude notes. You might write one daily, every week, or whenever you feel inspired. Consistency is key.

Reflect and Write: Before placing a note in the jar, take a moment to reflect on what you are grateful for. Write down your thoughts, expressing them in a positive and heartfelt manner.
Invite friends or family members to join in. They can add their own notes to the jar, creating a collective sense of gratitude.

Read Your Notes: Periodically, take some time to read the notes accumulated in the jar. This can be a powerful and uplifting experience, especially during challenging times.

Celebrate and Empty the Jar: Celebrate by reading all the notes at the end of the season or year. Consider emptying the jar and saving the notes in a scrapbook or special container.

Start Anew: If you wish, start a new Gratitude Jar for the upcoming season or year. You can continue this practice as a beautiful tradition.

If you want to get frisky, you can use the same idea but put it on your altar for needed petitions or prayers.

As I walk by each day, I think of a petition and put it in my bowl on my altar.

Mabon Altar Jar

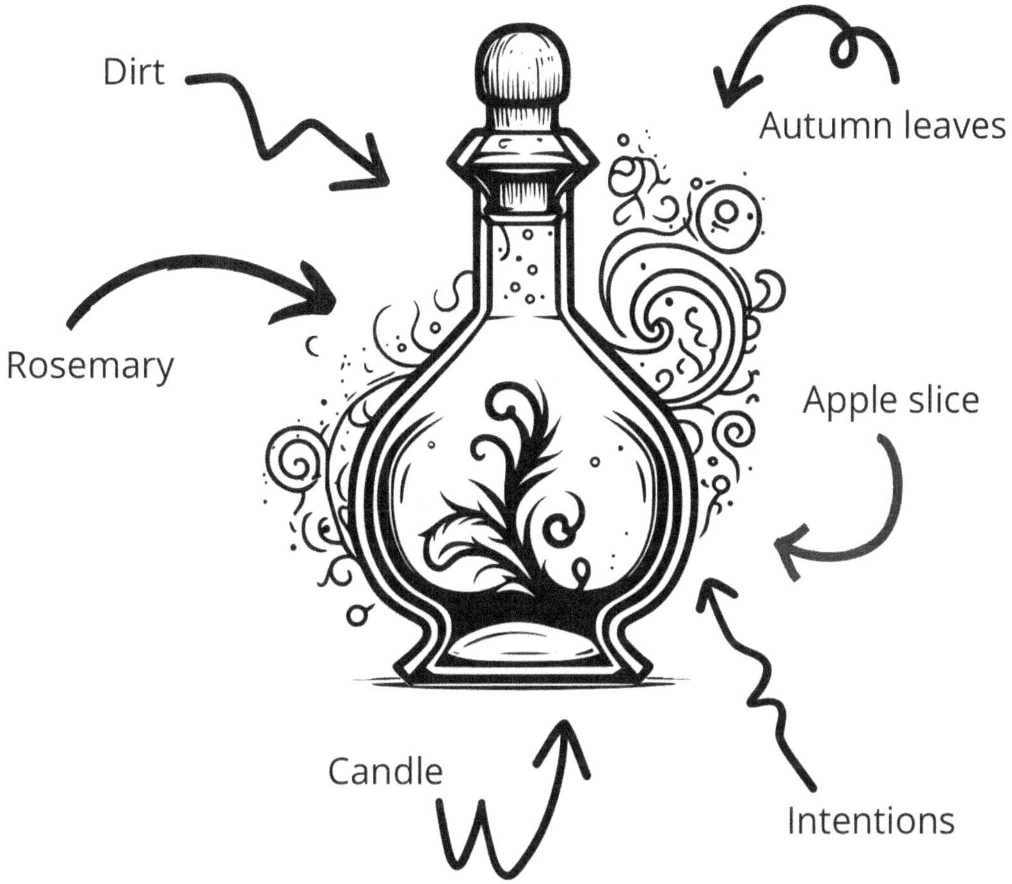

Dirt

Autumn leaves

Rosemary

Apple slice

Candle

Intentions

Mabon Simmer Pot

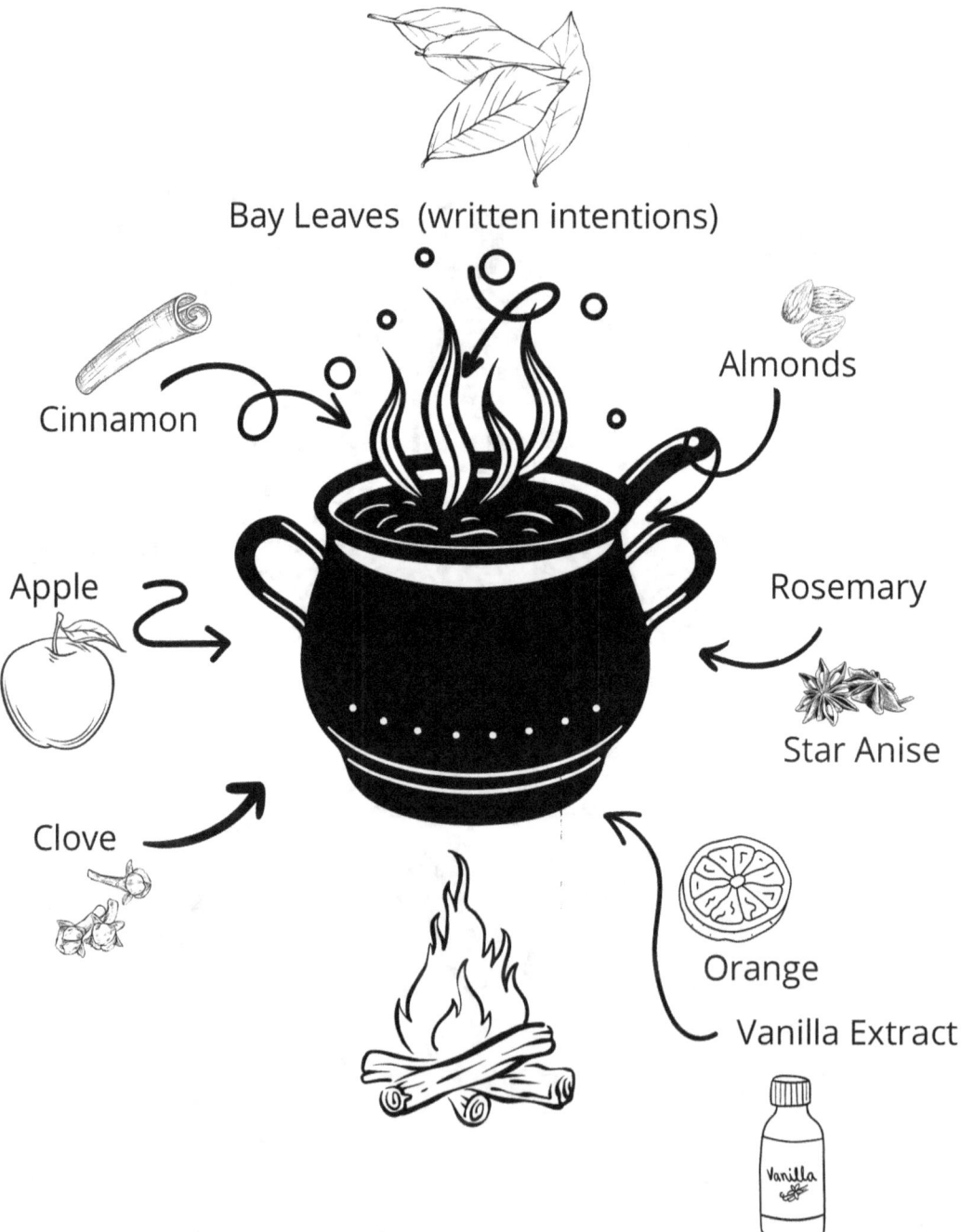

Bay Leaves (written intentions)

Almonds

Cinnamon

Rosemary

Apple

Star Anise

Clove

Orange

Vanilla Extract

Mabon Waxed Leaves

Waxed Fall Leaves Is there anything more beautiful than the shades of autumn leaves that fall to the ground during the autumnal equinox? If you admire the vibrant colors of fall, this craft is perfect for creating an inexpensive yet stunning look.

Ingredients:
Fall leaves
Paraffin wax

Directions:
Melt the paraffin wax in the mini crock pot or any other container and pour the melted wax onto a sheet.

Start dipping the leaves in the wax. Be careful not to let your fingers touch the hot wax while doing so.

Let the leaves stay there until the wax dries completely. It should take a minute or so.

You can make more than one coat on the leaves for a solid foundation. About 2 to 3 coats should be enough for this purpose.

Once they are done, you can place them wherever you would like.

Mabon Pine Cones

It is common around Mabon season, and combining pine cones and candy corn is the perfect craft for this festive da. Pine cones are great for decorating purposes, especially during the fall season. Combine this with beautifully applied paint and glitter; you have the perfect eye-catching decoration for your autumnal equinox festival.

Ingredients:
Pine cones
Parchment paper
Spray paint and glitter

Directions:
First, arrange the pine cones on a parchment sheet and heat them in the oven at low heat for about 30 minutes. This will help kill critters or insects that may have survived the harvest.

Start by painting the first layer using orange spray paint. Make sure you cover the whole pine cone with the color.

After the first coat has dried, take the white spray paint and spray the pine cone tip white.

Once the white coat has dried, hold the top of the pine cone and spray the bottom with yellow spray paint. Let the pine cones dry overnight, and then use Mod Podge and a brush to apply the glitter to them.

Put the pine cones in baskets or decorate the Mabon altar with them.

Mabon Garland

Apples have long been associated with the magical time of Mabon. They are used in food and for making various decor items. Garlands are one of the most common decorations during Mabon, and they add a touch of nature to your house or altar.

Ingredients:
Oranges (3 to 5)
Apples (2 to 3)
Bay leaves (15 to 20)
Cinnamon sticks (1 bag)
Twines (arm's length)
Embroidery needles Foil Cookie sheet Oven

Directions:
First, cut the oranges and apples into thin slices. Use a sharp knife to do this; otherwise, the slices will be uneven. When cut perfectly, the apples will resemble hearts, and the orange slices will be circular.

Place these slices between drying sheets and press to squeeze the juice out. This makes the drying process much more manageable.

Preheat the oven to high heat, and slide in the fruit slices arranged neatly on cookie sheets. Turn over the slices every few minutes to avoid burning.

Once the fruit slices are dried, line up the materials together and start threading a piece of twine through them.

Add the orange, apple, and cinnamon sticks to the garland, one at a time. Once done, hang it on your doors or simply on the wall.

Blessing Stones

Materials:
Smooth Stones
Acrylic paints or markers
Paintbrushes (if using paint)
Sealant (Optional)
A palette or dish (if using paint) egg carton is always good for this.

Directions:
Clean the Stones:
Choose Your Blessings: Reflect on the blessings or positive affirmations you want to infuse into the stones. These can be words, symbols, or simple images with personal meaning.
Paint or decorate each stone with your chosen blessings. You can paint words like "love," "joy," "peace," or symbols that represent positivity and personal growth.
Allow to Dry
Add Details (Optional): You can add details or accentuate your designs with fine-tip paintbrushes or markers.
Seal the Stones (Optional)
Charge with Intentions: Hold each stone and infuse it with positive intentions. Focus on your chosen blessings, sending good energy into each stone.
Place them in meaningful locations and arrange the blessing stones in areas where you'll see them often – on your desk, by your bedside, or in a bowl on your altar.

Tips:
Share the Blessings: Christmas is just around the corner.

Use in rituals or meditation by incorporating the blessing stones into your rituals, meditation, or mindfulness practices. Hold them during moments of reflection.

Mabon Candle

Apple Candles Again, as apples are closely associated with Mabon and Harvest goddess Demeter, and seeing that they are plentiful at this time of the year, Mabon wouldn't be Mabon without them. To make the most of these fruits, you should use as many as possible, not just in the grand Mabon feast but also in your crafts and decorations. One such craft can be these creative apple candles. The best part is that they are super easy to make! This craft doesn't even need a lot of supplies, time, or effort on your part, but it ends up being one of the most creative crafts on Mabon.

Ingredients:
Apples
Tea lights/Candles

Directions:
Take an apple, wash it, and dry it thoroughly. Red apples will match the theme perfectly, but green or yellow ones will work just as well.

Use a hole saw bit to drill out a circular hole the size of the candle top from the apple. Make sure you make an accurately sized hole to match your candle or tea light, or the craft will look uneven.

You can use a spoon to pry out the extra material from the hole you made.

Finally, place the candle inside the hole until it sits snugly inside. Light the candles and place them wherever you would like.

Mabon Wreath

Ingredients:
Acorns
Hot glue gun
Floral wreath

Directions:
Use the glue guns to glue the acorns to the straw or wooden wreaths individually. Make sure there are no gaps and that every space has an acorn.

Use ribbon to hang the wreath on your front door. You can spray-paint the acorns in any color you like.

Mabon Suncatcher

Leaves are a major symbol of the fall season and are seen all around the Mabon festivities. There are all kinds of creative and easy-to-make crafts involving leaves, and this one is no exception. This decor will showcase autumn's beauty using leaves of various colors, shapes, and sizes.

Ingredients:
Fall leaves
Laminator
Laminating sheets
Yarn
Hole punch
Rubber band
Scissors
Masking tape

Directions:
Go outside and collect some leaves and a three-foot-long stem from a bush. Ensure you cut off all the little twigs from the stick before bringing it home.

Make sure the leaves are straight and moist; do not collect dry or curled-up leaves.

Let the stick soak in warm water to make bending easier when you make the suncatcher.

While the stick is soaking, pick out the most beautiful leaves you have collected and place them in the middle of the laminating paper. Laminate away!

Bend the soaked stick slowly into a circle, gently so that the stick does not break. Tie the two ends together.

Cut the laminated sheet in a circular shape while keeping the leaf in the middle.

Punch holes in the edges of the sheet and use masking tape to hold the laminated leaf between the circular stick temporarily.

Thread the yarn through the punched holes and tie it around the stick to hold the laminated piece between the circles. Hang this sun catcher in direct sunlight to enhance the leaf's colors.

Autumn Sun Catchers

Materials:
Transparent Contact Paper
Assorted Fall Leaves
Tissue Paper (Optional)
Colored tissue paper in autumn hues can add extra vibrancy to your sun catcher.
String or Yarn

Directions:
Choose your design
Prepare the leaves if needed, and press the collected leaves between heavy books to flatten them. Ensure they are completely dry.
Cut contact paper into two equal-sized pieces of contact paper in the shape of your chosen design. Peel off the backing from one piece.
Arrange the leaves by placing them on the sticky side of the contact paper. You can create patterns or let them scatter randomly. If desired, add small pieces of colored tissue paper for extra vibrancy.
Secure the second layer once you've arranged the leaves, peel off the backing from the second piece of contact paper, and carefully place it over the leaves, sticky sides together. Press to seal.
Trim the edges of your sun catcher to refine the shape and create a neat border.
Add Details (Optional): Use a marker or pen to add details like veins on the leaves or any additional designs.
Punch a hole if you plan to hang your sun catcher, punch a hole at the top, and thread a piece of string or yarn through it.
You can just hang in a sunny window or a well-lit area.
Get frisky and experiment with shapes.

Tip: Change with the Seasons

Autumn Doll

This autumn dolly is made with natural materials connected with Mabon's theme. This cute piece will not only interest the little ones but also add a whimsical charm to your Mabon altar.

Ingredients:
Autumn leaves (red, orange, brown, green, and yellow shades)
Pine cone (small or medium-sized)
Acorn cap (large-sized)
Rusty-colored orange wool
White felt (1 ball)
String (small piece)
Hot glue gun

Directions:
First, prepare the doll's head with the white felt ball. You can also use a large cotton wool ball in its place.

Use the rusty orange wool to make the doll's hair by parting the wool into two parts.

Glue the hair on top of the white felt ball. Hold it until the glue has dried.

Take the acorn cap and use the glue gun to stick it on top of the doll's hair. Hold it in place until it is stuck.

Use the pinecone to make the doll's body. Place it upside down and add glue to the base of the pinecone. Stick the doll's head here and let it dry.

To make the doll's wings, take two bright-colored autumn leaves. Make sure that the leaves you pick are equal in size. Stick these to the back of the pinecone from the stem side.

Tie a string to the acorn's stem to hang the dolly wherever you want.

Mabon Corn Dolly

Mabon Corn Dolly Considered to be one of the most sacred symbols of Mabon, corn dollies have been historically significant throughout Wiccan and pagan traditions. Early practitioners believed that the spirit of the grain, or harvest, lived in the field with the crops. However, once all the crops were reaped, she no longer had a place to stay. So, the last sheaves were reaped and used to make corn dollies to preserve the harvest's spirit and keep her warm all winter. When spring came, the corn dolly would be put back into the earth to bring fertility to the land. Many of these traditions have remained almost the same throughout these years. Thus, the corn dolly still has spiritual significance and is a common part of Mabon rituals. They are easy to make and do not require more than three materials.

Ingredients:
Corn husk
String

Directions:
First, you need to soak the husks for a few hours
to make them more pliable. Once they
have soaked enough, take them out, and
Pat them dry with a towel.

Now, select 3 or 4 of the husks that are similar in size.
Tie a string around the narrow part of the husks.
Secure the knot twice, and then start folding the layers
downward.

Tie a string around the upper part of the husk
where her neck should be. Use another husk for
the arms. Roll the husk tightly and push the arms under her neck.

Use another piece of thread to tie her middle to resemble a torso. Now, take two long, thin husk pieces, tie them around her shoulders, and bring them to the front. This will be her shawl. Use another piece of string to secure her shawl to the front.

Quickly put the corn dolly configuration in the oven to dry the husks properly so they do not shrivel.

Take a stick and twigs to make a miniature broom for the corn dolly.

CHAPTER 13

Recipes
for
Mabon

Apple Cider

Ingredients:

12 apples (a mix of sweet and tart varieties)
1 orange, sliced
1 lemon, sliced
4 cinnamon sticks
1 tablespoon of whole cloves
1 tablespoon of whole allspice
1/2 cup of brown sugar (adjust to taste)
Water (magical if got some)

Directions:

Wash the apples thoroughly. Core and cut them into quarters, leaving the peels on.
Combine the quartered apples, orange slices, lemon slices, cinnamon sticks, cloves, and allspice in a large pot. Add enough water to cover the ingredients.
Bring the mixture to a boil over high heat. Once boiling, reduce the heat to low and let it simmer uncovered for 2-3 hours. The apples should become very soft and the flavors infused.

Mash and strain:

Stir in brown sugar to sweeten the cider. Adjust the amount based on your taste preferences. You can also add more sugar later if needed.
Return the strained cider to the stove and warm it over low heat. Do not bring it to a boil at this stage.
Serve Hot: Ladle the cider into mugs once it is warmed and perfectly flavored. Garnish with additional cinnamon sticks or orange slices, if desired.

Tip:

Leftover cider can be stored in the refrigerator for up to a week. Reheat on the stove or in the microwave before serving.

Spiced Apple Jam

Ingredients:
6 cups of apples, peeled, cored, and finely chopped
1/4 cup of lemon juice
1 cup of water
1 package (1.75 oz) of fruit pectin
1/2 teaspoon of ground cinnamon
1/4 teaspoon of ground nutmeg
1/4 teaspoon of ground cloves
5 cups of granulated sugar

Directions:
Sterilize your canning jars and lids by placing them in boiling water for 10 minutes or using your preferred method. Keep them warm until ready to use. Peel, core, and finely chop the apples. You should have about 6 cups of chopped apples.

Combine the chopped apples, lemon juice, and water in a large, non-reactive pot. Bring the mixture to a boil over medium heat, then reduce the heat and simmer until the apples are softened. Sprinkle the fruit pectin over the apple mixture, stirring continuously to prevent lumps. Add ground cinnamon, nutmeg, and cloves. Bring the mixture back to a boil.

Gradually add the granulated sugar to the pot, stirring constantly. Bring the mixture back to a rapid boil, stirring frequently to prevent sticking. Continue boiling until the jam reaches the gel point, which is typically around 220°F (105°C). You can test the gel point by placing a small amount of jam on a cold plate and checking if it wrinkles when pushed with your finger.

Once the jam reaches the gel point, remove it from the heat. Skim off any foam that may have formed on the surface. Carefully ladle the hot jam into the prepared sterilized jars, leaving about 1/4-inch headspace. Wipe the jar rims with a clean, damp cloth to ensure a proper seal.

Place the sterilized lids on the jars and screw on the metal bands until fingertip-tight. Process the jars in a boiling water bath for 10-15 minutes to ensure proper sealing. Once processed, remove the jars from the water bath and let them cool on a clean, dry towel. As they cool, you should hear the satisfying "pop" as the lids seal.

After the jars have cooled completely, press down on the center of each lid. If it doesn't pop back, the jar is sealed correctly. If it does pop back, refrigerate that jar and use it within a few weeks.

Label your jars with the date and type of jam. Store them in a cool, dark place.

Herb Infused Honey

Ingredients
1 cup of honey (raw and local honey works well)
Fresh herbs of your choice (rosemary, thyme, lavender, and mint.)

Directions
Prepare the Herbs: Rinse the fresh herbs thoroughly and pat them dry with a paper towel. For rosemary or thyme, you can leave the sprigs intact. If using lavender or mint, you may want to remove the leaves from the stems.

Combine Honey and Herbs: Place the fresh herbs in a clean, dry jar. Pour the honey over the herbs, ensuring they are fully submerged. The honey should cover the herbs completely.

Infusing Process: Seal the jar tightly and let it sit at room temperature for several days to allow the flavors to infuse. The duration of infusion depends on your taste preferences; you can start tasting the honey after 1-2 days.

Taste and Strain: Once the honey reaches your desired flavor intensity, strain out the herbs using a fine-mesh sieve or cheesecloth. Press the herbs gently to extract any remaining infused honey.

Transfer and Store: Pour the infused honey into a clean, airtight jar or bottle for storage. Ensure the container is completely dry to prevent any moisture that could lead to spoilage.

Labeling: Label the jar with the type of herb used and the date of infusion. This will make identifying and tracking the flavor profile easy over time.

Tips: Experiment with different herbs and combinations to discover your favorite flavors.
Ensure that the herbs are completely submerged in honey to prevent spoilage.
Store the infused honey in a cool, dark place to maintain its quality.

CHAPTER 14

Symbols
and
Shapes

Symbols

In many spells, symbols were imbued with profound meaning and power, serving as conduits for mystical energies and intentions. Often rich in esoteric significance, the spell caster carefully selected the symbols to represent specific concepts, deities, elements, or intentions. Whether inscribed on amulets, carved into ritual objects, or drawn in sacred spaces, symbols were believed to bridge the plain and the divine, unlocking hidden forces and facilitating the practitioner's connection to the spiritual realm. Each symbol carries layers of meaning, passed down through generations of practitioners, and their precise arrangement and invocation were crucial for the spell's efficacy. Through these symbols, ancient spellcasters sought to manifest their desires, protect against malevolent forces, and navigate the unseen forces of the cosmos.

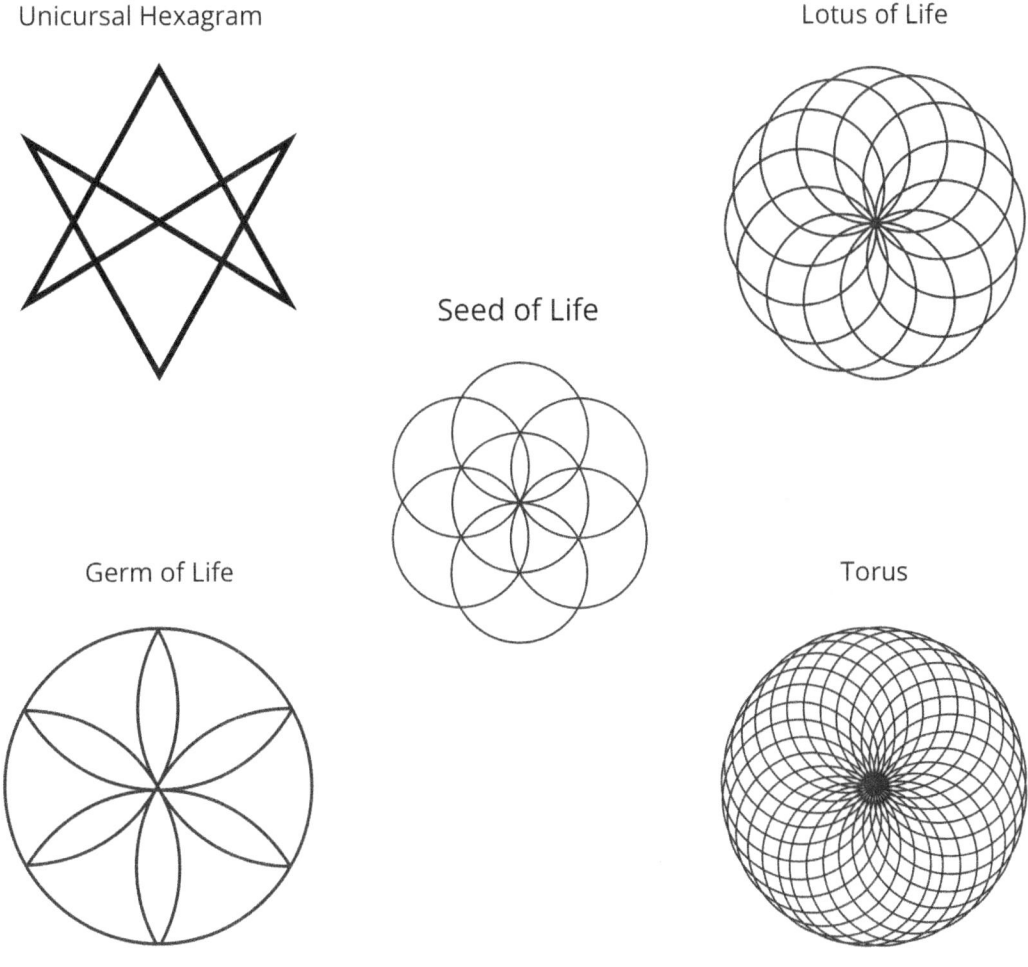

Unicursal Hexagram

Lotus of Life

Seed of Life

Germ of Life

Torus

Symbols

Merkaba

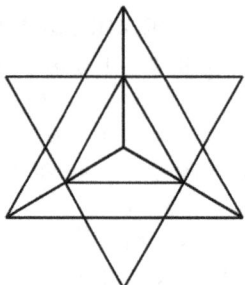

Double Spiral

Golden Spiral

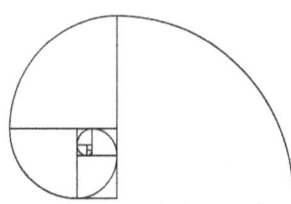

Fruit of Life

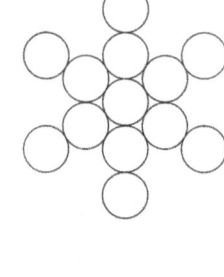

Mandala

Endless Knot

8-Pointed Star
(2 squares)

6-Pointed Star
(2 triangles)

Scared Geometry

Sacred geometry springs from the examination of patterns and relationships found in nature. On the surface that may sound a little dry, but when we look at how basic lines and curves come together to form the universe, it's like taking a wonderful look into the mind of creation.

The Fibonacci spiral and many other forms and patterns we talk about in sacred geometry arise from the Flower of Life, which is seen as the basis for all other patterns in the universe. The study of sacred geometry begins by drawing circles:

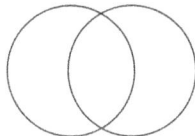
Vesica Piscis
Two intersecting circles form the vesica piscis, seen also in the chalice well symbol

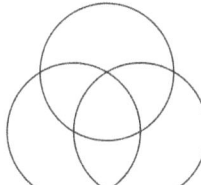
Triquetra
Where three spheres intersect, we see the triquetra, a symbol of sacred trinities

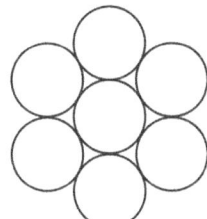
Genesis Pattern
The seed of life is also called the genesis pattern, where six intersecting circles signify the six stages of creation

Egg of Life
The egg of life takes this into three dimensions. The eight non-intersecting spheres can represent the cell division of an embryo

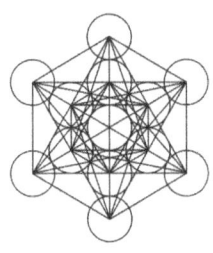
Metatron's Cube
In Metatron's cube, lines connect the centers of the circles in the fruit of life. The lines represent masculine energy, and the circle's feminine energy, so this pattern combines polarities into a unified creation

The 5 Platonic Solids

Sacred geometry involves universal patterns utilized in the design of every element of our reality. Mathematical ratios and proportions are evident in music, light, and cosmology. These foundational patterns of existence are believed to provide insight into the mysteries, laws, and lore of the universe.

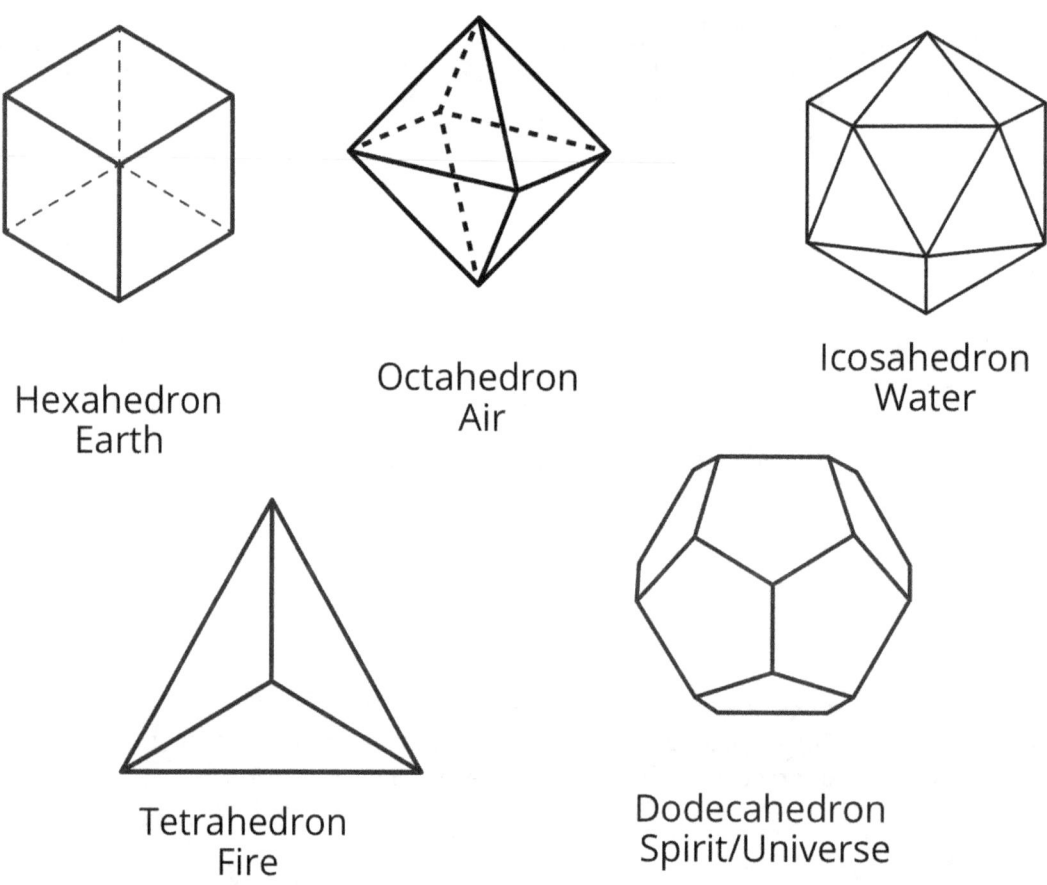

Hexahedron
Earth

Octahedron
Air

Icosahedron
Water

Tetrahedron
Fire

Dodecahedron
Spirit/Universe

Sacred Geometry

Tree of Life

It encloses within it various symbolism's, which are all linked to the concept of Cosmic Creation.

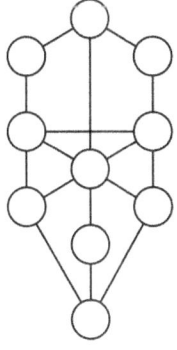

Yantra

They are geometrically sinuous figures that with their precise and particular shapes transmit serenity and positivity.

Yin Yang

The symbolic representation of two diferent counterparts: "Yin" the black and "Yang" the white.

Sri Yantra

The Sri Yantra represents the creation and equilibrium of the Universe.

Omnism

Omniest - A person who does not claim any one religion, practice or belief, but finds truth in them all.

Yoruba Traditions
"One who does evil to another does so to himself." - proverb

Atheism
"Treat others as you would want them to treat you and can reasonably expect them to want to be treated. Think about their perspective."
-The 10 Non-Commandments

Christianity
"Do unto others as you would have them do unto you."
-Matthew 7:12

Zoroastrianism
"Whatever is disagreeable to yourself, do not do unto others.
-Shayast-na-Shayast 13:29

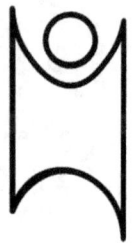

Humanism
"Before performing an action which might harm another person, try to imagine yourself in their position, and consider whether you would want to be the recipient of that action. If you would not want to be in such a position, the other person probably would not either, and so you should not do it."
-Adam Lee

Bahá'í Faith
"And if thine eyes be turned towards justice, choose thou for thy neighbour that which thou choosest for thyself."
-Tablets of Bahá'u'lláh

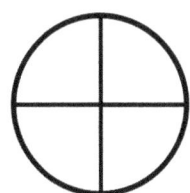

First Peoples
"Even though you and I are in diferent boats, you in your boat and we our canoe, we share the same river of life. What befalls me befalls you." -Oren Lyons, Turtle Clan, Seneca Nation

Jainism
"A man should wander about treating all creatures as he himself would be treated."
-Sutrakritanga 1.11.33

Islam
"By no means shall you attain righteousness unless you give freely to others of that which you love; and whatever you give, of a truth Allah knows it well."
-Qur'an 3:92

Wicca
"And it harm none, do
what thou wilt." - Wiccan Rede

Judaism
"What is hateful to you, do not do to your fellow: this is the whole Torah; the rest is commentary; go and learn."
-Babylonian Talmud

Sikhism
"As you see yourself, see others as well; only then will you become a partner in heaven."
-Sri Guru Granth Sahib Ji, 480

Hinduism

"This is the sum of Dharma
-duty: Do nothing unto others which would cause
you pain if done to you."
-Mahabharata 5:1517

Shinto

The heart of the person before you is a mirror. See there your
own form."

Confucianism

"Tse-kung asked, 'Is there one word that can serve as a
principle of conduct for life?' Confucius
-Doctrine of the Mean 13.3

Taoism

"Regard your neighbor's gain as your gain, and
your neighbor's loss as your own loss."

Buddhism

"All are afraid of the stick, all
fear death. Putting oneself in another's place, one should not hurt or
kill others."
-Dhammapada, verse 129

Unitarianism

"We affirm and promote respect for the interdependent web of all
existence of which we are a part."
-7th Principle

Take Care Of You

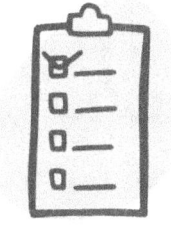

Intention/
Goal Setting + Planning

(Journaling,
Reading + Learning
Something New

Recreational
Creativity + Play

Tuning into your
Body, Mind, and Spirit

Recreating/Exploring
Your Environment

CHAPTER 15

Simmer Pots

Simmer Pots

In the world of spellwork, where the senses intertwine with intention, simmer pots have emerged as a captivating technique that marries the power of fragrance with the art of magic. Simmer pots, much like modern cauldrons, offer a unique and sensory-rich way to infuse spaces with intent, utilizing aromatic ingredients to conjure an atmosphere ripe for spells and manifestations. In this brief exploration, we'll uncover the transformative potential of simmer pots in spellwork, where the gentle dance of steam becomes a conduit for weaving intentions into the fabric of reality.

Mabon Simmer Pots

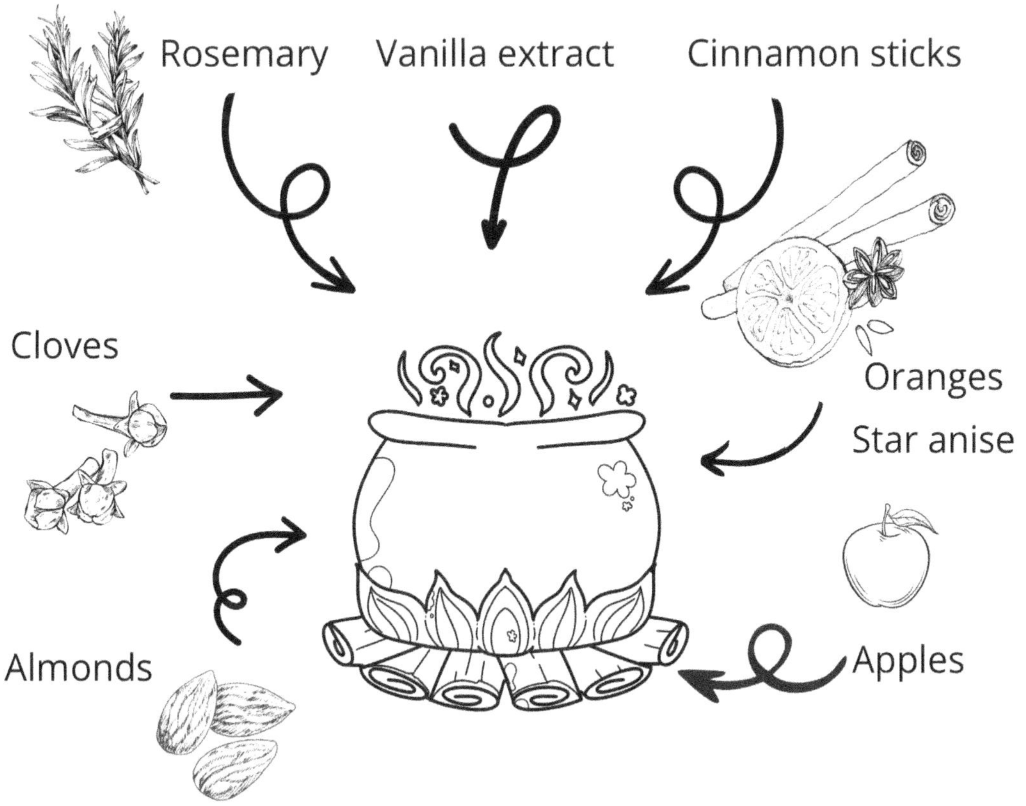

Rosemary   Vanilla extract   Cinnamon sticks

Cloves

Oranges

Star anise

Almonds

Apples

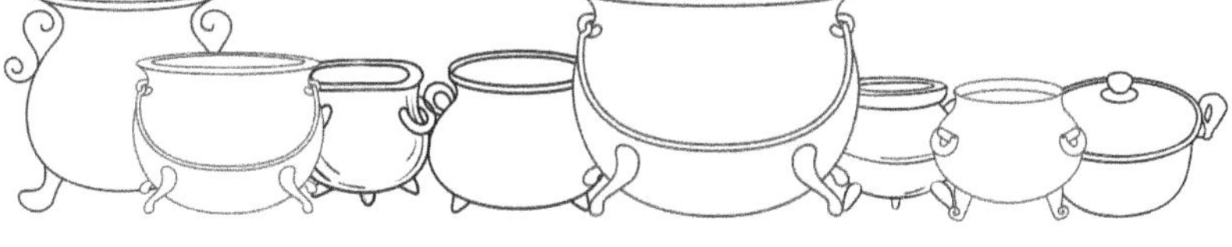

Prosperity Simmer Pots

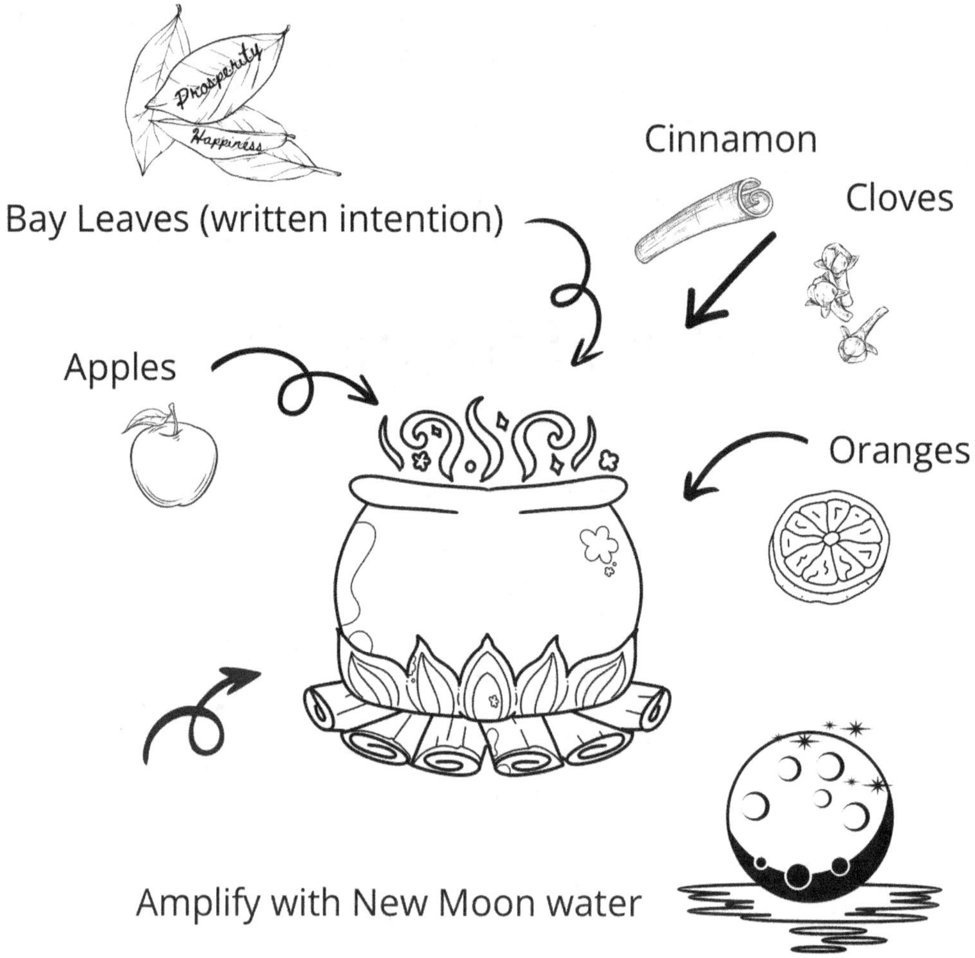

Bay Leaves (written intention)

Prosperity
Happiness

Cinnamon

Cloves

Apples

Oranges

Amplify with New Moon water

Calm Simmer Pot

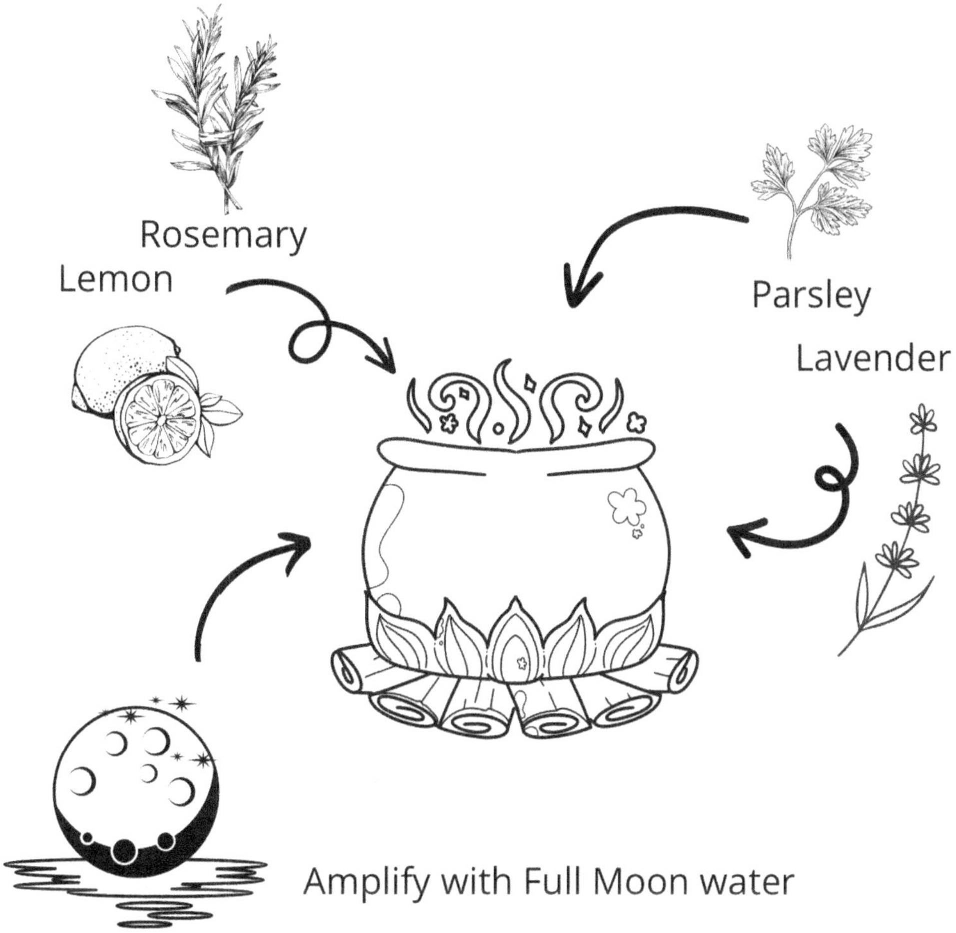

Rosemary

Lemon

Parsley

Lavender

Amplify with Full Moon water

Harvest Simmer Pot

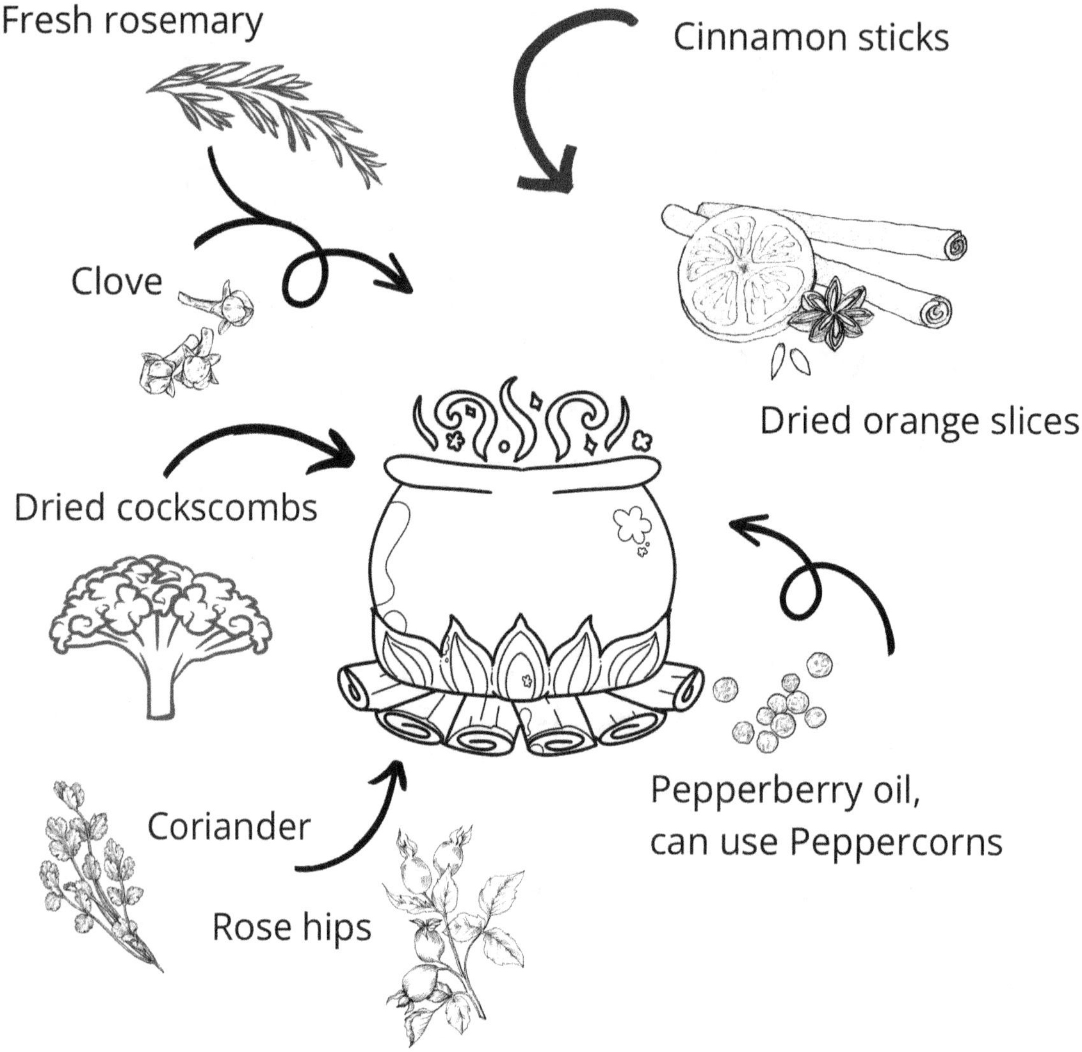

Fresh rosemary

Cinnamon sticks

Clove

Dried orange slices

Dried cockscombs

Coriander

Rose hips

Pepperberry oil,
can use Peppercorns

Love & Happiness Simmer Pot

Bay Leaves (written intentions on them)

Red Rose Petals

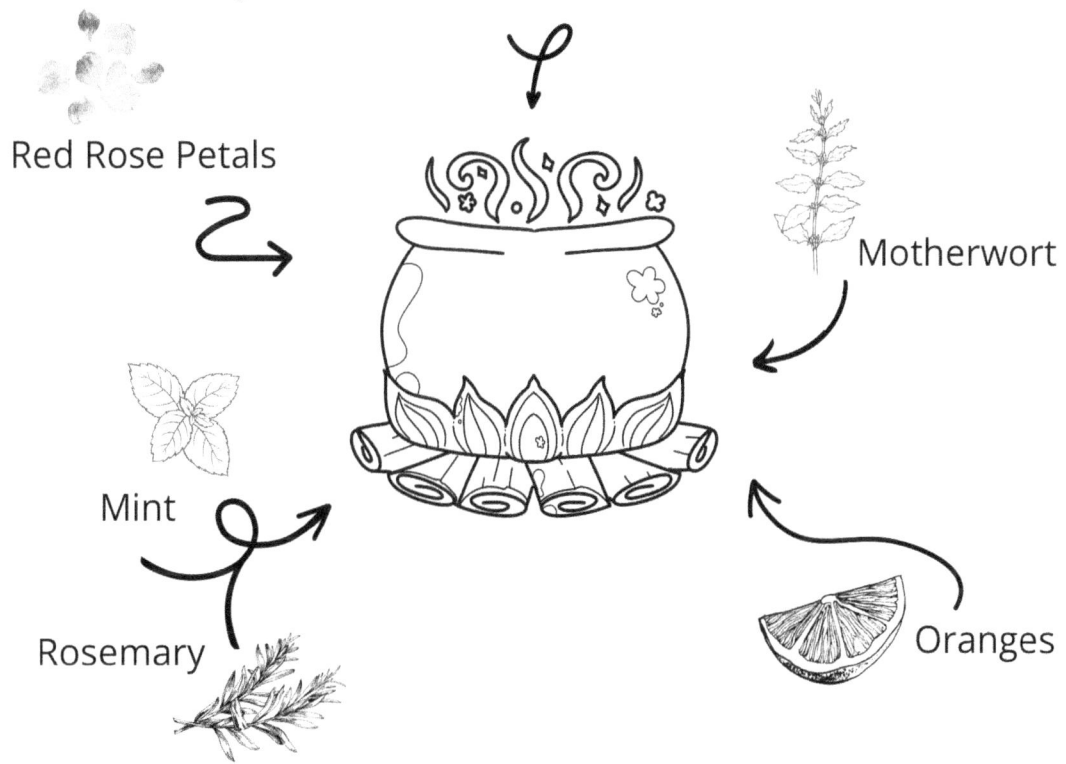

Motherwort

Mint

Rosemary

Oranges

Cleansing Simmer Pot

Bay Leaves (written intentions on them)

Allspice

Cinnamon

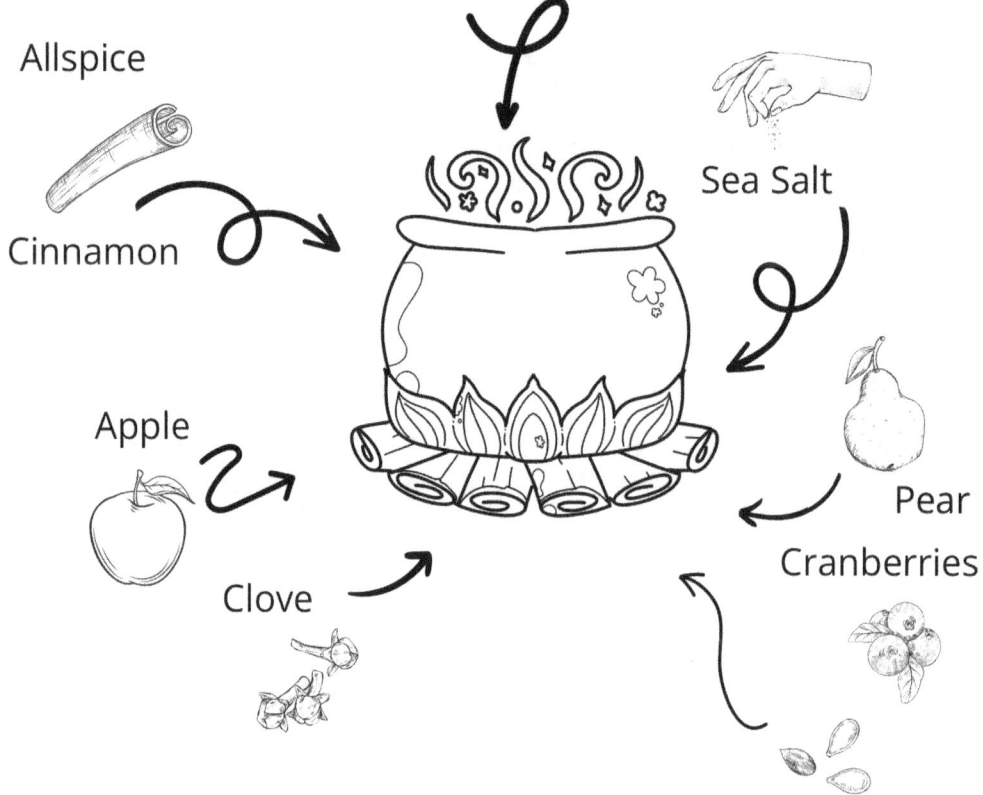

Sea Salt

Apple

Clove

Pear

Cranberries

Pumpkin seeds

Cold and Flu Fighter

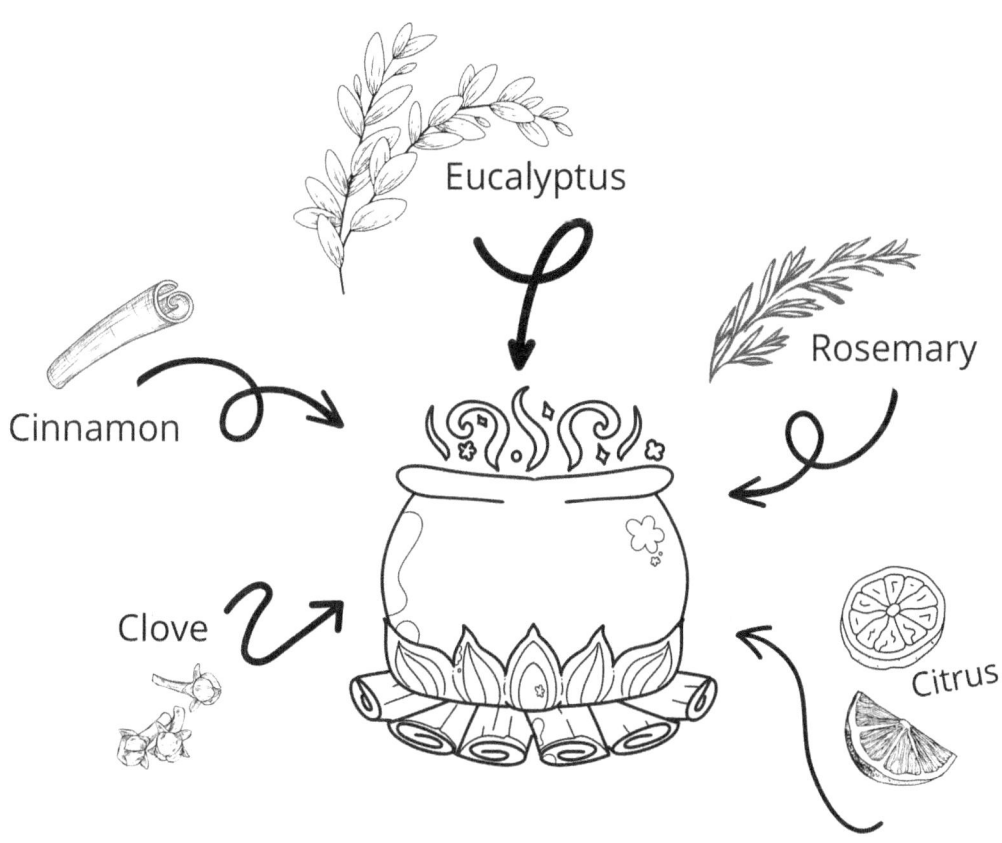

Eucalyptus

Cinnamon

Rosemary

Clove

Citrus

Spiritual Connection

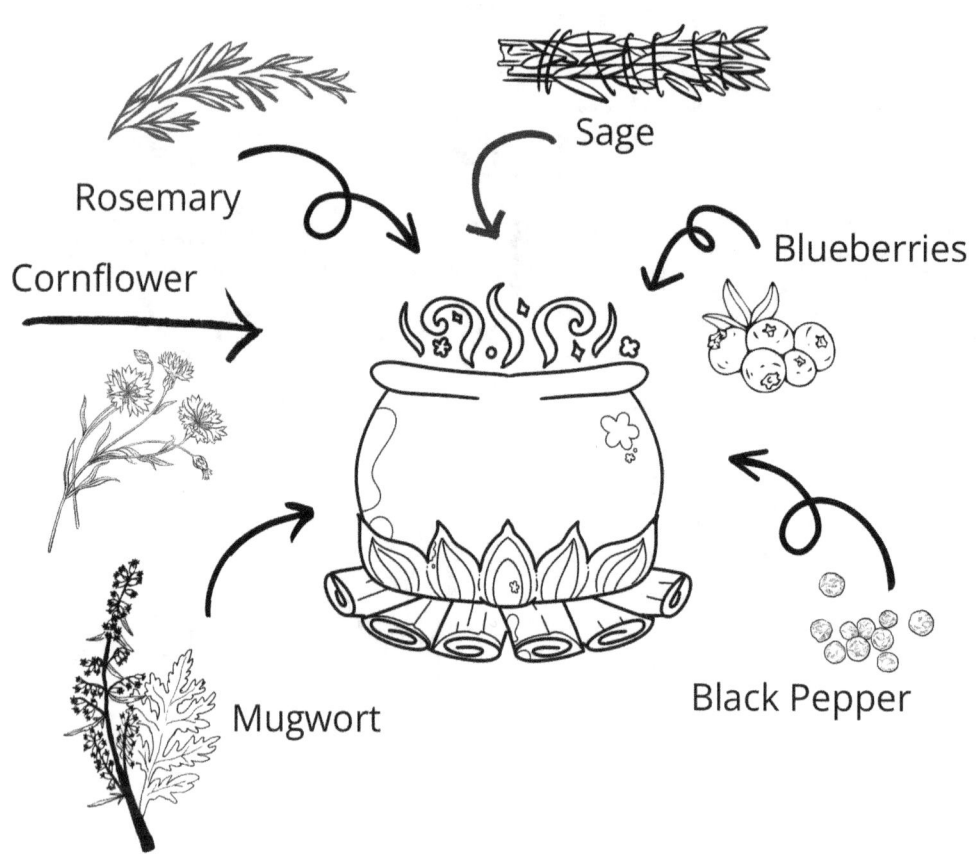

Rosemary

Sage

Cornflower

Blueberries

Mugwort

Black Pepper

CHAPTER 16

Spell Jars

Spell Jars

Introduction: Within the realm of spellwork, where intention meets ritual, one finds a fascinating and versatile tool known as the spell jar. These enchanting vessels encapsulate the essence of intention, allowing practitioners to blend their desires with tangible and visually captivating symbolic items. In this concise exploration, we will delve into the art of spell jars, understanding how these small, intricately crafted containers can serve as conduits for focused energy, manifestation, and personal transformation.

Protection & Positivity

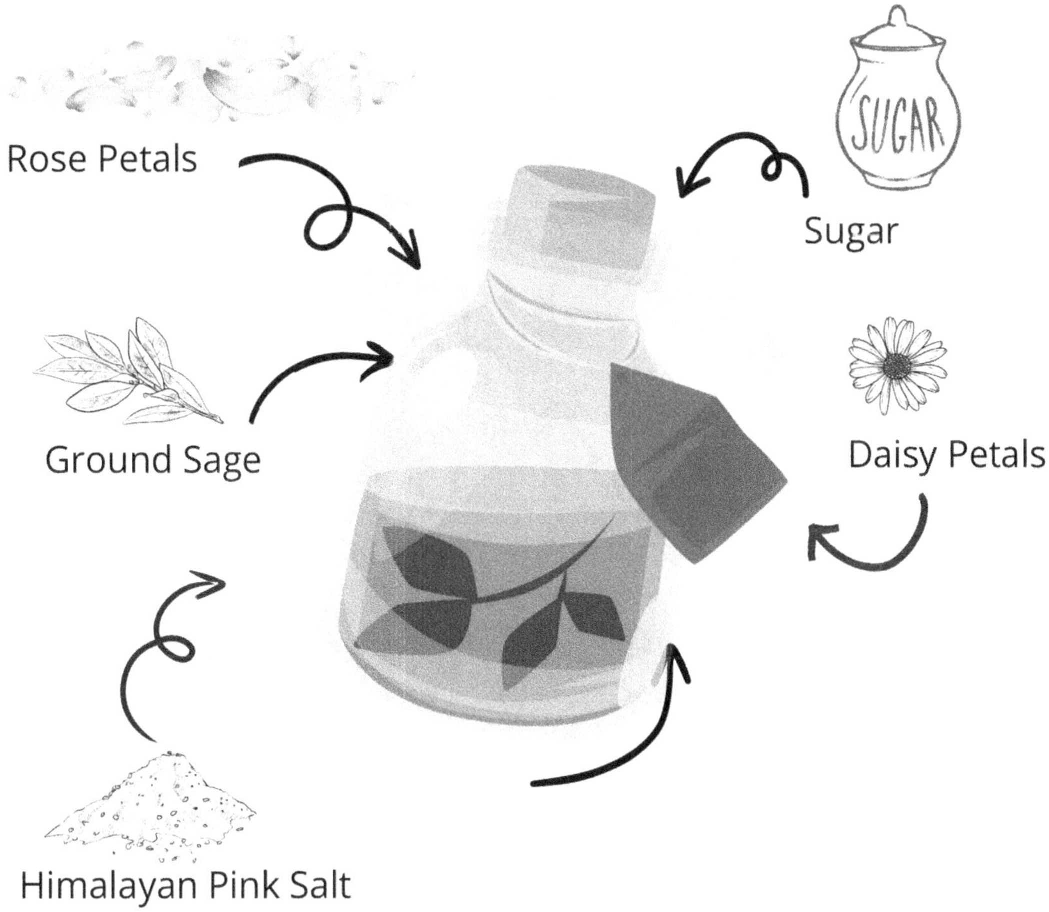

Rose Petals

Sugar

Ground Sage

Daisy Petals

Himalayan Pink Salt

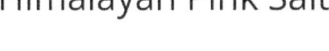

Motivation Spell Jar

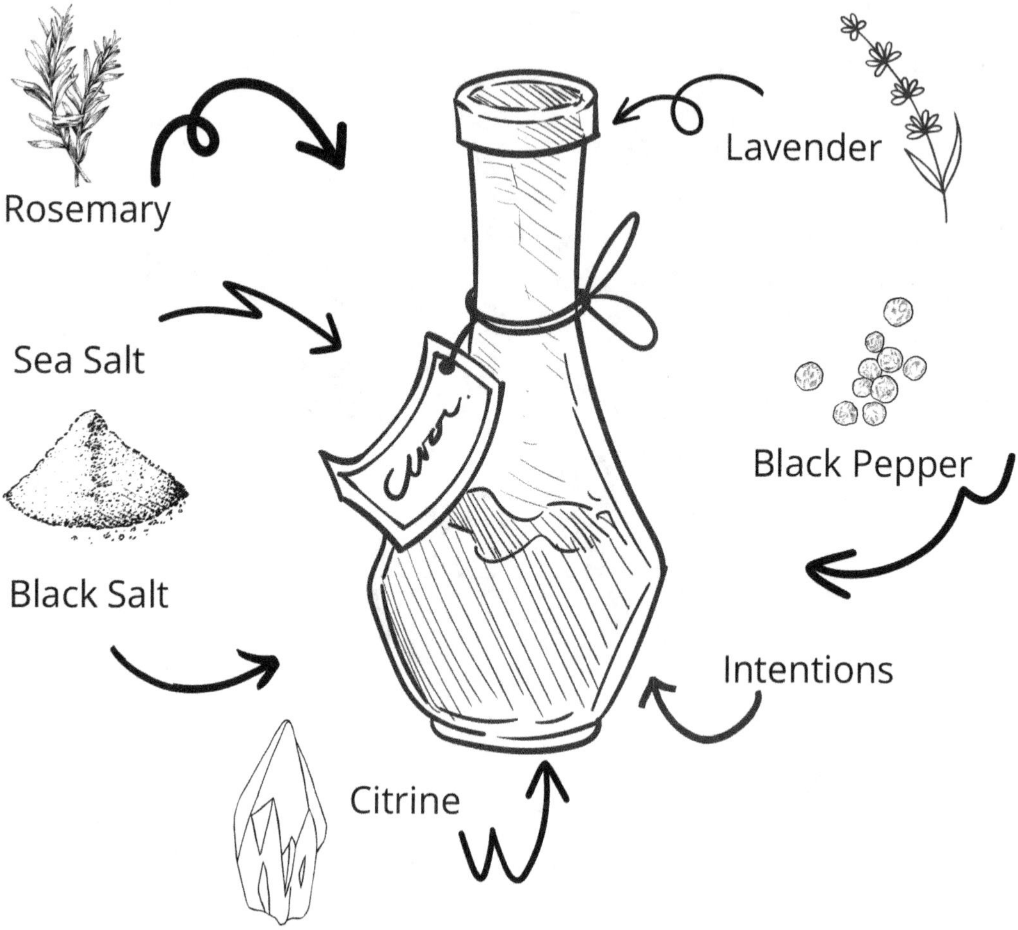

Rosemary

Lavender

Sea Salt

Black Salt

Black Pepper

Citrine

Intentions

Protection Spell Jar

Bay Leaves (written intentions on them)

Protect me

Safety

Cloves

Egg Shells

Lavender

Cinnamon

Incense Ash

Garlic Skins

Clear Quartz
(programmed with intentions)

Doorstep Rice Spell

Fill a jar with raw white rice without sealing it. Place the jar by the front door for protection. Remember that rice absorbs negative energy rather than repelling it. Replace the rice with fresh raw rice weekly. Avoid bringing old rice back into your home or cooking it. Dispose of it outside your home by burning, scattering, or throwing it away.

Anti-Anxiety Spell Jar

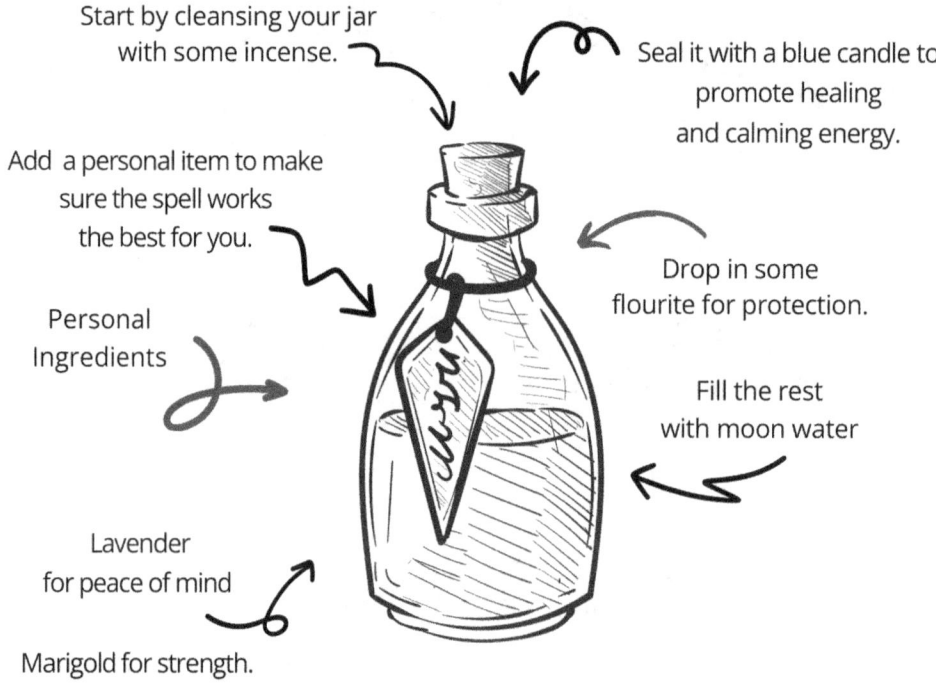

Start by cleansing your jar with some incense.

Seal it with a blue candle to promote healing and calming energy.

Add a personal item to make sure the spell works the best for you.

Drop in some flourite for protection.

Personal Ingredients

Fill the rest with moon water

Lavender for peace of mind

Marigold for strength.

CHAPTER 17

Candle
Magic

Candle Magic

The flickering glow of a candle flame is a potent tool of magic—a conduit between the material and spiritual realms. Candle magic is an ancient practice woven into the fabric of witchcraft, paganism, and many other traditions.

May your path be illuminated and your spirit enlightened with the burning flames.

The Significance of Candle Colors
In the dance of candlelight, the colors of the candle hold profound significance, each a vibrant expression of the energies we seek to invoke. When exploring candle magic, it is important to understand colors' symbolic power, guiding us on our journey of manifestation and spiritual awakening.

White: The pristine glow of a white candle symbolizes purity, clarity, and divine illumination.

Red: A fiery beacon of passion and vitality, the red candle ignites the flames of desire and action.

Green: Like the lush foliage of the earth, the green candle represents abundance, growth, and prosperity.

Blue: The tranquil hue of the blue candle invokes the calming energies of serenity, wisdom, and communication.

Yellow: Radiant as the sun's golden rays, the yellow candle embodies joy, creativity, and intellectual stimulation.

Purple: Regal and mysterious, the purple candle symbolizes spiritual insight, intuition, and divine guidance.

Black: The velvety depths of the black candle's flame contain the potent energies of protection, banishment, and transformation.

Orange: The vibrant hue of the orange candle radiates with the energies of creativity, vitality, and success.

Pink: Soft as the blush of dawn, the pink candle embodies the energies of love, compassion, and emotional healing.

As we adorn our altars with candles of myriad hues, let us honor the profound significance of color in our magical practices. Each flame becomes a vessel of transformation, carrying our intentions aloft on the wings of vibrant energy as we navigate the labyrinthine paths of the witch's wheel.

The Shapes of Candles

In candle magic, the shape of a candle is more than aesthetics; it is a language unto itself, speaking volumes of symbolism and intent.

Taper Candles: Elegant and slender, taper candles symbolize focus, direction, and spiritual ascension.

Pillar Candles: Solid and steadfast pillar candles embody stability, endurance, and foundation.

Tealights: Small yet mighty, tealights radiate with the energies of illumination, warmth, and intimacy.

Votive Candles: In a protective vessel, votive candles symbolize containment, protection, and introspection.

Figure Candles: Crafted in the likeness of human forms or symbolic shapes, figure candles embody the essence of their design. Whether representing individuals, deities, or abstract concepts, these candles serve as potent focal points for spellwork, channeling energy with precision and purpose.

Floating Candles: Drifting serenely upon the water's surface, floating candles evoke the fluidity of emotion, intuition, and subconscious exploration.

Container Candles: Nestled within vessels of glass or metal, container candles symbolize containment, protection, and preservation.

As we decorate our sacred spaces with candles of various shapes and sizes, let's pay tribute to the deep symbolism infused in their core. Every flame acts as a trigger for change, sparking the magic within us and lighting the way to spiritual awakening. Together, let's welcome the power of shapes into our mystical rituals, crafting spells of purpose and realization with elegance and insight.

Talking Candles
High, steady flame - Yes.
Low, steady flame - No.
Short, weak flame - No.
Dancing flame - Needs more focus. Re-ground, concentrate, and ask again.
Violently flickering flame - Strong no. Take this as a warning (if you are positive the flickering is not caused by any outside force).
Sputtering and crackling flame - There is more to your answer than a simple yes or no.
Dual-Flame - Thinking, wait for your answer.
Flame leaning to the left - Yes.
Flame leaning to the right - No.
Candle will not light - Now is not the right time to ask.
Candle will not go out - You are not done yet. There is more to your answer that you need to hear.
Candle goes out on its own before giving an answer - Now is not the right time to ask.

Candle Fragrances

Each scent carries memories, emotions, and energies, imbuing our rituals with layers of meaning. On the journey through the fragrant realms of enchantment, we will explore the significance of scent in the practice of candle magic.

Lavender: With its soothing aroma reminiscent of fields in bloom, lavender is a beloved ally in matters of tranquility, relaxation, and inner peace.

Sandalwood: Rich and earthy, sandalwood invokes the grounding energies of the earth, anchoring us to the present moment and deepening our connection to the sacred.

Rose: The timeless scent of rose evokes the essence of love, beauty, and divine femininity.

Patchouli: With its heady aroma of musk and spice, patchouli is a potent ally in matters of prosperity, protection, and sensuality.

Frankincense: Revered for millennia for its sacred properties, frankincense exudes an aura of sanctity, purification, and spiritual illumination.

Citrus: Vibrant and uplifting, citrus scents such as lemon, orange, and grapefruit infuse our rituals with the energies of joy, vitality, and optimism.

Cedarwood: Steeped in the wisdom of the ancients, cedarwood emanates the protective energies of the forest, warding off malevolent forces and creating sacred space.

Cinnamon: Spicy and invigorating, cinnamon ignites the fires of passion, creativity, and abundance.

Infusing rituals with these aromatic allies, each scent becomes a thread in the tapestry of spells, weaving intricate patterns of intention and invocation upon the winds of destiny. Embrace the transformative power of scent and journey deeper into enchantment and self-discovery.

Illuminating the Art of Spellcasting

At the heart of candle magic lies the ancient art of spellcasting—a sacred meeting of intention and manifestation, where the flicker of a flame becomes a conduit for realizing your deepest desires.

Setting Intentions: Spellcasting begins with clarity of intention—a focused desire or goal that serves as the guiding light of our magical endeavors. Each candle imbues itself with the essence of our intentions, infusing the flame with the energy of our desires and aspirations.

Creating Ritual: Central to spellcasting is ritual crafting, a sacred container for our magical workings, where intention meets action in a harmonious union of mind, body, and spirit. Through ritual, honor the ancient rhythms of the earth and the cycles of the moon, aligning with the forces of nature to amplify the potency of our spells.

Working with Correspondences: In the intricate web of spellcasting, every color, shape, fragrance, and symbol carries its unique vibration, aligning with specific intentions and energies. By harnessing the power of correspondences, we enhance the efficacy of our spells, weaving together elements that resonate harmoniously with our intentions to create potent magical recipes.

Empowering the Flame: As we light the candle, we ignite the spark of magic within, calling forth the elemental forces of fire to fuel our intentions and illuminate the path to manifestation. With each flicker of the flame, we offer our prayers to the universe, surrendering to the flow of energy and trusting in the wisdom of divine timing.

Visualization and Focus: As the candle burns, we enter into a state of focused meditation, visualizing our desires with crystal clarity and infusing them with the power of our will. Through the focused gaze of our mind's eye, we project our intentions into the flame, trusting in its transformative alchemy to manifest our desires in the physical realm.

Releasing and Letting Go: As the flame consumes the candle's wax, we must release our attachment to the outcome of our spells, trusting the manifestation process to unfold in its own time and way. With gratitude in our hearts and faith in the unseen forces that guide us, we surrender our intentions to the universe, knowing that they will be fulfilled in accordance with the highest good of all.

With each candle we light, may we be reminded of the infinite possibilities at our fingertips and the boundless power of the human spirit to shape our destiny with love, wisdom, and grace.

Decoding the Flames

The flame is more than just a source of light; it is a living symbol, a dynamic entity that communicates with us through its flickers, dances, and whispers.

Steady Flame: A steady flame, unwavering and strong, symbolizes stability, focus, and clarity of intention. It speaks of a harmonious alignment of energies, where our desires are firmly rooted in the fertile soil of our hearts, and our will is unwavering in its resolve.

Dancing Flame: A flame that dances and flickers with wild abandon evokes the energies of change, transformation, and movement. It signifies the presence of unseen forces at work, stirring the cauldron of creation and ushering in new beginnings and opportunities.

Sputtering Flame: An erratic and unpredictable sputtering flame signals disturbances in the energetic field and the need for purification and release. It may indicate the presence of stagnant or negative energies that require clearing or unresolved emotions that need to be addressed.

Tall Flame: A tall flame, reaching skyward with graceful determination, symbolizes strength, power, and the upward movement of energy. It signifies a surge of vitality and inspiration, propelling us toward our goals with unwavering confidence and resolve.

Low Flame: A low flame, flickering close to the wick with gentle intensity, speaks of introspection, introspection, and the need for rest and rejuvenation. It invites us to turn inward, listen to our soul's whispers, and replenish our inner reserves of strength and wisdom.

Split Flame: A split flame, dividing into two or more separate tongues of fire, suggests duality, polarity, and the need for balance. It reminds us of the interconnectedness of all things and the importance of honoring the light and shadow within ourselves and the world around us.

Colorful Flame: A flame that glows with vibrant blue, green, or purple hues signifies the presence of spiritual energies and divine guidance. It indicates a deepening connection to the higher realms and the awakening of psychic abilities and intuition.

Smokeless Flame: A flame that burns brightly without producing smoke embodies purity, clarity, and the absence of negativity. It signifies the presence of clear and aligned energies, free from obstacles or hindrances, and invites us to bask in the radiant glow of divine light and inspiration.

As we observe the flames that dance upon our candles, let us open our hearts and minds to the wisdom they impart, for in their flickers and dances lie the secrets of the universe and the keys to unlocking the mysteries of our souls.

Candle Spells

Abundance Blessing Spell
Ingredients: Green candle, Cinnamon oil, Bay leaf, Small piece of citrine or aventurine.
Instructions: Begin on the eve of Mabon, the autumn equinox. Anoint the green candle with cinnamon oil, focusing on drawing abundance into your life.
Light the candle and place it on your altar. Hold the citrine or aventurine in your hand, envisioning your goals and desires for abundance.
Write your intentions for abundance on the bay leaf and place it under the candle holder. Sit quietly, meditating on gratitude and abundance, allowing the candle to burn for at least 10-15 minutes.
Snuff out the candle, keeping the bay leaf and crystal on your altar until your desires manifest.

Harvest Blessing Spell
Ingredients: Orange candle, Patchouli oil, harvested fruits and vegetables (e.g., apples, pumpkins, grains)
Instructions: Set up your altar with the orange candle surrounded by the harvest produce. Anoint the candle with patchouli oil, infusing it with the season's energy.
Light the candle, focusing on gratitude for the abundance of the harvest.
Take each piece of produce in your hands, visualizing it as a symbol of prosperity and nourishment. Offer words of thanks for the Earth's bounty, expressing appreciation for the sustenance it provides.
Sit in quiet reflection, soaking in the energy of the harvest and allowing the candle to burn down completely.

Balance and Renewal Spell
Ingredients: White candle, Lavender oil, Feather
Light the candle, focusing on the energy of equilibrium as day
and night is of equal length during Mabon. Hold the featheFeatherour hand,
symbolizing the element of air and the gentle breeze
of change.
Close your eyes and visualize any imbalances in your life
being restored to harmony.
Whisper words of affirmation for renewal and balance,
feeling the lightness of spirit that comes with alignment.
Allow the candle to burn down completely, carrying your
intentions of balance and renewal out
into the universe.

CHAPTER 18

Divination

Divination

Divination is a practice deeply rooted in human history, spanning cultures and civilizations across time. At its core, divination is the art of seeking insight and guidance from mystical or supernatural sources to gain an understanding of the past, present, or future. It's a fascinating journey involving various methods, such as reading omens in nature, interpreting patterns in celestial bodies, or deciphering symbols through intricate tools like tarot cards, runes, and crystal balls. Divination offers us a unique perspective into the unknown, providing a glimpse into the threads of fate that weave through our lives. As we embark on this exploration, we will delve into divination's history, techniques, and cultural significance, fostering a deeper appreciation for the diverse ways societies have sought to connect with the hidden forces that shape our world.

Tarot Cards

Tarot is an intricate divination system comprising 78 cards divided into major and minor arcana. Heavily relying on classical mythology and symbolism, tarot allows one to receive answers to events by interpreting messages based on how the cards are dealt. This can be done utilizing card spreads like the classic Celtic cross or a simple three-card past, present, and future layout.

Oracle Cards

Less structured than tarot, oracle cards combine artwork and written interpretations, which can sometimes include exercises. They can be based on nearly any subject matter and are open to various styles and formats. They are perfect for guiding without the intricacies associated with tarot.

Draw Your Cards

There are multiple ways to select the cards for your reading. Cutting the deck with one hand and pulling the card on top is a simple, no-nonsense approach. Another way is to hold the deck in one hand and tilt it to reveal a gap; you can take the top card. Next, you can fan the cards out and choose the card your intuition pulls you to. Finally, draw a single card for a simple reading or several cards for what's known as a spread. Tarot spreads can speak more broadly to your situation. The more cards you use in a spread, the more in-depth the reading tends to be, but a big spread can be overwhelming for beginners.

After you choose your card(s), lay them down in your pattern for the spread. Now, you can gaze at them, pay attention to what comes immediately to mind, and then go from there.

Interpret the card(s) you draw.
Stay focused on the cards and the feelings you get, connect the cards to your senses, and write down what comes to mind. After your impressions are completely logged, look in the companion book for the general meaning of the cards you pulled. That's it. Eazy Peezey.

Seeking Inspiration

1-Where can I Look to find inspiration
2-An energy I need to reject to feel motivated
3-An energy I need to accept to feel inspired
4-Imagery on that card will fuel my inspiration
5-Why I am eager to feel inspired

Help and Guidance From Your Angels

Card 1 - A message from my angel
Card 2 - What this angel is helping me with
Card 3 - Something this angel wants me to know
Card 4 - The area of my life I'm learning these lessons
Card 5 - How this impacts my life
Card 6 - How this lesson makes me a better person

Moving Foreward

Card 1 - How should I start the process of moving forward
Card 2 - Which emotions do I have to fully feel before letting go
Card 3 - Something that is influencing my decisions
Card 4 - A quality I possess that will give me strength
Card 5 - Most important lesson I will learn from this experience
Card 6 - Where is the wind taking me next

Vibe Check

Card 1 - What is today's energy
Card 2 - What do I need to be aware of to help me navigate this energy

Strength and Weakness

Card 1 - What is my strength
Card 2 - What is my weakness

Comfort When Stressed

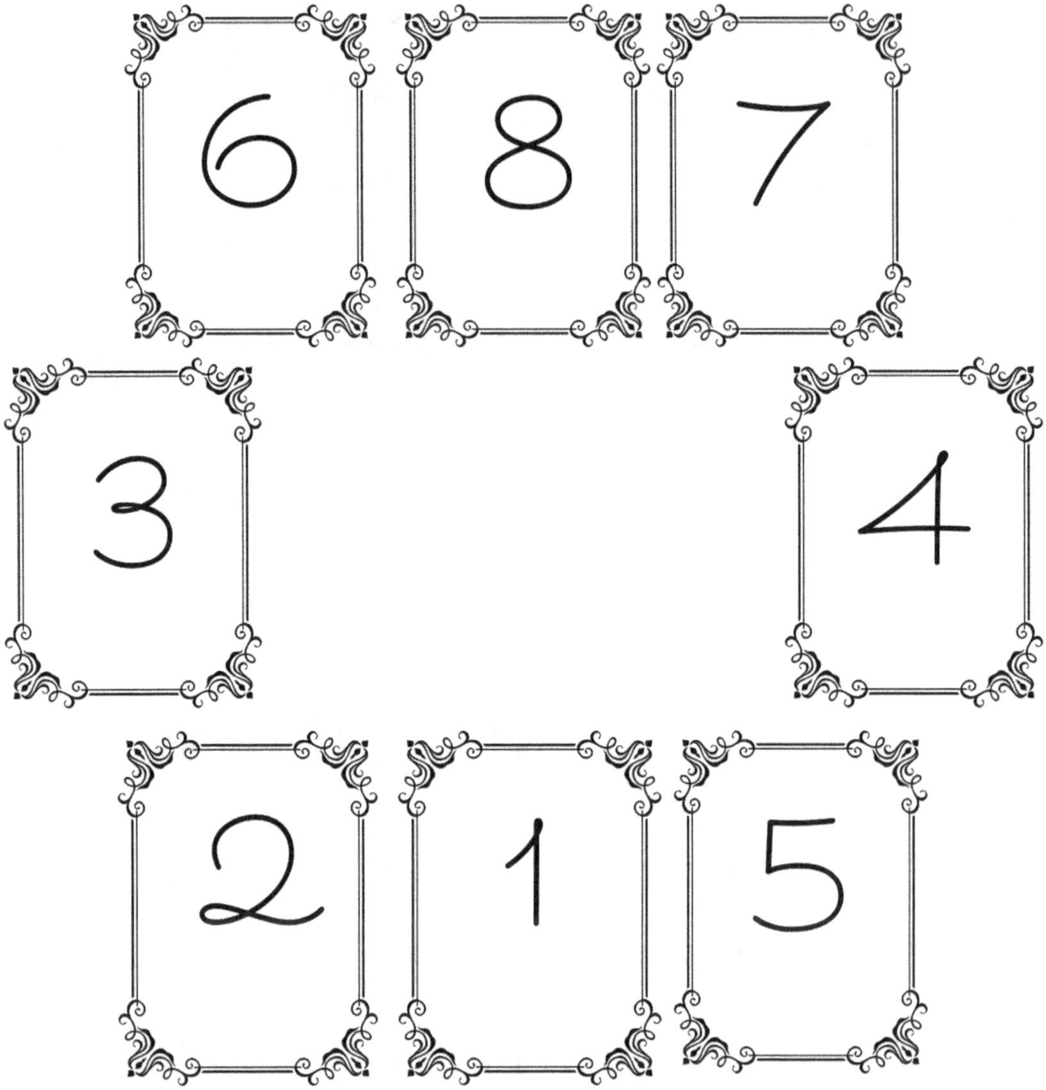

6   8   7

3   4

2   1   5

Card 1 - Your current situation
Card 2 - What's creating stress in your life
Card 3 - Something that can bring you comfort at the moment
Card 4 - Something inspiring or motivating to focus on right now
Card 5 - A way to resolve the stress or issue that is causing you stress
Card 6 - Someone or something that can offer you support.
Card 7 - Something to be hopeful about and look forward to
Card 8 - A near-future event

Prosperity

7	6	8
	4	5
2	1	3

Card 1 - Current financial situation

Card 2 - Financial lessons you have learned from the past

Card 3 - Financial issues you need to overcome presently

Card 4 - First step into improving your current situation

Card 5 - Money-making opportunities you may be overlooking

Card 6 - Who can help you currently

Card 7 - What do prosperity and good fortune look like to you, and methods to getting these things

Card 8 - Financial outcomes and advice for the near future.

Feeling Heavy

If you already know what is weighing you down, intentionally pull out a card or object that symbolizes your issue/situation instead of drawing a card.

Card 1 - What is weighing me down

Card 2 - How can I address this issue/situation in a healthy manner

Card 3 - What action(s) can I take to prevent this issue/situation from weighing me down in the future

Card 4 - What can I do to help lift some of this weight right now

Card 5 - Guiding Energies- this card relays any further messages you may need to hear

Friendship Spread

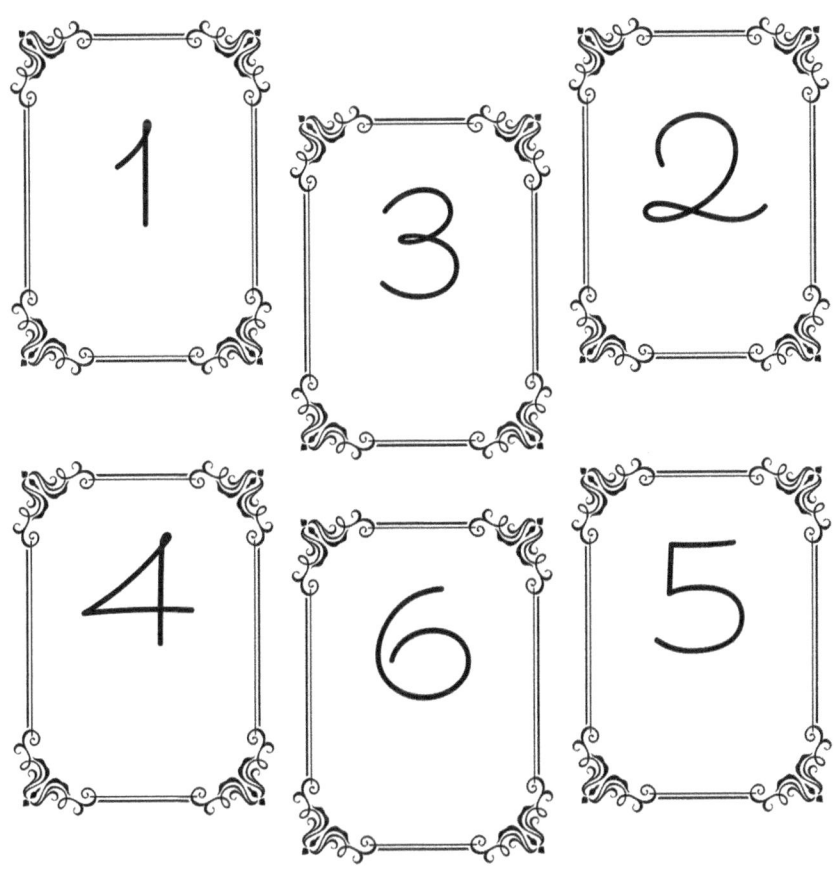

Card 1 - How you feel about the friendship
Card 2 - How they feel about the friendship
Card 3 - Problems in friendship
Card 4 - What you can do to help
Card 5 - What they can do to help
Card 6 - Likely outcome

The Daily Spread

Card 1 - Challenge for the day
Card 2 - Energy to use today
Card 3 - Energy to avoid today
Card 4 - Positivity for the day

Mabon

Card 1 - What part of my life is ready to flourish
Card 2 - How can I nurture this growth
Card 3 - What new seeds need to be planted now
Card 4 - What needs to be weeded out of my life

Autumn Equinox

Card 1 - What has to grow
Card 2 - What to keep
Card 3 - What to give
Card 4 - What to receive

Autumn Equinox

Card 1 - Where to focus my energy this season
Card 2 - Growth I'm bringing into Autumn
Card 3 - An obstacle of this season
Card 4 - Something to shed
Card 5 - Something to forgive
Card 6 - Something to harvest
Card 7 - Something to embrace

Mabon Offering

```
        ┌───┐
 ┌───┐  │ 2 │  ┌───┐
 │ 1 │  └───┘  │ 3 │
 └───┘         └───┘
        ┌──────┐
        │  My  │
        │Offerings│
        └──────┘
 ┌───┐  ┌───┐  ┌───┐
 │ 4 │  │ 5 │  │ 6 │
 └───┘  └───┘  └───┘
```

Place a small offering(s) in the center of your reading (examples: apple, crystal, herbs, something from nature, etc.); after reading, take and place it on your altar.

Card 1 - How should I be giving thanks for my "harvest"

Card 2 - What can I learn from the coming darkness

Card 3 - How can I best utilize these shorter days

Card 4 - How can I create more balance in my life

Card 5 - What must I shed for the coming season

Card 6 - What lessons have I learned from the year

Daily To Do

Card 1 - How can I feel grounded during the day ahead
Card 2 - Something I should make time for today
Card 3 - How can I embrace each moment and live in the present
Card 4 - How can I remain connected to Mother Earth today
Card 5 - A message from Mother Earth

Week Ahead

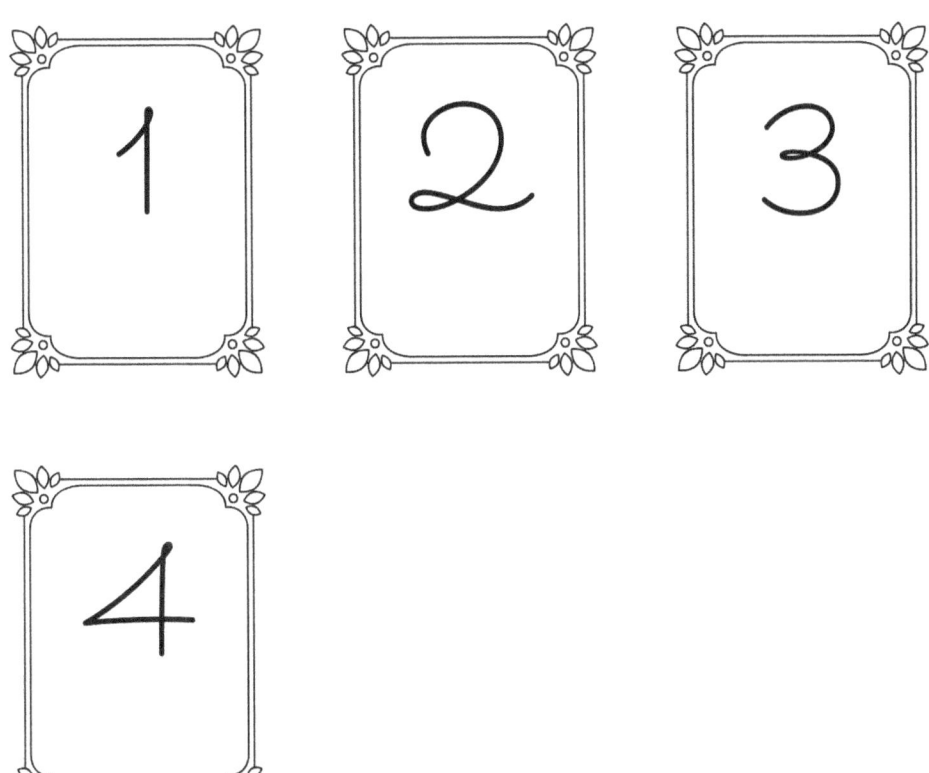

Card 1 - Expectations you have for the week ahead
Card 2 - Feelings to embrace throughout the week
Card 3 - Energy to bring with you into the week
Card 4 - Fears to leave behind you

Stress Reducer

Card 1 - The root of my current stress
Card 2 - The healthiest way to cope with this stress
Card 3 - Important lesson I am learning
Card 4 - Something I do not see clearly
Card 5 - How to avoid this problem in the future

Living Authentically

3

2   4

1   5

Card 1 - Card to describe me living authentically
Card 2 - What can I change to live more authentically
Card 3 - Why I feel called to live more authentically
Card 4 - A part of myself that feels neglected
Card 5 - How can I start honoring my authentic self

Theme

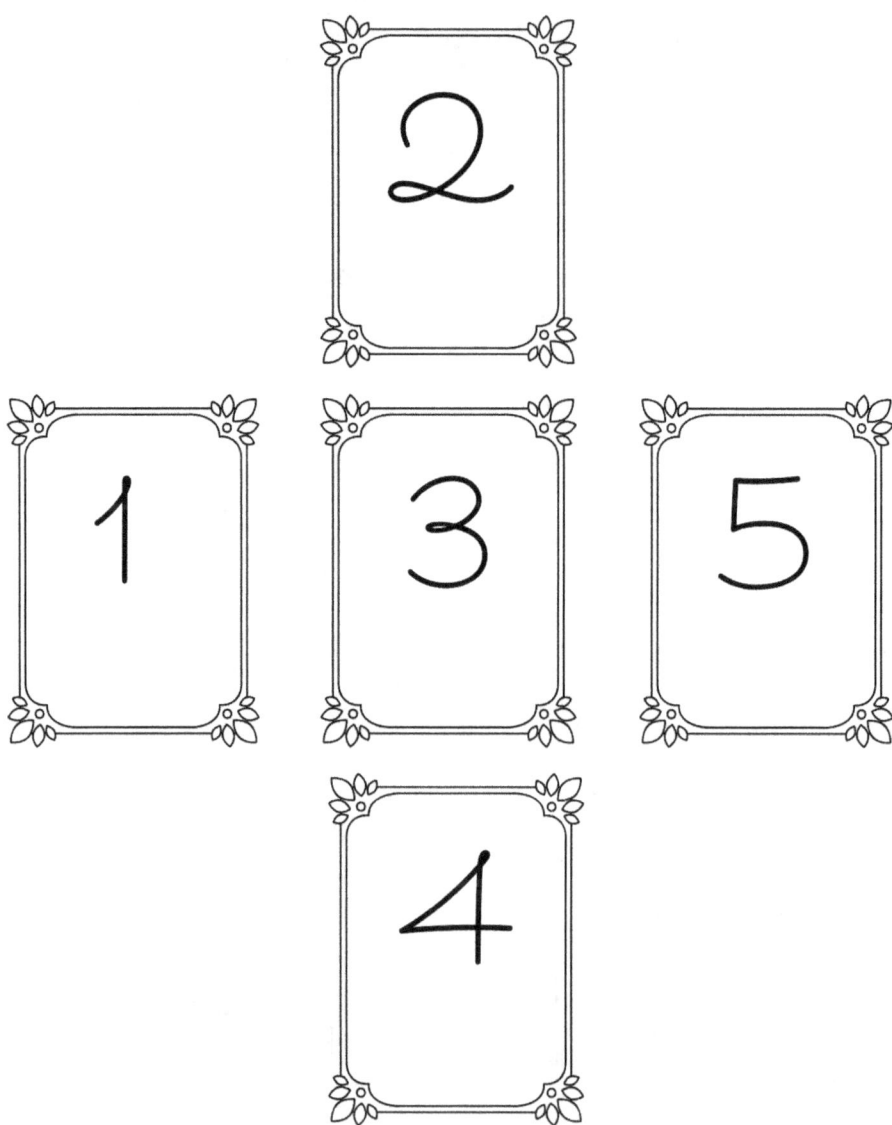

Card 1 - Yourself Now
Card 2 - Current Theme
Card 3 - Receding theme
Card 4 - Foundation theme
Card 5 - Upcoming theme

Sun Moon Stars

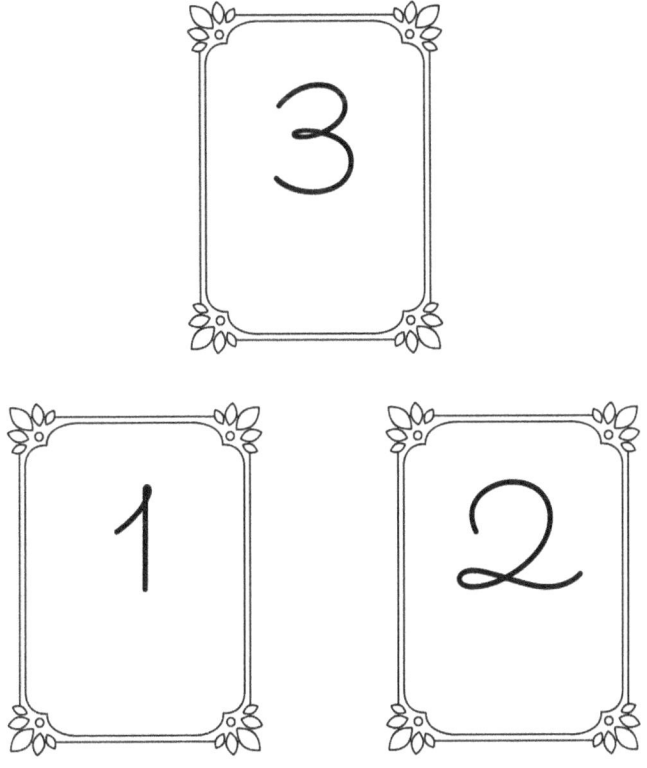

Card 1 - Sun: How others see you or project onto the world
Card 2 - Moon: A shadow aspect your subconscious is looking to assimilate
Card 3 - Stars: Your unique and possible untapped gift

Unlock Yourself

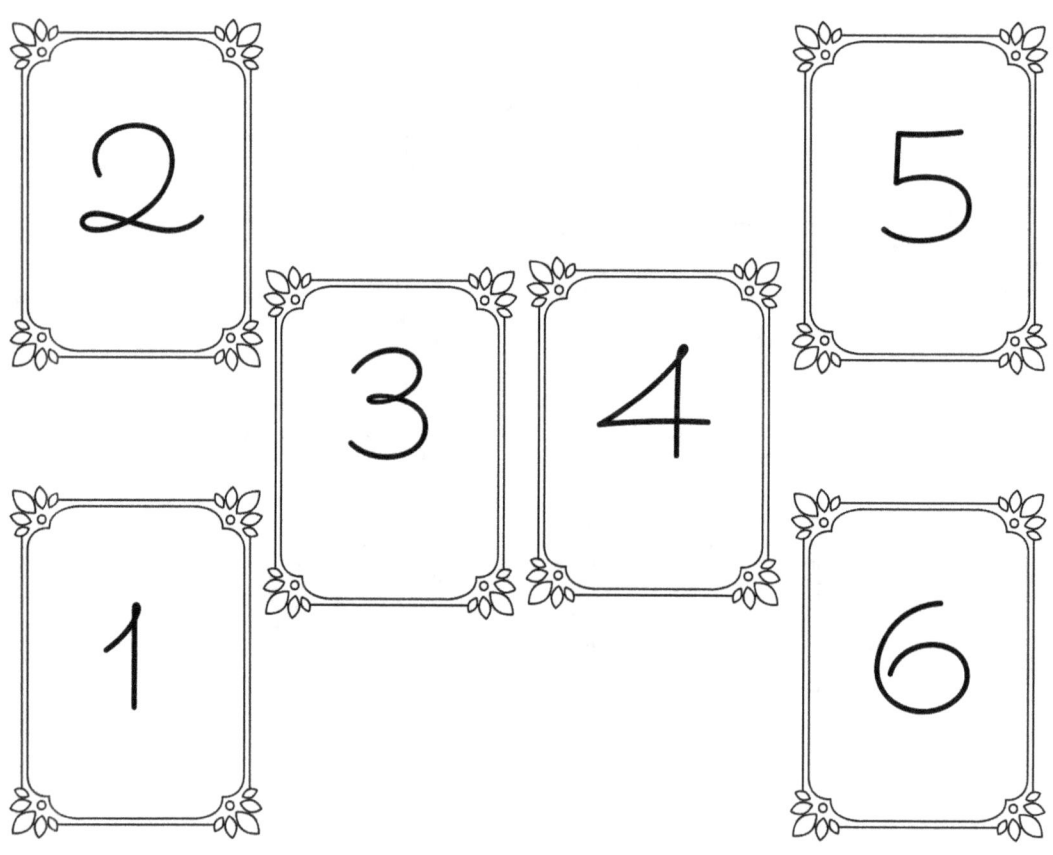

Card 1 - The true you
Card 2 - Your heart
Card 3 - Your mind
Card 4 - Your spirituality
Card 5 - Strengths
Card 6 - Weaknesses

CHAPTER 19

Energy

Energy: Yin

Zodiac: Cancer, Pisces, Scorpio, Taurus, Virgo
Solar System: Moon, Neptune, Venus
Rune:
Numbers: 1, 2, 4, 6, 7, 8, 10, 12
Color: Black
Tarot:
Trees: Apple, Beech, Birch, Cherry, Cypress, Elder, Elm, Horse Chestnut, Laurel, Magnolia, Mesquite, Mimosa, Myrtle, Palm, Poplar, Spindletree, Spruce, Sycamore, Willow, Yew
Misc. Plants: Aloe, Belladonna, Black Cohosh, Burdock, Cardamom, Coltsfoot, Cowslip, Dittany, Goldenrod, Henbane, Lady's Slipper, Lotus, Meadowsweet, Moonwort, Mullein, Myrrh, Orris Root, Patchouli, Reed, Sandalwood, Skullcap, Spikenard, Thornapple, Vanilla
Herb & Garden: Amaranth, Aster, Blackberry / Bramble, Catnip, Columbine, Comfrey, Daffodil, Daisy, Foxglove, Gardenia, Geranium, Grape, Heather, Hibiscus, Hyacinth, Iris, Ivy, Jasmine, Lady's Mantle, Lemon Balm, Lilac, Lily, Monkshood, Mugwort, Passionflower, Periwinkle, Poppy, Primrose, Raspberry, Rose, Sage, Solomon's Seal, Spearmint, Strawberry, Thyme, Valerian, Vervain Violet, Yarrow
Gemstones & Minerals: Agate (black with white veining, green, snakeskin, tree), Amazonite, Amethyst, Ametrine, Andalusite, Apophyllite, Aquamarine, Azurite, Beryl, Blue Lace Agate, Calcite, Celestite, Cerussite, Chrysocolla, Chrysoprase, Desert Rose, Diopside, Emerald, Iolite, Jade, Jasper (brown, green, ocean, pink), Jet, Kunzite, Labradorite, Lapis Lazuli, Larimar, Lepidolite, Lodestone, Malachite, Moonstone, Morganite, Moss Agate, Opal, Peridot, Petrified Wood, Quartz (blue, clear, green, tourmalated), Rose Quartz, Salt, Sapphire, Selenite, Smoky Quartz, Sodalite, Staurolite, Sugilite, Tourmaline (watermelon), Tsavorite, Turquoise
From the Sea: Coral, Cow, Mother-of-Pearl, Pearl
Metals: Copper, Lead, Mercury, Silver
Angel & Mythical Being: Dragon, Unicorn

Energy: Yang

Zodiac: Aquarius, Aries, Capricorn, Gemini, Leo, Libra, Sagittarius
Solar System: Mars, Pluto, Sun
Runes:
Numbers: 1, 3, 5, 7, 9, 11, 13
Color: White
Tarot:
Trees: Acacia, Alder, Ash, Aspen, Blackthorn, Cedar, Chestnut, Fir, Hawthorn, Hazel, Holly, Juniper, Linden, Locust, Maple, Oak, Olive, Palm (dragon's blood), Pine, Pomegranate, Rowan Walnut, Witch Hazel, Yew
Misc. Plants: Allspice, Anise, Asafoetida, Bamboo, Betony, Bittersweet, Blessed Thistle, Bloodroot, Cinnamon, Cinquefoil, Clove, Coriander, Cumin, Deer's Tongue, Eyebright, Flax, Frankincense, Galangal, Ginger, Ginseng, High John, Horehound, Mandrake, Mistletoe, Mustard, Nettle, Nutmeg, Pepper, Reed, Star Anise, Thistle, Wormwood
Herb & Garden: Agrimony, Anemone, Angelica, Basil, Bergamot, Borage, Broom, Carnation, Chamomile, Chrysanthemum, Clover, Dandelion, Dill, Fennel, Fern, Feverfew, Garlic, Goldenseal, Gorse, Heliotrope, Holy Basil, Honeysuckle, Lavender, Lily of the Valley, Lovage, Marigold, Marjoram, Morning Glory, Pennyroyal, Peony, Peppermint, Rosemary, Rue, Saffron, St. John's Wort, Snapdragon, Sunflower, Sweet Woodruff
Gemstones & Minerals: Agate (banded, black, brown, fire, red, red-banded, snakeskin), Amber, Amethyst, Ametrine, Andalusite, Apache Tears, Aventurine, Beryl (golden), Bloodstone, Calcite (orange, red), Carnelian, Cat's Eye, Chrysoberyl, Citrine, Diamond, Fluorite, Garnet, Hematite, Herkimer Diamond, Jasper (leopard skin, red, yellow), Lodestone, Obsidian, Onyx, Opal, Pyrite, Quartz (clear, rutilated), Rhodochrosite, Rhodonite, Ruby, Sard, Sardonyx, Serpentine, Sphene, Spinel, Staurolite, Sunstone, Tanzanite, Tiger's Eye, Topaz, Tourmaline (red, watermelon), Zircon
From the Sea: Coral (red)
Metals: Aluminum, Antimony, Brass, Gold, Iron, Mercury, Steel, Tin
Angel or Mythical Being: Dragon, Phoenix, Unicorn

Brainwaves

Brainwave States: How do we begin perceiving energy beyond our five primary senses? Radios work by transmitting on different hertz frequencies. By tuning in to the right channel with the appropriate frequency on your radio, you are able to perceive that once unperceivable frequency. Like radio waves, our brains produce subtle electrical impulses generated by masses of neurons communicating to each other for particular activities that we are engaged in and create specific states of consciousness. Each brainwave state is named after a Greek letter and is measured by the cycles per second called hertz. There are five brainwave states: gamma, beta, alpha, theta, and delta. Each one is distinguished by their hertz cycle, though there's an area of overlap. By learning to alter our brainwave states, we learn to alter our consciousness.

GAMMA—38–42 hertz: Once thought to be random brain noise, the mysterious gamma is the fastest brainwave state. Researchers have found that gamma is highly active when in universal love and transcendental states of consciousness associated with enlightenment. Some Tibetan Buddhist monks and some Indian yogis are able to display this brainwave state while meditating.

BETA—12–28 hertz: Beta occurs while we're awake, alert, and concentrating on something. This is the most common brainwave state that we engage in as humans. Excitement, anxiety, stress, decision-making, critical thinking, and focused attention are associated with beta.

ALPHA—7.5–13 hertz: Alpha occurs while we're relaxed, meditating, visualizing, and daydreaming. Alpha has access to the subconscious mind and occurs when we are receiving information passively, such as learning. Alpha is the state of consciousness that is most associated with psychic ability and the state of consciousness linked with hypnosis.

THETA—4–7 hertz: Theta occurs before and after sleep. It is associated with light sleep, deep meditation, deep dreaming, vivid imagery, and high levels of inner awareness. In theta, we become completely unaware of the external world.

DELTA—1–3 hertz: Delta occurs during periods of deep, dreamless sleep and is associated with the deepest states of meditation. Healing and regenerating are associated with this state of consciousness, which is why deep sleep can be deeply healing.

Types of Energy Healing

There are many types of energy healing modalities, each with its own unique approach and benefits. Depending on your needs and intentions, some may be more aligned with your individual energy system than others.

Reiki is a healing technique that uses universal energy to restore balance and harmony. The practitioner directs this energy to where it is needed most by placing their hands near or on the body. During a session, recipients may feel the release of stuck emotions, relaxation, and peace.

Acupuncture is a practice that uses energy pathways called meridians to restore balance and harmony. Practitioners believe that by inserting needles into specific points along these meridians, they can unblock any stagnation and restore the flow of health and wellness. Community acupuncture is growing in popularity thanks to its lower cost and easier access for many folks.

Massage is one of the oldest and most common forms of energy healing. The therapist uses their hands to move energy around your body. This can help promote relaxation, improve blood and lymphatic circulation.

Reflexology is a type of massage that uses pressure points on the feet, hands, and ears to promote healing. Reflexologists believe that these pressure points correspond to different parts of the body. By massaging or applying pressure to these points, we can encourage energy to flow freely and restore balance.

Craniosacral therapy is a light touch treatment that uses gentle hands-on techniques to examine the movement of fluids in and around the central nervous system. This therapy can help relieve stress, tension headaches, and neck pain. Craniosacral is also known to help restore balance and wellness after traumatic injuries.

Yoga is an ancient healing modality that uses movement, meditation, and the chakra system to support healing and well-being. Some popular styles of yoga that focus on energy healing include Kundalini, Iyengar, and Vinyasa.

Qigong (pronounced chi gong), is a system of energy healing that uses movement, breathwork, and visualization to open and balance the energy pathways in the body. Qigong is thought to improve health and help relieve stress, anxiety, and pain. Read our article about the many benefits of this ancient healing art.

Ecstatic Dance, a relatively new form of energy healing, ecstatic dance uses movement and music to open the body, mind, and spirit. During an ecstatic dance session, participants move freely to express their emotions and connect with their inner power. This type of dance is thought to release blocked energy, clear the mind, and boost self-confidence. See Ecstatic Dance classes in San Diego >>

Sound healing uses sound and vibration to restore balance and harmony in the body. By listening to certain sounds or music, you can stimulate different parts of the body, promote relaxation, and improve mental clarity.

Shamanic healing uses plant medicines and intentional ceremonies to restore balance to the body, mind, and spirit. Shamanic healers use tools like the drum, prayers, and rituals to help shift energy and restore health.

CHAPTER 20

At a Glance Chakras

Crown Chakra
Sahasrara
Represents spiritual consciousness and transformation.

Third Eye Chakra
Ajna
Responsible for spiritual communication, awareness, and perception.

Throat Chakra
Visuddha
Governs self-expression, communication, and the ability to speak one's truth.

Heart Chakra
Anahata
Governs people's love for themselves and those around them, supporting empathy, compassion, and forgiveness.

Solar Plexus Chakra
Manipura
Represents confidence, self-esteem, and personal power.

Sacral Chakra
Svadhisthana
It supports emotional and physical health aspects and governs many of the body's fluids (from the sex organs, the bladder, and the kidneys).

Root Chakra
Muladhara
Good health in the body, a sense of connection to the Earth, and a feeling of support and stability in the physical world.

Chakra Symbols

Crown Chakra:
To Know and Understand

Third Eye:
To See

Throat Chakra:
To Speak and Be Heard

Heart Chakra:
To Love and Be Loved

Solar Plexus Chakra:
To Act

Sacral Chakra:
To Feel and Desire

Root Chakra:
To Be Here and To Have

CHAPTER 21

Correspondence
Flowers and Herbs

These worksheets can help you organize and personalize correspondences for your Sabbat celebration. You can use them to research and document correspondences that are meaningful to you and your unique way of celebrating the Sabbat. Feel free to add other herbs and flowers to personalize your unique celebration of this Sabbat. In addition, there is a section on how to dry herbs and make an infusion oil.

Foraging Calendar

January, February, and March
Chickweed, Common Mallow Leaves, Common Sorrel, Cowberry, Crow Garlic, Dandelion Root, Garlic Mustard, Ground Elder, Hairy Bittercress, Nettles, Pignut, Sheep's Sorrel, Silver Birch Sap, Wild Garlic, Winter Cress, and Wood Sorrel

April, May, and June
Beech Leaves, Borage, Broom, Chickweed, Cleavers, Common Poppy, Dandelion Leaves and Roots, Dog Rose Flowers, Elderflower, Garlic, Mustard, Ground Elder, Hawthorn Blossom, Hops, Nettles, Pignuts, Sheep's Sorrel, Spearmint, Sweet Cicely, Watercress, Wild Garlic, Wild Thyme, Wood Sorrel, and Yarrow

July, August, and September
Acorns, Apples, Beech Nuts, Bilberries, Blackberries, Burdock, Chamomile, Chickweed, Chicory, Cleavers, Common Mallow, Dandelion Leaves and Flowers, Elderberry, Fat Hen, Garlic, Mustard, Gooseberries, Hawthorn Berries, Hazelnuts, Horseradish, Juniper Berries, Nettle, Plums, Rowan Berries, Sheep's Sorrel, Spearmint, Sweet Chestnuts, Sweet Cicely, Walnuts, Wild Cherries, Wild Strawberries, Wild Thyme, Wood Sorrel, and Yarrow

October, November, and December
Chestnuts, Chickweed, Crab Apples, Hawthorn Berries, Horseradish, Nettles, Rosehips, Sheep's Sorrel, Sloes, Spearmint, Sweet Chestnuts, and Walnuts

I live in the North Eastern United States; you may find different species depending on where you live.

Indoor Herbs

Growing Schedule

January + February
Start perennial herb seeds indoors.

March + April
Start annual herb seeds indoors.
Pinch perennial herbs.

May + June
Move perennial herbs outdoors.
Pinch annual herbs.
Set overgrown annuals outdoors.
Second seeding of annual herbs.

July + August
Pinch second planting of annuals.
Take root cuttings of perennials.

September + October
Move perennial herb cuttings to soil indoors.

November + December
Grow + harvest perennial herbs.
Move large perennial herbs to larger pots.

Doorstep Rice Spell

Fill a jar with raw white rice without sealing it. Place the jar by the front door for protection. Remember that rice absorbs negative energy rather than repelling it. Replace the rice with fresh raw rice weekly. Avoid bringing old rice back into your home or cooking it. Dispose of it outside your home through burning, scattering, or throwing away.

Dehydrate Herbs

When you have more than enough fresh herbs for spells, the best way to keep them is in their dehydrated form.

Sun Dry
It's called sun-dry, but do NOT dry herbs under the sun. Place in a warm spot, but avoid direct sunlight.

Air Dry
A very common method to dry herbs. It is the cheapest and most natural way of preserving your fresh herbs.

Microwave Dry
This is the fastest way, and it keeps your herbs greener.

Oven Dry
It is quicker than air and sundry, but herbs will cook a little, removing some of the potency and flavor.

Food Dehydrator
An efficient way to quickly dry and preserve the flavor and medicinal value of fresh herbs.

Infusions

Exploring the Art of Infusion: Techniques and Methods for Infusing Plant Matter
Infusion is a process that involves soaking plant matter in a liquid to create a flavored medium. This can be achieved using a variety of liquids, including water, alcohol, oil, or sweet solutions. Two primary methods of making infusions are cold and hot, each producing a unique flavor profile. Cold infusions are less bitter and have a fresh flavor, while hot infusions are more intense and offer quicker results.

How to make infused vodka, vinegar, and water. Infused vodka is made by adding flavoring agents to vodka and letting it sit for several days or weeks before straining out the solids. Infused vinegar follows the same method and can create vinaigrettes or a refreshing beverage called a "shrub." Infused water is a simple way to flavor water by adding sliced fruits or vegetables.

Several infusions include extracts, tinctures, glycerine, decoctions, and tisanes, each with a unique preparation method. Extracts, for example, are cold infusions typically concentrated and made with alcohol. Tinctures, on the other hand, are strong infusions used for medicinal purposes. Glycerine is a popular alternative to alcohol for those who are sensitive to it. Decoctions require simmering plant material for an extended period, while tisanes are hot herbal infusions used to differentiate herbal beverages from teas made exclusively with Camellia sinensis plant leaves.

There are two methods for infusing herbs or flowers into carrier oils: the solar infusion method and the slow infusion cooker method. For the solar method, fill a mason jar with herbs, cover them with carrier oil, and place them on a sunny windowsill for 2-6 weeks before straining the oil. For the slow-cooker method, fill a mason jar with herbs, cover them with carrier oil, place them in a slow cooker with water, and let the mixture infuse for 10-12 hours before straining the oil. Store the oil in a cool, dark place.

Freezing herbs is a simple method to keep them fresh throughout the year. This involves chopping the herbs, blending them with olive oil, and storing them in freezer bags or ice cube trays. This method is also suitable for making DIY baby food.

Freezing Herbs

Freezing is an excellent method to preserve herbs; you'll have fresh herbs for the whole year. You can have whatever you want whenever you want:-)

Cut up your chosen herb and add 2-3 tablespoons of olive oil.

Put in blender and blend for 3- 4 minutes.

Put in freezer storage bags to use throughout the year.

Or, if you will use them soon, you can put them in an ice cube tray for later.

My daughter does this with her DIY baby food, which works great.

Kitchen Herbs to use for Magic

Pepper: banish spells, protection

Cloves: prosperity, friendship

Rosemary: love, lust

Thyme: approval, money, purification

Garlic: healing, protection

Bay: wishes, psychic work

Mint: love, money, healing

Cinnamon: cleansing, success

Basil: money, purification, love, protection

Salt: protection, purification

Acorn Magic

The acorn (or oak nut)is the nut of the oak tree and its close relatives.

Between midsummer and through autumn, a dried acorn worn as an amulet around the neck brings a youthful glow, good luck, and protection. If gathered on a full, they are said to attract Fairies, welcoming enchantment throughout the following month. They promote wisdom and prosperity if placed near a window; acorns banish illness and loneliness when carried in a pocket.

Acorns are symbols of security, abundance, and luck. They can protect homes from lightning and draw money when placed on windowsills during a full moon. Planting one under the light of the moon can bring prosperity to you and your home. Acorns are associated with new life, fertility, strength, and protection. They can also be used in charms to bring back lost love or ward off illness. Label two acorn caps with your and your crush's names, then float them in the water to determine if you're meant to be.

Acorns pair well with rose quartz, carnelian, and jasper
Carry an acorn to banish loneliness
Wear as an amulet around your neck for protection
Place in your window to attract prosperity & luck
Put it in your car to ward off getting lost
Pick up the first acorn you find in autumn and carry it in your purse or pocket all through fall and winter.
It will protect you from negativity, prosperity, and good luck through the dark months.
Then come spring, return it to nature as a "thank you" for all its assistance.

Acorns
Quercus Robur
Folk Name: Oaknut

Magical Properties
Strength
Protection
Wisdom
Security
Abundance
Counteracts Loneliness
Draws Good Luck
Preserves the Illusion of Youth.

Draw or Paste your herb here

Physical Properties & Essential Oil
It Is/It May:
Improve Gut Health
Rich in Antioxidants
Good Source of Fiber
Aid Healthy Bones
Help to Control Blood Sugar
Provide Energy
Good for the Metabolism
Good for the Skin

Use Caution: Acorns contain a high level of tannins, which can make them bitter and unpalatable. Additionally, acorns must be processed before they can be consumed, as they contain a small amount of hydrocyanic acid which can be toxic in large quantities.

I trust in the healing properties of herbs, allowing them to support my physical, emotional, and spiritual well-being.

Allspice

Pimenta dioica
Folk Names: Jamaica Pepper, Myrtle Pepper, Pimenta, and Pimento

Magical Properties
Draws Luck and Money
Prosperity
Increase Virility
Relieve Mental Tension
Create a Sense of Peace and Quiet
Increase Determination

Draw or Paste your herb here

Physical Properties & Essential Oil
It Is/It May:
Boost the Immune System
Aid Digestion
Support Healthy Heart Function
Improve Blood Circulation
Relieve Cramps and Spasms
Relieve Insomnia
Reduce Inflammation
Help with Weight Management
Reduce Gas and Bloating
Manage Blood Sugar Levels

I am guided by the ancient wisdom of herbal traditions, honoring the cycles of the earth.

Apple

Pyrus spp
Folk Name: Fruit of the gods, Silver branch, Tree of love

Magical Properties
Love
Divination
Making wands (wood)
Tarot reading
Scrying
Garden magic
Immortality

Physical Properties
It May:
Prevent cancer
Diabetes
Dysentery
Fever
Heart problems
Warts
Vitamin C-deficiency condition called
scurvy

As I brew herbal teas, I infuse each sip with intention, nourishing my body and soul.

Basil

Ocimum basilicum
Folk Names: Albahaca, American Dittany, "Our Herb," St. Joseph's Wort, Sweet Basil, and Witches Herb

Magical Properties

Bring wealth
Luck
Prosperity
Abundance
Harmony
Divination
Success
Peace
Courage
Strength
Stress
Purification
Happiness
Love
Travel

Draw or Paste your herb here

Physical Properties & Essential Oil
It Is/It May:

Treat snakebites
Help inflammation
Help to Reduce High Blood Sugar
Help to Reduce High Blood Pressure, albeit very briefly
Help to Relieve Anxiety and Stress
May Prevent Memory Loss Caused by Aging
Increase your Ability to Think and Reason

I honor the ancestors who passed down the knowledge of herbal medicine, carrying on their legacy with reverence.

Bay

Laurus nobilis
Folk Names: Daphne, Bair, Bay Laurel, Grecian Laurel, Laurel, Laurier Sauce, Noble Laurel, Roman Laurel, and Sweet Bay

Magical Properties

Protector of Homes
Attract Prosperity
Ward off Negative Energies
Enhance Intuition
Psychic Abilities
Dreams
Amplify your Intentions

Physical Properties & Essential Oil
It Is/It May:

Relieve Gastrointestinal Discomfort
Relieve Diarrhea
Regulate Amenorrhea
Act as a Stimulant
Act as a Diuretic

I am surrounded by the protective energy of herbs, shielding me from negativity and harm.

Bay Laurel

Laurus nobilis
Folk Names: Sweet Bay, Daphne, Apollo's Bay, Noble Laurel

Magical Properties: Bay laurel is associated with protection, success, and divination. Bay leaves are often used in rituals for psychic awareness and to attract positive energies. Bay laurel is considered a symbol of honor and accomplishment.

Draw or Paste your herb here

Physical Properties & Essential Oil
It Is/It May: Bay leaves are used in traditional medicine for their mild diuretic and digestive properties. Bay laurel essential oil may be employed for its antimicrobial effects.

I embrace the magic of Mabon, working with herbs to manifest my intentions and desires.

Blackberry

Rubus
Folk Names: Bly, Bramble, Bramble Berry, and Brummel

Magical Properties
Protection
Prosperity
Abundance
Nourishing
Soothing
Symbolizes Life
Pagan Fairy Fruit
Attract Wealth (leaves)

Physical Properties & Essential Oil
It Is/It May:
Help Stop Bleeding (leaves)
Treat bowel Problems
Improve Brain Health
Treat Sore Throats

I trust in the intuitive wisdom of my body, knowing which herbs will serve me best during this season.

Broom

Cytisus scoparius
Folk name: Link, genista, banal, Scotch broom

Magical Properties
Sacred to the Sun
Symbolize the Sun
Purification
Protection
Divination

Draw or Paste your herb here

Physical Properties & EO
It May:
Urinary support

As I create herbal sachets, I infuse them with love and positivity, spreading their healing energy throughout my space.

Cedar

Cedrus spp.
Folk Names: Lebanon Cedar, Tree of the Gods, Cedrus

Magical Properties:
Cedar is revered for its purifying qualities and is often used to cleanse spaces of negative energies. It is associated with protection, strength, and grounding. Cedar is used in rituals to create a sacred and spiritually charged atmosphere.

Physical Properties & Essential Oil
It Is/It May: Cedarwood essential oil, derived from the wood of cedar trees, has been used in aromatherapy for relaxation and stress relief. It is also believed to have antimicrobial properties.

With each herb I harvest, I am reminded of the abundance and generosity of the natural world.

Cinnamon

Cinnamomum spp.
Folk Names: Sweet Wood, Cinnamomum, Gui Zhi

Magical Properties: Cinnamon is associated with warmth, prosperity, and success. It is often used to attract abundance, enhance psychic abilities, and bring positive energy into a space. Cinnamon is also considered a powerful herb for love and passion.

Draw or Paste your herb here

Physical Properties & Essential Oil
It Is/It May: Cinnamon has been studied for its potential benefits in blood sugar regulation and as an antioxidant. It is also used traditionally for digestive issues.

I am in tune with the cycles of growth and decay, knowing that each herb serves a purpose in the grand tapestry of life.

Frankincense

Boswellia spp.
Folk Names: Olibanum, Frank, Luban

Magical Properties: Frankincense is considered a sacred resin with powerful spiritual properties. It is often used in rituals to enhance spiritual connection, meditation, and purification. Frankincense is associated with consecration and creating a sacred atmosphere.

Physical Properties & Essential Oil

It Is/It May: Frankincense has been used traditionally for various medicinal purposes, including anti-inflammatory effects. It is sometimes used in aromatherapy and may have potential applications in joint health.

I cultivate a deep connection with the earth, respecting the plants and their medicinal properties.

Garlic

Allium sativum
Folk Names: Stinking Rose, Ajo, Poor Man's Treacle, and
Stinkweed

Magical Properties
Protective
Ward off Evil Spirits
Good Luck
Protect against Infections

Draw or Paste your herb here

Physical Properties & Essential Oil
It Is/It May:
Immune-Boosting Properties
Aid Cardiovascular Health
Improve Cholesterol Levels
Detoxify Heavy Metals in the Body

I am aligned with the energy of Mabon, embracing the magic of herbs to enhance my spiritual journey.

Myrrh

Commiphora spp.
Folk Names: Didthin, Mirra, Bowl, Gum Myrrh

Magical Properties: Myrrh is linked to transformation, purification, and healing. It is used in rituals to banish negative energies, promote spiritual growth, and enhance meditation. Myrrh is also believed to have protective properties.

Physical Properties & Essential Oil It Is/It May: Myrrh has a long history of use in traditional medicine for its anti-inflammatory and antimicrobial properties. It has been used for oral health, wound healing, and respiratory conditions.

I am open to receiving the healing energies of herbs, allowing them to cleanse and purify my spirit.

Marigold

Tagetes

Folk Name: Maribel, Arely, Mariel, Mirabelle, Emerald

Magical Properties

Prosperity
Blessings
Purification
Peace
Meditation
Youth
Calming
Sleep
Energy
Clearing
Joy
Healing
Inspiration
Money

Draw or Paste your herb here

Physical Properties
It May:

Anti-inflammatory
Soothes Anxiety
Reduces Stress
Boosts Immune system
Relieves Menstrual Cramps
Treats Nausea
Indigestion
Soothes Stiff Muscles
Promotes Good Sleep
Helps Skin Irritation
Soothes Sore Throat

As I work with herbs, I am filled with gratitude for the abundance of the harvest.

Pine

Pinus spp.
Folk Names: Longleaf Pine, Yellow Pine, Sweet Pine

Magical Properties: Pine is connected to endurance, purification, and rebirth. The evergreen nature of pine trees symbolizes vitality and eternal life. Pine is often used to cleanse spaces, promote healing, and attract positive energy.

Physical Properties & Essential Oil It Is/It May: Pine has been used in traditional medicine for its high vitamin C content, providing immune system support. Pine resin may also have antimicrobial properties.

I am attuned to the seasonal shifts, harnessing the power of herbs to align myself with Mabon.

Rose

Rosa spp.
Folk name:

Magical Properties
Associated with both gods of love,
Aphrodite and Eros
Attracting love
Prophetic dreams
Calm Stress
Reduce family feuds
Divination

Draw or Paste your herb here

Physical Properties & EO
Rose Essential Oil is the most
often used for mental health.
It May:
Sedative, Stress relieving, and Anti-
depressive
Planet - Venus

With each herb I gather, I connect deeply with nature, embracing its healing energies.

Walnuts

Juglans spp
Folk Name:

Magical Properties
Weather Working
Abundance
Insight
Healing
Focus
Wealth
Creativity
Motivation

Physical Properties & Essential Oil
It Is/It May:
Improve Heart Health
Reduce the Risk of Cancer
Improve Brain Function
Reduce Inflammation
Strengthen the Immune System
Improve Bone Health
Help to Sleep Better

I honor the wisdom of the earth, utilizing herbs to enhance my spiritual practices during Mabon.

Herb/Flower

Folk Names:

Magical Properties

Physical Properties & Essential Oil
It Is/It May:

Quicky Herb Reference

Agrimony – ancient herb of healing, restoration, and benevolent protection
Alfalfa – good fortune, money magic, healing and cleansing infusions
Angelica – warding and banishing, angelic magick, and summoning strength
Astragalus - vital energy, protection (shielding), promoting health, mental clarity, and concentration
Basil - blessings, love, money, and happiness
Bay Leaf – confers wisdom, strength, visions, and a sacred herb of Apollo
Bearberry – psychic awareness, dreams, courage, smudging, and offerings
Birch Bark – new beginnings, psychic protection, strength, and devotion
Blessed Thistle – consecration, protection, healing, and cleansing by fire
Blue Sage – smudging, meditation, relaxation, ancestral wisdom, and peace
Blue Vervain – spells of love and advancement, astral travel, and initiation
Burdock Root – warding, cleansing, uncrossing, and counter-magic
Calendula – solar rites, divination, remembrance, and honoring the dead
Catnip – love-drawing, relaxation, trance work, and feline magic
Cedar – ancient wisdom, protection, maturity, strength, and power
Cinnamon – passion, shielding, quick success, spirit evocation, fire magic
Cinquefoil (Five Finger Grass) – for the five blessings: health, money, love, power, and wisdom
Coltsfoot – divination, visions, love magic, and healing from within
Comfrey – healing, restoration, lucky herb of travelers and gamblers
Damiana – lust, sex magic, psychic abilities, energy work, and spirit quests
Dandelion – wishes, divination, calling spirits, charisma and success
Devil's Claw - protection, exorcism, banishing spells, keeping away evil, and confounding enemies
Dill - sexual love, luck, protection against sorcery and disease
Dittany of Crete – a rare herb from Greece, renowned for love magick, manifestation, and spirit contact
Elderberry – hidden wisdom, Crone magic, banishing, and Faery offerings
Eucalyptus – cleansing, healing, ritual baths, rites of Mercury and Air
Fennel Seed – psychic protection, counter-magic, confidence, and adaptability
Feverfew – flower renowned for its curative properties, and a magickal "fix-all"
Galangal – strength and power, victory, luck, hex-breaking, and male potency
Ginger – fiery herb of passion, success, and personal power
Hawthorn Berry – fidelity, shielding, clarity, ancestor, and Faery magic
Hibiscus – love and passion, independence, and confidence
Horehound – mental clarity, dispelling illusion, quick action, and healing
Hyssop – purification, innocence, blessings, sacred baths and washes
Irish Moss – financial luck, folk remedies, safety during travel, and sea magic
Jasmine – love, dreams, divination, sensuality, luxury and kindness
Juniper Berry – good luck, prosperity, masculine energy, and protection at home
Juniper Leaf – purification, protection, bringing luck, and exposing the truth

Lavender – love and attraction, purification, relaxation, and restful sleep
Lemon Balm – tranquility, attraction, fidelity, teamwork, and harmonious home
Lemon Peel – cleansing, purifying, boosting energy, sweetness and charm
Licorice Root – domination, advantage over others, passion, power, and persuasion
Lobelia – spirit communication, love and weather magic, trance, blessings and curses
Mandrake – legendary magical herb for love magic, protection, and curses
Marjoram - protection, married love, calming the mind, and easing grief
Marshmallow Root – love charms, psychic powers, protection, and drawing good spirits
Meadowsweet – a sacred flower of Spring, the Maiden, and the Underworld
Mistletoe – good luck, love, and money spells, and many traditional charms
Mugwort – scrying, divination, psychic ability, lucid dreaming, and Lunar magic
Mullein – protection, illumination, courage, hedge-crossing, and Crone magic
Nettle – courage, consecration, protection, healing, and deterring evil
Orange Peel – uplifting and centering Solar herb of joy, blessings, and good luck
Orris Root – charms of love, persuasion, popularity, charisma and success
Patchouli – love and sex magic, attraction, fertility, and rites of Earth
Pennyroyal – calmness, endurance, patience, dispelling anger, and warding
Peppermint – healing, purification, psychic awareness, love and energy
Pine - persistence, moderation, prosperity, and good health
Raspberry Leaf – love and enjoyment, tempting others, and divination
Red Sandalwood – is used in incense for meditation, healing, and trance work
Rose – charms of love and beauty, harmony, divination, and Goddess rites
Rosemary – cleansing, purification, vitality, wisdom, and protection
Rue – warding, exorcism, cleansing, love-drawing, and protective charms
Spearmint – love, psychic ability, cleansing, renewal, and house blessing
Star Anise – clairvoyance, good luck, psychic dreams, and travel charms
Thyme - beauty, strength, courage, and a favorite herb of Faeries
Valerian – warding, enemy spells, transmuting negativity, and feline magic
Vervain – Old World herb of wisdom, healing, and second sight
White Sage – cleansing, house blessing, meditation, and healing
White Willow Bark – solace, wisdom, long-lasting love, divination, and Lunar magic
Wild Lettuce – visions, trance, dream magick, enthrallment and sleep
Witch Hazel – comfort and healing, wisdom, protection, and soothing of anger
Wood Betony – herb of St. Bride, used in charms against ill luck, anxiety, and despair
Wormwood – psychic vision, spirit evocation, hexes and curses, and reversal magic
Yarrow – ancient medicinal flower used for courage, divination, and good fortune

Herbs by Intention: Prosperity

Basil
Bay
Calendula Cinnamon
Chamomile
Clover
Cloves
Comfrey
Dandelion
Dill
Frankincense
Honeysuckle
Lemongrass
Mint
Myrrh
Poppy Seeds
Rose Hips
Rosemary
Sandalwood
Star Anise
Thyme
Verbena

Herbs by Intention: Grounding

Ashwagandha
Basil
Cinnamon
Chamomile
Damiana
Ginger
Hawthorn
Hibiscus
Kava Kava
Lemon Balm
Lavender
Mint
Oregano
Passionflower
Rosemary
Skullcap
Thyme
Valerian

Herbs by Intention: Love

Basil
Calendula
Carnation
Cinnamon
Cumin
Daisy
Fennel
Jasmine
Lavender
Lovage
Marjoram
Mint
Mugwort
Oregano
Patchouli
Rose
Rosemary
Thyme
Vervain
Yarrow

Herbs by Intention: Healing

Basil
Lavender
Cayenne
Mint
Pepper
Lemon Balm
Chamomile
Orris Root
Cinnamon
Parsley
Cloves
Peppermint
Dill
Rose
Fennel
Rosemary
Feverfew
Sandalwood
Thyme
Turmeric

Herbs by Intention: Protection

Agrimony
Juniper
Benzoin
Lilac
Basil
Marjoram
Bay Leaf
Mugwort
Black Pepper
Mistletoe
Catnip
Mullein
Clove
Myrrh
Coriander
Rose
Dandelion
Rosemary
Dill
Rowan
Fennel
Sage
Hawthorn
Sandalwood
Holly
Vervain
Lavender
Wormwood

CHAPTER 22

Crystals

Cleansing vs. Charging

Cleansing:
Removes past energies
Item is restored to its natural state
Crystal-like quartz and selenite can cleanse other crystals/tools

Charging:
Adds purpose or intention
Programs a tool for a specific energy
Charged crystals can be used to add energy to other items

Cleansing Methods

Cleansing with Water
Water Bath
Cleansing With Moonlight
Cleansing With Sound
Cleansing With Sunlight
A few crystals never need cleansing. For example, citrine, kyanite, and selenite are self-cleaning. Clear Quartz and Carnelian cleanse other crystals.
Check with which ones are safe in water

Energize and Charge

Quartz Points
Sunlight
Moonlight
Plants
Herbs

Cleansing vs. Charging

Cleansing

Removes past energies
Item is restored to its natural state
Crystal-like quartz and selenite can cleanse other crystals/tools

Charging

Adds purpose or intention
Programs a tool for a specific energy
Charged crystals can be used to add energy to other items

Cleansing and Energize	**Energize and Charge**
Cleansing with Water	Quartz Points
Water Bath	Sunlight
Cleansing With Moonlight	Moonlight
Cleansing With Sound	Plants
Cleansing With Sunlight	Herbs

A few crystals never need cleansing. For example, citrine, kyanite, and selenite are self-cleansing. Clear Quartz and Carnelian cleanse other crystals.
Be sure to check which ones are safe in water.

Grounding Spell with Hematite

Let Go of Troubles: Hematite serves as a versatile stone for grounding and balancing energy.

Select a hematite stone that resonates with you. In a tranquil setting, confide in the stone, articulating each of your troubles one by one. Once you've shared all your concerns, bury the hematite in a location away from your home. As the Earth absorbs the negativity stored within the stone, your troubles will diminish, and your problems will ease.

Crystal Shapes

Clusters
radiates unity throughout the space and charges other crystals

Pyramids
anchoring crystal and powerful for manifesting desires

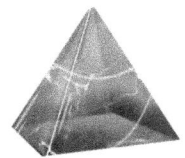

Cubes
consolidates energy, grounding & meditation, and connect to the energy of the Earth

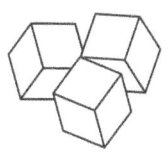

Double Terminated
absorb negative energy, grounding, break down old patterns, and promotes psychic ability

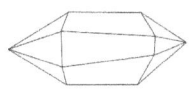

Twin
grounding & harmonizing energies, and balances yin & yang energies

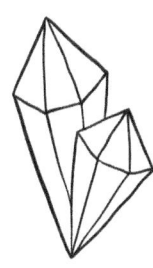

Points
concentrates & directs energy

Crystal Shapes

Wand
healing rituals,
moving &
directing energy

Egg
healing, fertility,
and
balance

Spheres
emits energy
equally
from all direction,
and
ideal for scrying

Druzy
charging, relaxation &
harmony, purify &
amplify body's
natural healing
properties

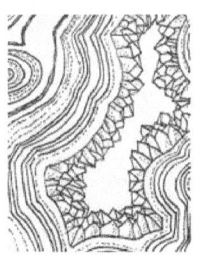

Geode
amplifies,
conserves &
releases energy,
and
Internal healing

Isis
feminine energy,
healing
emotional
hurt and distress

Choosing the Shape of Your Crystal

1 - Look up the energetic properties of your crystal.

2 - Consider the shape and if it offers benefits, such as enhancing any of the properties you are interested in.

3 - Consider if the crystal shape suits your chosen way of working with the stone.

Crystal Grids

To create a crystal grid, first, decide on your intent. You can choose from Love, Travel, Wealth, or Joy. Next, select a layout that aligns with your intent. You can choose from Health, Growth, Intuition, Flower, Connection, Seed, Balance, Metatron's Cube, Energy, Fibonacci sequence, or Abundance.

After selecting your layout, choose crystals that align with your intention. Trust your intuition when selecting the crystals, as there are no right or wrong stones. You will need a center crystal, which can be any stone, but a point will be more powerful for directing your intention straight up into the universe. Then select a selection of points or tumbles to align with your intention.

To set up the surrounding stones in your crystal grid, start from the outside and move inwards. As you place each crystal, make sure you keep your intention in mind. If you want, you can activate your grid by using a quartz point to circle each of the stones to connect them energetically.

Here are some examples of crystals and their properties that you can use:

Quartz: Master healer, Amplifier
Citrine: Happiness stone, Abundance
Tourmaline: Protective stone
Adventurine: New beginnings, Abundance
Rose Quartz: Nurturing stone, Love
Lapis/Sodalite: Communication stone, Expression
Amethyst: Healing stone, Calming, restorative.

Within the sacred geometry of my crystal grid, I lay the foundation for a spell of love and healing. Each carefully placed crystal serves as a conduit, channeling the energy of the cosmos into the earthly realm. At the center of this arrangement, I place the soft, pink glow of rose quartz, its gentle vibrations radiating outward like ripples on a tranquil pond. As I trace the intricate lines of the grid, I imbue each crystal with my intentions, infusing them with the power of love.

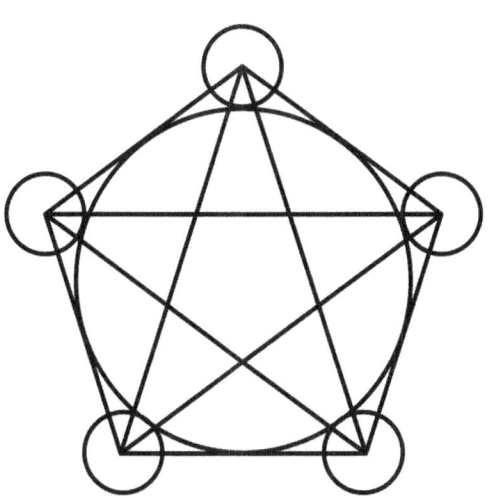

Seed of Life

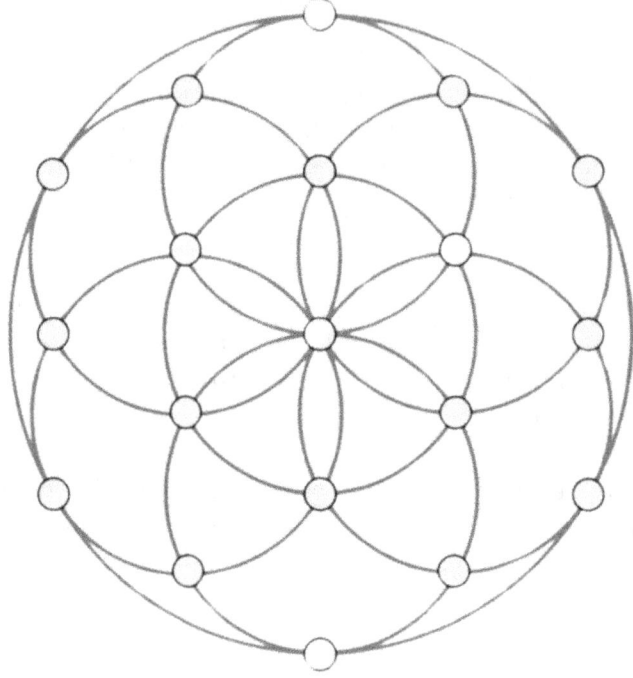

Metatron's cube

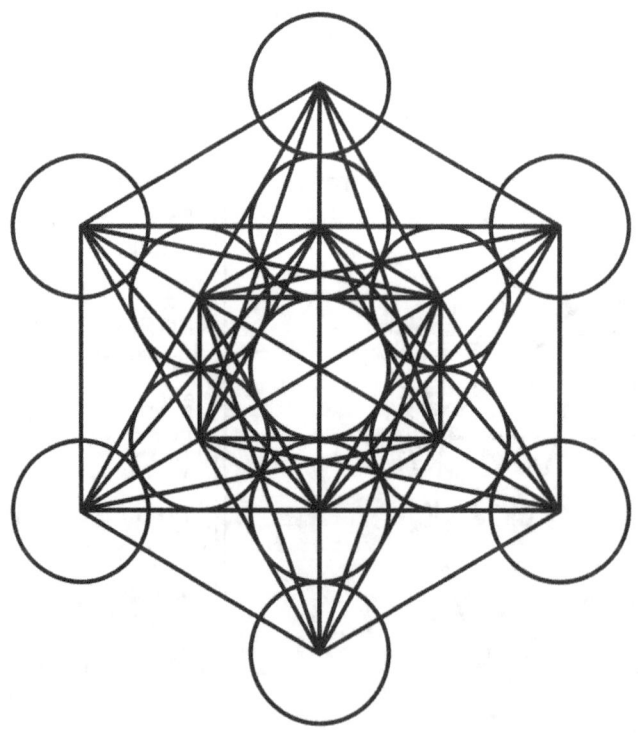

Antimony

Magical Properties
Self-confidence
Development
Amplifying power
Courage
Regulates internal frequencies
Increase clairvoyance

Classification -
Origin - Germany, China, France, Italy, Japan, Romania.
Rarity - It is uncommon to find a vein of antimony stone in its natural state.

Crystal Pairs With -
Don't Mix With - The stone must not come into contact with water, salt, or ammonia.
Cost -
Got it from -
Planets - Pluto
Chakra - All chakras
Signs - Scorpio, Capricorn
Notes:

Identification
Color(s) - Lustrous gray
Transparency -
Lustre -
Crystal System - Orthorhombic
Chemical - (Sb2S3)

As Mabon arrives, I embrace the balance of light and darkness within myself.

Apache tears

Magical Properties
Creativity
Opportunities
Transformation
Protection
Courage
Meditation
Confidence
Knowledge
Empathy
Channeling
Grounding
Clairvoyance

Classification -
Origin - United States
Rarity -

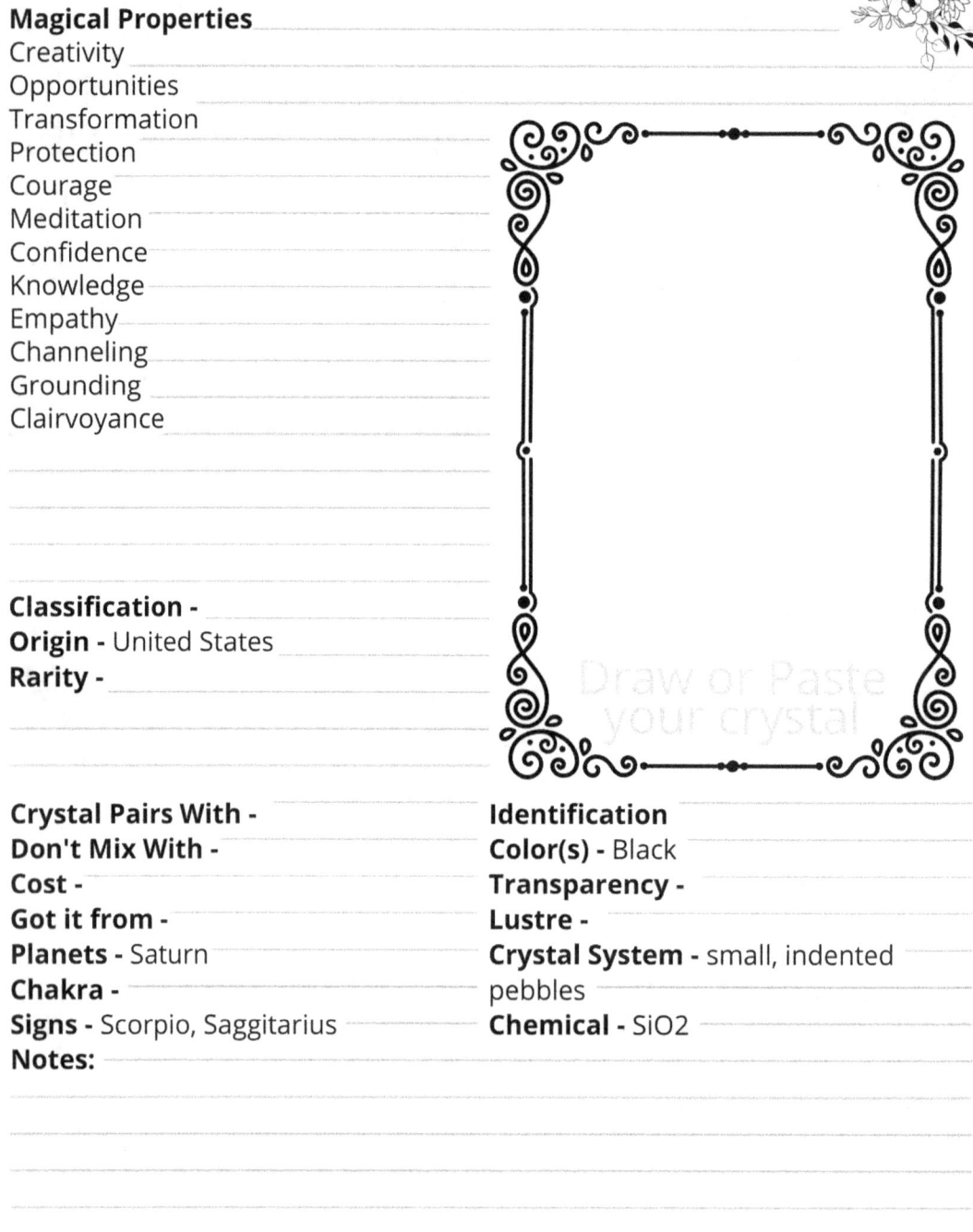

Draw or Paste
your crystal

Crystal Pairs With -
Don't Mix With -
Cost -
Got it from -
Planets - Saturn
Chakra -
Signs - Scorpio, Saggitarius
Notes:

Identification
Color(s) - Black
Transparency -
Lustre -
Crystal System - small, indented pebbles
Chemical - SiO2

With the guidance of crystals, I attract abundance and prosperity.

Azurite

Magical Properties
Spirit Guides
Angels
Higher Self
Aids the 6 "Clairs"
Mental clarity
Memories
Peace and harmony
Relieves aggravation
Facilitate meditation

Classification
Origin
Rarity

Crystal Pairs With
Don't Mix With
Cost

Got it from:
Notes:
Planets - Jupiter, Mercury
Chakra **-** Third eye, Crown
Signs - Sagittarius

Identification
Color(s) Dark blue
Transparency
Lustre
Crystal System -
Chemical

I am open to receiving the wisdom and guidance of the crystals during this sacred time.

Benitoite

Magical Properties
Heals diseases related to the brain.
Revitalize the brain
Powerful psychic development
Warrior energy
Joy, happiness, and beauty
Self-reflective meditation
Astral travel or communication with
divine realms

Classification -
Origin - One mine in California
Rarity - Very rare

Draw or Paste
your crystal

Crystal Pairs With -
Don't Mix With -
Cost -
Got it from -
Planets -
Chakra - Third eye and Crown
Signs - Virgo
Notes:

Identification
Color(s) - Deep blue, Blue, violet-blue,
colorless, and rarely pink
Transparency -
Lustre -
Crystal System - Hexagonal
Chemical - $BaTi(Si_3O_9)$

**During Mabon, I connect deeply with nature and feel the earth's wisdom
guiding me.**

Black Obsidian

Magical Properties
Truth-enhancing
Deep soul healing
Protection
Relieves stress and tension
Absorbs negative energy
Gives clarity of emotions
Blocks psychic attacks
Removes negativity influences
Calming
Compassion
Strength
Prophesy
Helps with shadow self & brings them
to the forefront to be acknolgeked
Breaks through mental barriers
Dissolves mental conditioning

Classification cooled molten lava
Origin
Rarity

Crystal Pairs With
Don't Mix With   water
Cost
Got it from

Notes: Base chakra
Scorpio Sign

Identification
Color(s)
Transparency
Lustre
Crystal System
Chemical

Put by the bed or under your pillow to draw out mental stress and tension.

Black Tourmaline

Magical Properties
Retrograde
Security and stability
Creativity
Protection
Clearing
Grounding
Purification
Cleansing
Mastering Fear
Transmutation of Negative Energies

Classification -
Origin - Germany
Rarity -

Draw or Paste
your crystal

Crystal Pairs With - Selenite and Rose Quartz
Don't Mix With - Saltwater
Cost -
Got it from -
Planets - Saturn
Chakra - Root
Signs - Capricorn
Notes:

Identification
Color(s) - Black
Transparency -
Lustre -
Crystal System -
Chemical - $Na(Fe2+3)Al6(Si6O18)$ $(BO3)3(OH)3(OH)$

Crystals are my companions, enhancing my intuition and surrounding me with loving energy.

Bloodstone

Magical Properties
Abundance
Alignment
Organization
Smooth energy flow
Generosity
Idealism
Good fortune
Purification

Crystal Pairs With Many
Don't Mix With
Cost

Got it from:
Notes:
Planets - Mars
Chakra **-** Base
Signs - Aries, Libra, Pisces

Identification
Color(s) -
Transparency -
Lustre -
Crystal System -
Chemical

I am deeply connected to the earth and all living beings, and I honor and respect them.

Bronzite

Magical Properties
Strength
Love & Relationships
Opportunities
Transformation
Protection
Courage
Channeling
Grounding
Self-Discipline
Leadership
Focus
Determination
Self Discovery
Growth

Classification -
Origin - Brazil, Czech Republic,
Madagascar, Austria, and USA.
Rarity - Common

Draw or Paste
your crystal

Crystal Pairs With -
Don't Mix With -
Cost -
Got it from -
Planets -
Chakra - Sacral, Root
Signs - Virgo
Notes:

Identification
Color(s) - brown
Transparency -
Lustre -
Crystal System -
Chemical - $(Mg, Fe^{2+})_2[SiO_3]_2$

As I meditate with crystals, I connect deeply with my inner self, gaining insight and clarity.

Celestite

Magical Properties
Retrograde
Meditation
Creativity
Psychic Abilities
Calming and Patience
Dreams
Clarity
Cleansing
Angelic Communication
Attunement With Higher Realms
Communication With Higher Realms
Elimination Toxins
Lucid Dreaming
Communication
Resolution

Classification -
Origin - Madagascar
Rarity - Extremely rare

Crystal Pairs With -
Don't Mix With -
Cost -
Got it from -
Planets - Venus, Neptune
Chakra - Etheric, Crown, Third eye
Throat
Signs - Gemini
Notes:

Identification
Color(s) - Blue, Light Blue
Transparency - Transparent
Lustre -
Crystal System - crystallizes as small
prismatic shards
Chemical - SrSO4

I embrace change with grace and acceptance, knowing that it is part of the cycle of life.

Clear Quartz

Magical Properties
Amplify spells/crystals
Clears away stagnant energy
Cleansing
Healing
Positive vibes
Programmable
Can substitute for any crystal

Classification
Origin
Rarity

Draw or Paste
your crystal

Crystal Pairs With   **Identification**
Don't Mix With   Color(s)
Cost   Transparency
Got it from   Lustre
                                Crystal System
Notes: Crown Chakra   Chemical
Leo Sign
Archangel Raziel

I trust in the divine timing of the universe, knowing that everything happens for a reason.

Cobra Jasper

Magical Properties
Relaxation
Contentment
Compassion
Nurturing
Consolation
 Tranquility
Healing
Completion

Classification
Origin
Rarity

Draw or Paste your crystal

Crystal Pairs With
Don't Mix With
Cost

Got it from:
Notes:
Planets -
Chakra - Base Chakra, Heart Chakra, Crown Chakra
Signs -Leo, Virgo, Scorpio

Identification
Color(s) -
Transparency -
Lustre -
Crystal System -
Chemical -

I release all past hurt and forgive myself and those who have wronged me.

Dalmation Jasper

Magical Properties
Amplify herbal remedies
Good focus
Prosperity
Protective charm against financial
scams
Encourage teamwork
Determine which friends

Classification
Origin
Rarity

Draw or Paste
your crystal

Crystal Pairs With

Identification

Don't Mix With

Color(s) -

Cost

Transparency -

Lustre -

Got it from:

Crystal System -

Notes:

Chemical -

Planets -Earth
Chakra - Root chakra
Signs - Virgo

I am filled with love and compassion for myself and others.

Eclogite

Magical Properties
Strength
Leadership
Spiritual Awakening
Soothing
Sexuality
Sense of Purpose
Selflessness
Self Discovery
Self- Healing
Action
Courage
Confidence
Compassion
Claiming Wholeness

Classification -
Origin - Norway, China, Germany, Austria, and the United States
Rarity - incredibly rare

Crystal Pairs With - Rose Quartz, Rhodonite, Kunzite, Rhodochrosite or Pink Opal
Don't Mix With -
Cost -
Got it from -
Planets - Earth
Chakra - Heart, Solar Plexus, Sacral, Root
Signs - Scorpio
Notes:

Identification
Color(s) - Red, Green
Transparency -
Lustre -
Crystal System -
Chemical - n{(Mg, Ca, Fe2+, Mn2+)3(Al, Fe3+, Cr3+, V3+)2(SiO4)3} p{(NaaCabFe2+cMgd) (AleFe3+fFe2+gMgh)Si2O6}

I am grateful for the blessings of the season, finding joy and fulfillment in the simple pleasures of life.

Emerald

Magical Properties
See visions
Truth
Protect against unwanted spells
Ward off unwanted enchantment
Creativity enhanced

Classification
Origin
Rarity

Draw or Paste
your crystal

Crystal Pairs With
Don't Mix With
Cost

Identification
Color(s) -
Transparency
Lustre -

Got it from:
Notes:
Planets -
Chakra - Crown
Signs - Aries

Crystal System -
Chemical -

I am open to receiving divine guidance and wisdom, and I trust in the universe to provide for me.

Flourite

Magical Properties
Sports
Decisions
Balance
Clarifying
Protection
Grounding
Cleansing
Balancing Polarities
Life's Purpose
Mental Enhancement
Self-Discipline

Classification -
Origin - South Africa, China, Mexico, Mongolia, the United Kingdom, the United States, Canada, Tanzania, Rwanda, and Argentina
Rarity -

Crystal Pairs With - Obsidian
Don't Mix With -
Cost -
Got it from -
Planets - Mercury
Chakra - Crown, Third Eye, Throat Heart, Solar Plexus, Sacral, and Root
Signs - Libra, Capricorn, and Pisces
Notes:

Identification
Color(s) - Blue, Green, Colorless, Purple, Black, Yellow, and Pink
Transparency -
Lustre -
Crystal System -
Chemical - CaF2

I feel a deep connection with the universe's insights by using crystals.

Gold

Magical Properties
Honor
Wealth
Happiness
Composure
Stabilize the emotions
Alleviate tension and stress
Amplify positive feelings

Classification -
Origin - Found almost everywhere
Rarity -

Draw or Paste your crystal

Crystal Pairs With - Jet, Colemanite, Citrine, Lepidolite, Bronzite, Lithium Quartz, Blue Phantom Quartz, Aragonite, Smoky Quartz, or Magnetite
Don't Mix With -
Cost -
Got it from -
Planets - Jupiter
Chakra - Third eye and Crown
Signs - Aries, Cancer, Leo, and Sagittarius
Notes:

Identification
Color(s) - Gold
Transparency -
Lustre -
Crystal System -
Chemical - Au

I am open to receiving the abundance that the universe offers me during the Mabon season.

Golden Topaz

Magical Properties
Power
Personal Will
Peace of Mind
Opportunities
New Beginnings
Motivation
Prosperity
Meditation
Mental Enhancement
Mastering Fear

Classification -
Origin - Brazil, Chelyabinsk, Russia, and the Topaz Mountains in western Utah
Rarity -

Crystal Pairs With - Garnet
Don't Mix With -
Cost -
Got it from -
Planets - Mars
Chakra - Solar Plexus
Signs - Saggitarius, Pisces, Leo
Notes:

Identification
Color(s) - Pale Yellow, Orange
Transparency -
Lustre -
Crystal System - Vertical hexagonal crystals
Chemical - $Al_2(SiO_4)(F, OH)_2$

With crystals and Mabon's energy combined, they guide me toward a season of balance, gratitude, and self-discovery.

Heliodor

Magical Properties
Trauma
Transformation
Strength
Stress Relief
Longevity
Spiritual Awakening
Soothing
Sense of Purpose
Selflessness
Self Discovery
Self- Healing
Self-Discipline
Resolution

Classification -
Origin - Ukraine, Sri Lanka, Namibia,
Brazil, Finland, Russia, and
Madagascar.
Rarity - One of the rarest beryllium
silicates on Earth

Draw or Paste your crystal

Crystal Pairs With - Clear Quartz
Don't Mix With -
Cost -
Got it from -
Planets - Jupiter
Chakra - Solar Plexus
Signs - Leo
Notes:

Identification
Color(s) - Pale Brass, Pale Yellow,
Green, Yellow
Transparency -
Lustre -
Crystal System -
Chemical - $Be_3Al_2(Si_6O_{18})$

My heart is filled with joy and gratitude when I experience the magic of crystals.

Iolite

Magical Properties
Psychic Abilities
Dreams
Communication
Meditation
Past Lives
Cleansing
Attunement
Higher Self
Inner Vision
Attunement With Higher Realms
Communication With Higher Realms
Self- Healing
Lucid Dreaming

Classification -
Origin - Brazil, Madagascar,
Burma, and India
Rarity - Common

Crystal Pairs With -
Don't Mix With -
Cost -
Got it from -
Planets - Saturn
Chakra - Third Eye, Crown
Signs - Taurus, Sagittarius, Libra
Notes:

Identification
Color(s) - Blue, Violet
Transparency -
Lustre -
Crystal System -
Chemical - $(Mg, Fe)2Al3(AlSi5O18)$

With each crystal grid I create, I amplify my intentions and manifest my desires.

Irnimite

Magical Properties
Psychic Abilities
Dreams
Transformation
Synchronicity
Channeling
Attunement
Ascension
Higher Self
Wisdom
Inner Vision
Angelic Communication
Attunement With Higher Realms

Classification -
Origin - Khabarovsk Krai region
of eastern Russia.
Rarity - Extremely rare

Draw or Paste
your crystal

Crystal Pairs With - Moldavite
Don't Mix With -
Cost -
Got it from -
Planets - Saturn
Chakra - Crown, Third eye Throat
Signs - Scorpio, Cancer, Pisces
Notes:

Identification
Color(s) - Blue, White, Brown
Transparency -
Lustre -
Crystal System - crystallizes in mass
formation
Chemical -

I honor the ancient traditions of Mabon, celebrating the harvest and giving thanks.

Jadeite

Magical Properties
Health-strengthening
Improve longevity
Absorb negative energy
Emotional healing
Dreamwork
Connecting with higher realms

Classification -
Origin - Myanmar, New Zealand,
Canada, Taiwan, Guyana, Surinam,
southern Europe, Russia and China.
Rarity -

Crystal Pairs With -
Don't Mix With -
Cost -
Got it from -
Planets -
Chakra - Heart Chakra
Signs - Aries, Taurus, Gemini, Libra
Notes:

Identification
Color(s) - Many
Transparency - Translucent
Lustre -
Crystal System -
Chemical - NaAlSi2O6

Mabon's energy fills me with harmony, helping me find equilibrium in all aspects of my life.

Kambaba Jasper

Magical Properties
Inner peace
Tolerance
Focus during meditation
Intention setting
Release negative thoughts
Increase prosperity
Increase money flow

Classification
Origin
Rarity

Draw or Paste
your crystal

Crystal Pairs With Many
Don't Mix With
Cost
Got it from:
Notes:
Planets - Saturn
Chakra - Heart
Signs - Capricorn

Identification
Color(s) Blue and Green
Transparency
Lustre
Crystal System -
Chemical

I release negativity and invite positivity into my life, harnessing the energy of the crystals

Kyanite

Magical Properties
Balance Aura
Calming Emotions
Divine Guidance
Aid Communication with Archangels
Protection
Healing
Telepathy

Classification
Origin
Rarity

Crystal Pairs With Many
Don't Mix With
Cost
Got it from:
Notes:
Planets - Earth and Uranus
Chakra **-** Crown, Third Eye, and Throat
Signs - Virgo, Aquarius, Pisces

Identification
Color(s) Blue
Transparency
Lustre
Crystal System - Triclinic
Chemical

I welcome the blessings of Mabon into my life, embracing its transformative power.

Lava Rock

Magical Properties
Vitality
Protection
Luck
Love
Calming

Classification
Origin
Rarity

Draw or Paste
your crystal

Crystal Pairs With   **Identification**
Don't Mix With   Color(s)
Cost   Transparency
Got it from   Lustre
                            Crystal System
Notes: Lava beads are porous   Chemical
and
can absorb essential oils

I honor the cycles of nature, aligning myself with the energy of Mabon.

Leopard Skin Jasper

Magical Properties
Courage
Mentally brave
Confidence
Increase agility
Sparks creative problem-solving

Classification
Origin
Rarity

Draw or Paste
your Crystal

Crystal Pairs With
Don't Mix With
Cost

Got it from:
Notes:
Planets - Venus
Chakra - Root, Sacral, and Heart Chakra
Signs -Capricorn and Leo

Identification
Color(s) -
Transparency -
Lustre -
Crystal System -
Chemical -

I am aligned with the cycles of the earth and the seasons of the year.

Magnesite

Magical Properties
New Beginnings
Motivation
Meditation
Luck and Good Fortune
Living in the Present Moment
Life Path
Leadership
Intention Enhancement
Inspiration
Insight
Growth
Expanded Awareness
Enlightenment

Classification -
Origin - Portugal, Bolivia, Australia, Chile, Sweden, France, Canada, and the USA.
Rarity -

Draw or Paste your crystal

Crystal Pairs With
Don't Mix With -
Cost -
Got it from -
Planets - Earth
Chakra - Crown, Third Eye, Throat, Solar Plexus, Sacral, and Root
Signs - Aquarius, Capricorn, Aries, and Virgo
Notes:

Identification
Color(s) - Black, Brown, and Grey
Transparency -
Lustre -
Crystal System - Octahedral, and dodecahedral crystals
Chemical - $Fe^{2+}Fe^{3+}_2O_4$

I let go of negative energy and welcome the healing vibrations of crystals.

Mookaite Jasper

Magical Properties
Strength
Stability
Quiets the mind
promote goal reaching
Self Confidence
Inner strength
Removes challenges
Encourage versatility

Classification
Origin
Rarity

Crystal Pairs With
Don't Mix With
Cost
Got it from:
Notes:
Planets - Saturn
Chakra - Root, solar plexus, navel
Signs - Capricorn

Identification
Color(s) Red, yellow, mauve
Transparency
Lustre
Crystal System -
Chemical

I am attuned to the natural rhythms of the earth, finding peace and tranquility in Mabon.

Morganite

Magical Properties
Selflessness
Nourishing and Rejuvenation
Nurturing
Passion
Peace of Mind
Physical Healing
Purification
Relaxation
Resolution
Self- Healing
New Beginnings

Classification -
Origin - Brazil, China, Australia, France, and the United States.
Rarity -

Crystal Pairs With - Rose Quartz, Green Calcite, and Pink Opal
Don't Mix With -
Cost -
Got it from -
Planets - Venus
Chakra - Heart
Signs - Libra
Notes:

Identification
Color(s) - Pink
Transparency -
Lustre -
Crystal System -
Chemical - Be3Al2(Si6O18)

Draw or Paste your crystal

I feel empowered when my thoughts and instincts are enhanced by crystals and guided by inner wisdom.

Moss Agate

Magical Properties
Growing Love
New beginnings
Trust
Release old fears
New lease on life
Grounding
Drawing strength from nature
Connecting with Fairie
New business/prosperity
Luck

Classification
Origin
Rarity

Crystal Pairs With
Don't Mix With
Cost
Got it from

Notes:
Cancer and Virgo Signs

Identification
Color(s)
Transparency
Lustre
Crystal System
Chemical

As the leaves change, so do I, growing and evolving with each season.

Musgravite

Magical Properties
Relieve stress
Boost positive energy
Bring joy
Peace of mind
Healing chronic ailments

Classification -
Origin - Musgrave Ranges, South
Australia
Rarity - Extremely rare

Draw or Paste
your crystal

Crystal Pairs With -
Don't Mix With -
Cost -
Got it from -
Planets -
Chakra - Heart chakra
Signs -
Notes:

Identification
Color(s) -
Transparency -
Lustre -
Crystal System - Trigonal
Chemical - Be(Mg, Fe, Zn)2Al6O12

With each crystal I hold, I amplify my intentions and manifest positive change.

Onyx

Magical Properties
Retrograde magic
Decisiveness
Strength
Protection
Confidence
Knowledge
Clearing
Purification
Cleansing
Self-Discipline
Wisdom
Focus
Self Discovery

Classification -
Origin - Mexico, Argentina, Brazil, Australia, South Africa, Madagascar, India, and the United States.
Rarity -

Crystal Pairs With - Quartz or Selenite
Don't Mix With -
Cost -
Got it from -
Planets - Earth, Mars, and Saturn
Chakra - Third eye, Solar Plexus, and Root
Signs - Leo
Notes:

Identification
Color(s) - Black
Transparency - Opaque
Lustre -
Crystal System -
Chemical - SiO2

I feel that crystals bring a lot of love and positivity into my life.

Orbicular Jasper

Magical Properties
Nurturing Protective
Encourage patience
Release emotional blockages
Soothing past sorrows

Classification
Origin
Rarity

Draw or Paste
your crystal

Crystal Pairs With
Don't Mix With
Cost

Got it from:
Notes:
Planets - Earth
Chakra - Heart Chakra
Signs -Capricorn

Identification
Color(s) -
Transparency -
Lustre -
Crystal System -
Chemical -

I can manifest my desires and creating my own reality.

Painite

Magical Properties
Spiritual, Emotional, and Physical
Healing
Healthy flow of energy
Clearing of the subliminal mind

Classification -
Origin - Myanmar
Rarity - Extremely Rare

Crystal Pairs With - Moldavite and
Herkimer Diamonds
Don't Mix With -
Cost -
Got it from -
Planets - Earth
Chakra - Chakra opener
Signs -
Notes:

Identification
Color(s) - Deep garnet red
Transparency - Transparent
Lustre - Vitreous luster
Crystal System - pseudo-orthorhombic
Chemical -

As the days grow shorter, I ignite my inner light and shine with renewed purpose.

Petalite

Magical Properties
Relaxing and calming down
Connecting with your guides
Healing the whole body, mind & spirit
Bringing magic and miracles
Boosting the immune system
Relieving stress and anxiety
Protecting from negative energy
Clearing your auric field
Releasing emotional baggage
Removing energetic cords and blocks

Classification -
Origin - Kalgoorlie, Western Australia, Minas Gerais, Brazil, Namibia; Manitoba, Canada, and Zimbabwe.
Rarity -

Draw or Paste your crystal

Crystal Pairs With -
Don't Mix With -
Cost -
Got it from -
Planets - Pluto
Chakra - Crown, Third eye, Heart
Signs - Leo, Pisces
Notes:

Identification
Color(s) - colorless, pink, grey, yellow, yellow grey, to white
Transparency -
Lustre -
Crystal System -
Chemical - LiAlSi4O10,

I find that my crystals have the ability to cleanse, renew, and uplift my spirit.

Picasso Jasper

Magical Properties
Creativity,
Digestive System,
Endocrine System, Enthusiasm,
Eye Health,
Grounding, Mental Clarity,
Metabolism, Neurological
Protection, Recovery,
Relationships,
Spirits, Spiritual Realms, Stress,
Transition, Weight Loss

Classification -
Origin - Huánuco, Peru
Rarity -

Crystal Pairs With - Barite, Mangano Calcite, Pyrite, and Rhodonite.
Don't Mix With -
Cost -
Got it from -
Planets - Mars, Venus
Chakra - Root, Sacral, and Heart
Signs - Taurus and Leo
Notes:

Identification
Color(s) -
Transparency -
Lustre -
Crystal System -
Chemical - SiO2

I feel a flow of spiritual energy within me, guided by the power of crystals.

Red Jasper

Magical Properties
Fertility
Deter bad luck.
Healing
Balance
Courage
Strength

Classification
Origin
Rarity

Draw or Paste
your crystal

Crystal Pairs With
Don't Mix With
Cost

Got it from:
Notes:
Planets - Mars
Chakra - Root and Sacral chakra
Signs -Aries

Identification
Color(s) -
Transparency -
Lustre -
Crystal System -
Chemical -

I release all fear and doubt and embrace the unknown with excitement and curiosity.

Rose Quartz

Magical Properties
Peace
Harmony
Acceptance
Trust
Love
Healing
Empathy
Intimacy
Romance
Who doesn't need self-love

Classification
Origin
Rarity

Draw or Paste your crystal!

Crystal Pairs With
Don't Mix With Sun
Cost
Got it from

Notes: Heart Chakra
Taurus and Leo Sign
Archangel Ariel

Identification
Color(s)
Transparency
Lustre
Crystal System
Chemical

I am grounded like the roots of the ancient trees, rooted in the energy of the earth.

Selenite

Magical Properties
Resolution
Clarity
Enlightenment
Transformation
Clearingaway anger/negativity
Positivity
Past-Life regression
Psychic abilities
Calm & stress relief
Meditation
Healing
Cleanses/charges other crystals

Classification
Origin
Rarity

Draw or Paste
your crystal

Crystal Pairs With
Don't Mix With Salt and water
Cost
Got it from

Notes: Delicate

Identification
Color(s)
Transparency
Lustre
Crystal System
Chemical

With each passing day, I am filled with gratitude for the abundance of the harvest season.

Sunstone

Magical Properties
Rest
Self-Healing
Humor
Cheerfulness/positivity
Self-confidence/self-esteem
Temperament
Self-love

Classification
Origin
Rarity

Draw or Paste
your crystal

Crystal Pairs With
Don't Mix With
Cost
Got it from

Notes: Sacral Chakra
Libra and Pisces Signs

Identification
Color(s)
Transparency
Lustre
Crystal System
Chemical

I embrace the balance of Mabon, finding harmony in my life.

Tanzanite

Magical Properties

Psychic Abilities
Intuition
Meditation
Truth
Higher Self
Wisdom
Alignment of Chakra
Expanded Awareness
Attunement With Higher Realms
Communication With Higher Realms
Communication with Guides
Astral Travel

Classification -
Origin - Tanzania
Rarity -

Draw or Paste
your crystal

Crystal Pairs With - Hematite
Don't Mix With -
Cost -
Got it from -
Planets -
Chakra - Crown, Third Eye, Throat
Heart
Signs - Gemini
Notes:

Identification
Color(s) - Blue, Light Blue
Transparency -
Lustre -
Crystal System -
Chemical - [Ca2][Al3](Si2O7)
(SiO4)O(OH)

Just as the leaves fall, I release what no longer serves me during this Mabon season.

Tiger Iron

Magical Properties
Self Discovery
Living in the Present Moment
Longevity
Manifestation
Mastering Fear
Motivation
New Beginnings
Personal Will
Power
Self-Discipline

Classification -
Origin - Western Australia
Rarity -

Draw or Paste
your crystal

Crystal Pairs With -
Don't Mix With -
Cost -
Got it from -
Planets - Earth
Chakra - Root, Sacral, Solar plexus
Signs - Leo
Notes:

Identification
Color(s) - Pale Yellow, Pale Brass, Silver, Brass-Yellow
Transparency -
Lustre -
Crystal System -
Chemical - n{Fe2O3} p{SiO2}

I am attuned to the energy of the crystals, allowing their healing power to flow through me.

Topaz

Magical Properties
Relaxation
Inner Peace
Inner Vision
Interdimensional Communication
Intuition
Living in the Present Moment
Mental Enhancement
Psychic Abilities
PTSD
Resolution
Self-Discipline
Self- Healing
Self Discovery

Classification -
Origin - Brazil and Zimbabwe
Rarity -

Draw or Paste
your crystal

Crystal Pairs With -
Don't Mix With -
Cost -
Got it from -
Planets - Mercury
Chakra - Third Eye and Throat
Signs - Saggitarius
Notes:

Identification
Color(s) - Blue, Light blue
Transparency -
Lustre -
Crystal System - Vertical hexagonal crystals
Chemical - $Al_2(SiO_4)(F, OH)_2$

I use the power of crystal energy and intention to bring my dreams to fruition.

Turquoise

Magical Properties
Travel
Balance
Communication
Empathy
Truth
Stress Relief
Higher Self
Expansion
Expanded Awareness
Inner Peace
Self- Healing
Peace of Mind
Emotional Understanding

Classification -
Origin - Turkey, United States
Rarity - Common

Crystal Pairs With -
Don't Mix With -
Cost -
Got it from -
Planets - Venus, Neptune
Chakra - Throat
Signs - Scorpio, Sagittarius, Pisces
Notes:

Identification
Color(s) - Blue, Pale yellow, Light Blue
Transparency -
Lustre -
Crystal System -
Chemical - $CuAl_6(PO_4)_4(OH)_8 \cdot 4H_2O$

Each crystal I work with is a sacred tool, helping me to manifest my intentions.

Vanadinite

Magical Properties
Meditation
Channeling
Grounding
Self-Discipline
Focus
Manifestation
Determination
Bridging the Spiritual and Physical
Worlds
Organization
Channeling and Grounding Higher
Vibrations
Self Discovery
Sexuality

Classification -
Origin - Morrocco, Mexico, and
the U.S.A.
Rarity - Rare

Crystal Pairs With - Carnelian or
Zincite
Don't Mix With -
Cost -
Got it from -
Planets -
Chakra - Third Eye, Solar Plexus
Sacral, Root
Signs - Virgo
Notes:

Identification
Color(s) - red, orange, and brown
Transparency -
Lustre -
Crystal System - Prismatic
Chemical - Pb5(VO4)3Cl

Draw or Paste
your crystal

I am filled with abundance and prosperity, in harmony with the energy of Mabon.

Crystal Name

Magical Properties

Classification -
Origin -
Rarity -

Draw or Paste
your crystal

Crystal Pairs With -
Don't Mix With -
Cost -
Got it from -
Planets -
Chakra -
Signs -
Notes:

Identification
Color(s) -
Transparency -
Lustre -
Crystal System -
Chemical -

I am open to receiving the abundance that the universe offers me during the Mabon season

If you want to bring beauty and serenity into your home discreetly without drawing attention, consider crafting crystal bowls. These elegant pieces can serve as both decorative items and tools for spells and other mystical practices.

Grab and Go Combos

Insight
rosemary, lemongrass, nutmeg, orange, aquamarine, howlite, or clear citrine.

Wisdom
parsley, thyme, chamomile, cumin, yellow quartz, and, lapis lazuli

Money
ginger, patchouly, dill, spearmint, gold, malachite, moss agate, and pearl

Peace
cumin, lavender, violet, marjoram, amazonite, blue lace agate, and silver

Relations
pansy, rose, valerian, moss agate, peridot, and sapphire

Love
vanilla, apple, clove, lavender, rose, amber, calcite, moonstone, and rose quartz

Banishing
clove, dragon's blood, garlic, hot pepper, obsidian, jet, and smoky quartz

Protection
angelica, frankincense, sandalwood, amber, carnelian, citrine, and petrified wood

Travel
dill, caraway, fennel mustard, malachite, moonstone, or tiger's eye

Communication
mint, turquoise, tiger's eye, and sodalite

Success
rosemary, saffron, bay, pyrite, clear quartz, and selenite

Courage
horseradish, basil, chives, nettle, pepper, tigers eye, carnelian, and pyrite

Happiness
cinnamon, mint, thyme, lavender, rose quartz, amethyst, citrine, and clear quartz

Health
cinnamon, coriander, eucalyptus, rosemary, sage, thyme, agate, amethyst, jade, and sunstone.

Binding
spiderwort, witch hazel, knotweed, agrimony, and jet

Grab and Go Crystals

Abundance crystals
citrine
clear quartz
amazonite
pyrite
adventurine
tiger's eye

Breaking Bad Habits crystals
amethyst
carnelian
garnet
hematite
lepidolite
citrine

Productivity crystals
tourmaline
green aventurine
pyrite
amazonite
citrine
smoky quartz

Mindfulness crystals
malachite
citrine
obsidian
turquoises
calcite
carnelian

Healing crystals
clear quartz
lapis lazuli
rose quartz
amethyst
aquamarine
garnet

Motivation crystals
pyrite
carnelian
amethyst
bumblebee
unakite
citrine

Friendship crystals
rose quartz
lapis lazuli
emerald
carnelian
blue lace agate
unakite

Happiness crystals
amazonite
amethyst
tourmaline
citrine
clear quartz
smoky quartz

Protection crystals
labradorite
amethyst
tourmaline
smoky quartz
obsidian
prehnite

Manifestation crystals
rose quartz
green jade
sodalite
citrine
selenite
amethyst

Lucky crystals
pyrite
green jade
tiger's eye
citrine
labradorite
carnelian

Work crystals
tourmaline
amethyst
rose quartz
pyrite
selenite
aventurine

Stress Relief crystals
lepidolite
amethyst
rose quarts
fluorite
sodalite
aquamarine

New Start crystals
aventurine
citrine
kyanite
rutile quartz
moonstone
labradorite

Grab and Go Crystals

New Home crystals
tourmaline
amethyst
rose quartz
clear quartz
sodalite
citrine

Anxiety crystals
moonstone
labradorite
rose quartz
amethyst
clear quartz
aquamarine

Love crystals
rhodonite
garnet
moonstone
sodalite
rose quartz
selenite

Letting Go crystals
Rutilated Quartz
Fire Quartz
smoky quartz
serpentine
black obsidian
rose quartz

Student crystals
amethyst
carnelian
fluorite
howlite
tiger's eye
clear quartz

Confidence crystals
citrine
carnelian
rose quartz
red jasper
orange calcite
tiger's eye

Relaxation crystals
amethyst
celestite
fluorite
tourmaline
angelite
howlite

Spirituality crystals
Fluorite
white howlite
labradorite
aura quartz
blue obsidian
amethyst

Creativity crystals
carnelian
amethyst
smoky quartz
clear quartz
citrine
tiger's eye

Trauma crystals
amazonite
lepidolite
fluorite
black line jasper
rose quartz
mangano calcite

Mental Clarity crystals
amethyst
hematite
apatite
sodalite
fluorite
citrine

Animal crystals
amethyst
smoky quartz
selenite
rose quartz
carnelian
agate

Crystals for breakups
rose quartz
malachite
pyrite
septarian
rhodonite
amethyst

Communication crystals
fluorite
kyanite
amazonite
sodalite
smokey quartz
lapis lazuli

Good Sleep crystals
amethyst
clear quartz
hematite
howlite
agate
moonstone

Grab and Go Crystals

Energy crystals
clear quartz
ruby
orange calcite
amethyst
carnelian
fuorite

Plant crystals
moonstone
tourmaline
aventurine
amethyst
clear quartz
malachite

Driving crystals
amethyst
rose quartz
tourmaline
malachite
carnelian
jasper

Crystals for breakups
rose quartz
malachite
pyrite
septarian
rhodonite
amethyst

Crystals for the bath
rose quartz
carnelian
tiger's eye
citrine
amethyst
clear quartz

Crystals for bedroom
celestite
rose quartz
labradorite
selenite
smoky quartz
howlite

I put them in bowls and up high so the wieners don't get into them. I usually add some salt and lavender, and rose quartz to all of them, but whatever feels right or even gives comfort. So you do you, Boo.

I pair selenite and rosemary for protection and cleansing

I pair rose quartz with (duh) roses for love and forgiveness.

I pair amethyst and chamomile for anxiety and stress relief

I pair garnet and pine for commitment and longevity

I pair black tourmaline and sage for dissolving negativity

I pair citrine with bay leaf for manifestation magic

I pair green adventure and basil for good fortune

I pair carnelian and cinnamon for sparking creativity

I pair moonstone and jasmine for harnessing confidence

CHAPTER 23

Magical Water

Magical Water

Water is a revered element with transformative and purifying properties, making it sacred to life. In the realm of spirituality and magic, different types of magical water hold immense power and are utilized for various purposes. Each enchanted kind of water has unique qualities, making it a versatile tool for spellwork, rituals, and energetic practices. Moon water offers soothing and healing properties, while holy water is potent and protective. These enchanted waters serve as conduits for intention and manifestation.

When combined with intention, visualization, and focused energy, the power of water is amplified in magic and spirituality. These different types of magical water serve as potent tools that allow practitioners to connect with the natural forces and energies around us. Whether seeking healing, protection, purification, or manifestation, the versatile uses of magical water offer a profound connection to the mystical realms.

Magical Water Properties

Rain Water: Growth and rebirth spells, cleansing, scrying, altar water, and ritual baths.

Storm Water: Vitality, self-esteem, courage, mental strength, strengthening spells, and protection.

Dew Water: Healing, beauty, eyesight, love, fertility, working with the fae, and cleansing.

Snow Water: Unthaw a situation, transformation, balance, peace, consecrating, and endings.

Moon Water: Charging, blessing or cleanse, bath rituals, powering spells, healing magic, curses, and hexes.

Sun Water: Protection, healing, clairvoyance, happiness, fertility, and creativity.

River Water: Moving on, focusing energy, warding, breakthrough, power, and charging.

Sea Water: Cleansing, banishing, protection, emotional balance, healing rituals, and manifestation.

Spring Water: Growth, holy water, cleansing, abundance, potions, and beauty.

Lake Water: Peace, joy, contentment, relaxation, self-reflection, and self-discovery.

Wellwater: Healing, wishes, intuition, manifestation, connection to otherworldly beings.

Swamp Water: Banishing, binding, hexing, cursing, and reversing.

Use clean, filtered water like distilled or spring water to add more magic to your recipes.

Rain Water

Catch the rainwater any time of day and bottle it up for your craft usage. Good for rebirth, cycles, transformation, cleansings, protection, altar water, ritual baths, peace, tranquility, purification, scrying, divination, and asperging.

Lake Water

Good for peace, happiness, contentment, joy, relaxation, reflection, personal journey, and growth.

Swamp Water

Good for revenge magic, binding, hexing, curses, and banishing

Dew Water

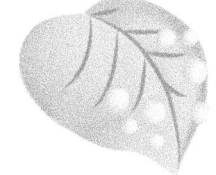

Collect dew water during the morning from windows, leaves, or flowers. Good for healing, cleansing, beauty, love, passion, fertility, and fae magic

Well Water

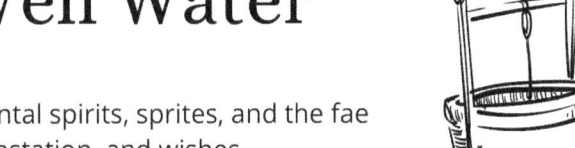

Good for connecting with elemental spirits, sprites, and the fae healing, intuition, scrying, manifestation, and wishes.

Spring Water

Good for growth, cleansing, abundance, fae work, love, fertility, healing, positivity, strength, purify altars, divination tools, endurance and grounding

Spiritual Water Properties

Fast Luck - Brings fast luck, money luck, quick outcomes, and aids manifestation.

Love Water - It brings love and resonates with love, harmony, and compassion.

7 African Powers - Draws strength from the 7 African Orishas.

Protection - Protects you, your space, your place, and your things.

Road Opener - Removes obstacles, brings new opportunities, and opens pathways.

Peruvian FL Water- Help with spiritual work, purification, rituals, and cleansing.

Destroy Everything - Destroys all conditions, jinxes, and curses and removes all things that do not serve you.

Attraction or Come To Me - Attracts the things you want, need, or desire in your life.

Tobacco Water - Draws spirits of nature, helps communication between worlds, and honors ancestors.

Success & Prosperity - Attracts success, abundance, money, and positivity.

Florida Water - It brings protection, spiritual cleansing, and positive vibes.

Florida Water Recipe

Ingredients:
16 oz of vodka
3-5 tablespoons of floral water (orange, rose, lavender, etc.)
8 drops of Lavender EO
10 drops of Lemon EO
10 drops of Orange EO
5 drops of Bergamot EO
5 drops of Cinnamon EO
5 drops of Clove EO
3 drops of Benzoin EO
Fresh rose petals and fresh rosemary (optional)

Directions:
Add your vodka and floral water to a bowl and smell each EO before adding it to your bowl. Let your nose and spirit tell you if you should add more or less than the recipe.
Combine all ingredients in a spray bottle.
Shake well before each use.
Remove rose petals and rosemary if you wish.
Keep your customized Florida Water on hand, too.

Worry Water

Water is the essence of life. It has the ability to absorb the emotions and feelings that we release into it. You can perform an energy transmutation ritual to release stress and anxiety from your body by sharing your secrets, fears, and worries with a pool of water. After releasing your emotions, pour the water down the drain or onto the Earth, making sure not to pour it directly onto plants. This will help you transform your negative energy into a more neutral state.

A Prayer for Grounding
Read out loud slowly for more calm energy.

Dear Universe, I ask you to ground me now and help me feel stable, safe, and secure in my mind, body, and spirit. I place a hand on my heart and one on my stomach. I take three deep breaths and exhale completely to reel in that tranquil energy of rooting. I feel myself being slowly anchored in angelic light. This light pours softly through the top of my head, down to my third eye, then my throat and heart, my sacral chakra, and all the way to the top of my legs. This calm light moves to my knees and then flows down to the top of my feet. Gently, it goes to the bottom of my feet and exits out through my toes. Thank you for helping me feel grounded, relaxed, and my divine best self.

CHAPTER 24

I Got a Jar of Dirt!

Types of Dirt and Their Magical Uses

Graveyard
Traditionally used in divination, cursing, love, and protection spells.
Avoid collecting from an unclean spirit's grave for most workings.
Leave an offering in exchange for the dirt.
Try to collect from an ancestor's grave to ensure the energy you are collecting is safe.

Churchyard
Traditionally used for many intentions and spells:
Healing
Prosperity
Purification
Protection
Mending relationships
Justice workings

Crossroad
They are traditionally used in road-opening spells.
Used in journeying to the underworld, as it helps open the gate to the other realms.
They are used as offerings to guardians and gods of the crossroads: Hecate, Hermes, Papa Legba, etc.

Backyard
Traditionally used in workings for the family, home, and property:
Purification
Protection
Peace
Collect from the 4 corners of the property if possible.

Graveyard

Working with Graveyard Dirt: Traditional Use in Healing, Protection and Prosperity Spells.

Graveyard dirt has long been used for its mystical properties, particularly in healing, protection, and prosperity spells. However, following specific guidelines when collecting graveyard dirt is essential to avoid negative energies. Here are some tips:

Avoid collecting dirt from the grave of an unwell spirit. Always leave an offering in exchange for the dirt gathered. Collecting dirt from ancestors' graves rather than from unknown ones is recommended. By following these guidelines, you can safely and effectively work with graveyard dirt in your practice.

Churchyard

Churchyard dirt is a versatile substance that can be utilized in magic and witchcraft for various purposes. Some of the most popular intentions and spells include:

Healing
Prosperity
Purification
Protection
Mending relationships
Justice workings

Crossroads

The Power of Crossroads Dirt in Road Opening Spells. Crossroads dirt has been used in road-opening spells for years and is particularly helpful in journeying to the underworld. This is because it helps to open the gate to other realms. Additionally, it's a great offering to guardians of the crossroads, such as Hecate and Papa Legba.

Leave

Things to leave at the crossroads for power or ritual.

Offerings
Spiritual offerings and prayers can be left at the crossroads to show thanks or strengthen your relationships with spirits. Be sure to leave appropriate offerings for the particular spirits you are working with or for the specific prayer/work.

Active Spells
The crossroads is a perfect place to anchor spells related to the power of that crossroads. Burying a spell designed to work long term here will allow the work to stay strong and progress without being actively worked at home.

Spell Remains
Most spellwork remains can be buried, burned, or left at the crossroads. This brings their energy to full completion. It lets any leftover prayer or intent in the work's plants, petitions, or other remains be fully and safely released. Use mindfully.

Take

Things to take from the crossroads for spells or charms.

Dirt
Crossroads dirt brings the power of manifestation from the crossroads. Dirt from male crossroads is excellent to manifest customers to a business. Dirt from a divine crossroads mixed into a garden or field attracts good spirits and increases harvest.

Stones
Crossroads stones carry the power of the crossroads itself with them. Pregnant women can carry stones from a female crossroads to protect the baby.
Stones from damned crossroads may be left in a house, yard, or field to curse it and make it barren.

Coins
Coins found at the crossroads are especially powerful. Silver coins found here protect from haunting nightmares and evil spirits. Copper coins protect one who carries them from love spells and binding. You may leave coins on purpose to pick up later, but found is always best.

CHAPTER 25

Witch Words

Witch Words

Altar - A sacred space of devotional or ritual work. This space is usually a table, shelf, or corner where offerings are presented to spirits and where one may perform rituals or spell work.

Animism - The belief that objects, places, and creatures all possess a distinct spiritual essence or soul.

Arcane - From the Latin for "hidden" or "secret." The term is often applied to mystical secrets, and the word arcanum is used in alchemy and arcana in Tarot.

Aspect - An archetype of a deity or entity. A form, facet, or persona of a deity. In astrology, an aspect is an angle planets make to each other in a chart.

Asperge - To cleanse and purify a space. This is usually done by spraying water around a room or using an herbal bundle to cleanse the area.

Astral Plane - The multi-dimensional plane within the astral realm where one can travel using their astral body.

Athame - A double-edged knife with a black handle, usually used in ceremonial magick and traditional Wiccan practices. It is associated with masculine energy and the elements of fire and air.

Besom - A broom made of twigs tied around a stick. Used in cleansing rituals and to invite beneficial energies to a space.

Blot - A communal event where animal sacrifice is used as an offering to a deity or god. Members of the ritual feast on the sacrifice in celebration. In today's age, sacrificing a live animal is less common; there will be lots of good food and wine in its place.

Book of Shadows - Personal notebook kept by a practitioner of magick to record their work. This would include spellwork, rituals, personal wisdom, dreams, and observations.

Boline - A small sacred knife used to cut items during a ritual. In contrast to the "Athame", a "Boline" usually has a white handle.

Broom closet - One who practices Magick or follows a pagan lifestyle and keeps that aspect of their life to themselves. Being "In the broom closet" means you practice in secrecy from your friends and family.

Burning Times - A name given to the days of the Reformation, Inquisition, etc., when Witches were tried and executed by inquisitors, sometimes burned at the stake.

Casting the circle - To project a circle or cone of energy where the practitioner will contain the energy generated by their ritual or magick.

Cense - To perfume something ritually with the odor of burning incense, such as a room, person, or object.

Charge - Intentionally passing specific energy or intention to an object, person, or space. Items that have been charged are sacred or consecrated for a particular purpose.

Charm - From the Latin carmen meaning "song, incantation," but came to be a generic term referring to any type of magick. As a noun, it commonly refers to a small object that protects its wearer from evil. As a verb, it commonly refers to the act of using magick to exert control over a person.

Conjure - Originally had to do with the taking of oaths. Its Magickal associations came when it was used to refer to binding demons to one's will. In time, "conjurer" became a generic term for a magick user.

Coven - A group of witches is called a Coven. A witch's magickal family may be considered their coven if they have formed a group to perform magick alongside each other.
Covenstead - A meeting space for witches to gather as a Coven.

The Craft - Refers to Witchcraft as a whole. One who follows the path of witchcraft follows the path of the craft.

Craft name - A name chosen by the practitioner for themselves within the magickal and spiritual community. This name can be a representation of
their craft, abilities, interests or can sometimes be given to them by other
members of their coven or elders.
Deosil - The clockwise motion of directing energy during a spell or ritual. This can be done with your hand, a wand, a knife, etc.

Dianic - A Wiccan type of group within the Goddess tradition, focused on female experience and empowerment, sometimes linked to feminism and led by women.

Drawing down - Invoking a Goddess into one who possesses the ability and strength to handle the deity's energy. Drawing refers to divination using mistletoe, where a high-ranking political/religious class in some ancient Celtic cultures.

Eclectic - One who shapes their practices from many different cultures and belief systems. Someone who follows their own experimental journey rather than dedicating themselves to one predefined path.

Elder - One who has reached old age within the Pagan community. This person will typically guide and share their wisdom with others.

Elementals - Personified spirits of each Element. Traditionally: Gnomes, Undines, Sylphs, and Salamanders.

Esbat - Meeting of a coven outside of the Sabbats, where healing, feasts, psychic work, and rituals take place, sometimes in the Full Moon but not necessarily.

Esoteric - From Ancient Greek esoteriks, "belonging to an inner circle." It often refers to occult orders and belief systems like Gnosticism, Kabbalah, and Rosicrucianism, whose teachings are not shared outside of a group of initiates.

Equinox - This happens twice a year when the duration of the day is equal to the duration of the night (12 hours each). The equinoxes occur around March 2st and September 21st and correspond to spring and autumn.

Evil Eye - A particular look or stare that is believed to bring bad luck for the person at whom it is directed, for reasons of envy or dislike. It is a curse or legend believed to be cast by a malevolent glare and usually given to a person when they are unaware.

Familiar - An entity that has a spiritual bond with a Witch on a higher plane, sometimes said to shape-shift into a physical being such as a companion animal.

Familiars and a Pet...NOT the same thing. Nor should you want your beloved pet to be your Familiar. For a modern witch to lay claim to a Familiar spirit, the animal must have made a pact with the witch.

Great Rite - Wiccan ritual involving symbolic sexual intercourse (actual sex or symbolic) with the purpose of drawing energy from the powerful connection between a male and a female participant.

Green Witch - A practitioner who works with plants, flowers, and herbs, and studies herbalism, botany, and folk magick. Green Witches talk to nature for guidance and respect for every living being. Green Witchcraft is the discipline of tuning into the energies of Earth through herbs. It's an important piece in the puzzle of working with the Five Elements of Nature: Air, Water, Fire, Earth, and Spirit.

Kindred - Members of a community gather for mutual benefit and to share their beliefs.

Left-hand path - A type of practice that pursues the empowerment of the self over nature or any spiritual order. It focuses on the strength and will of the practitioner rather than on the communion or alignment with Divinity or nature.

Magic or Magick - Some prefer to use the term "Magick" to differentiate it from stage magic performed by illusionists. The word "magic" has its roots in Magh, which meant "to be able, to have power", later found in Latin magice, meaning sorcery. The correct term for stage magic is "illusionist," as it is not actual Magic but rather an illusion of Magic. Aleister Crowley chose to use Magick with a -k for his practices and rituals. The term has since been re-popularized by those who have adopted elements of his teachings, but not everyone.

Otherkin - Those who believe they have an aspect within them that is non-human. Examples: Vampires, werewolves, fairies, shape-shifters, etc.

Pendulum - A handheld device, usually a crystal or metal piece hung on a chain, used to receive yes or no answers.
Polytheism - The belief in many gods. A polytheist may worship multiple gods in their craft.

Quarters - The four corners and/or watchtowers associated with each cardinal direction in a magickal circle. They are symbolic structures called upon to guard over a circle during a ritual. The Four Quarters are spirits that rule over each direction: North, East, South and East. Each is associated with one of the four classical elements: Earth, Air, Fire, and Water.

Reconstructionist - One who tries to recreate a single pre-Christian tradition, emphasizing historical accuracy over eclecticism, usually with a few exceptions.

Rede - From Middle English, meaning "advice" or "counsel", the Wiccan Rede provides the key moral system for Wiccans; "An it harm none, do what thou will".

Runes - The Scandinavian alphabet is mainly used today for divinatory purposes. Runes are usually inscribed on small stones.

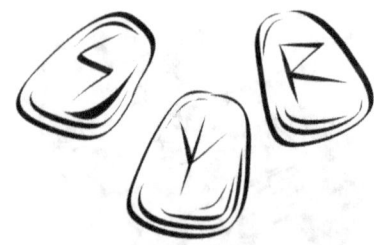

Sabbat - Each of the eight Wiccan holidays is celebrated in a calendar year. The first sabbat is Yule, and then comes Imbolc, Ostara, Beltane, Litha, Lammas, Mabon, and Samhain. These festivals are considered sacred days and it's tradition to celebrate them in good company.

Shadow Work - The shadow represents the repressed aspects of the personality that are rejected by the ego. Shadow work is an introspective practice where we face our pain instead of fighting it.

Sigil - A magickally charged seal, symbol, or glyph used in spells or charms.

Solstice - The time when the sun reaches its highest or lowest point at noon, resulting in the shortest and longest days of the year, typically around June 21-22 and December 21-22.

Summerland - A place beyond the material plane, similar to an afterlife, where souls go between incarnations.

Tradition - The beliefs, structures, history, rituals, and techniques followed and passed on for generations by a specific group of Pagans.

Warlock - From Old English for "traitor, liar, oath-breaker." It was sometimes used to refer to a person who was in league with the devil, and from there, it evolved (mainly in fictional work) into a male equivalent of "witch."

Wiccaning - Blessing a child or a newborn into the world by those who are part of the Wiccan community. A Neopagan ritual analogous to the christening or baptism of an infant.

Smudging

Smudging is a sacred ritual practiced by various Indigenous American tribes, involving the burning of specific herbs (such as white sage, cedar, or sweetgrass) to cleanse and purify spaces, objects, and individuals.

Cultural Significance: Smudging holds deep spiritual and cultural significance for Indigenous American communities, who believe it helps to dispel negative energies, promote healing, and maintain balance and harmony.

Differentiation: It's important to note that smudging is distinct from "smoke cleansing," which is a more general practice used in various spiritual and cultural traditions for similar purposes but may not necessarily involve the same rituals, beliefs, or cultural contexts.

Spirit Animals

Description: Spirit animals are an integral part of the spiritual beliefs and practices of many Indigenous American tribes. They are believed to be guides, protectors, or sources of wisdom and strength for individuals and communities.

Cultural Specificity: The concept of spirit animals is deeply rooted in the cultural and religious traditions of certain Indigenous American tribes. While other cultures may have similar beliefs about animal symbolism, the specific practice of connecting with spirit animals is exclusive to these Indigenous communities.

Belief Exclusivity: According to Indigenous American beliefs, one's spirit animal is determined by their ancestry, personal experiences, and spiritual connections within the tribe. It is not something that individuals outside of these communities typically have or claim.

Chakras

Description: Chakras are energy centers or focal points within the subtle body, according to Hindu and Buddhist spiritual traditions. They are believed to be located along the spine and correspond to different aspects of physical, emotional, and spiritual well-being.

Cultural Significance: The concept of chakras is integral to Hindu and Buddhist spiritual practices, including yoga, meditation, and energy healing. Each chakra is associated with specific qualities, elements, colors, sounds, and spiritual lessons.

Practices and Techniques: Within Kundalini yoga and other spiritual disciplines, various practices such as breathwork, visualization, meditation, mantra chanting, and mudras are used to balance and activate the chakras, promoting physical health, emotional harmony, and spiritual awakening.

Egg limpia

Egg limpia, also known as "egg cleansing," is a South American folk practice used for spiritual cleansing and healing. It involves the use of a raw egg to absorb negative energies or illnesses from a person's aura or energy field.

Cultural Significance: Egg limpia is deeply rooted in the cultural and spiritual traditions of South American folk medicine and shamanic practices, where it is believed to restore balance and remove blockages in the body's energy system.

Geographical and Cultural Context: Egg limpia is primarily associated with South American cultures and is part of their indigenous healing traditions and folk practices.

Karma

Karma is a concept originating from Hinduism and later adopted by Buddhism, referring to the law of cause and effect. It suggests that the intentions and actions of an individual influence their future experiences and circumstances, either positively or negatively.

Cultural Origin: Karma is deeply rooted in Hindu and Buddhist philosophy and spirituality, where it serves as a moral and spiritual principle guiding ethical behavior, personal development, and the cycle of reincarnation.

Belief System:

Karma is central to the belief systems of Hinduism and Buddhism, shaping notions of morality, justice, and spiritual evolution within these religions.

Spirituality For Beginners

Spirituality is about experiencing what's beyond the physical and using that knowledge to improve your life and the lives of others. It's not about relying on second-hand information but finding the truth for yourself.

As you develop spiritually, you'll gain psychic abilities, expand your existence beyond the mundane, and make better decisions. With intention and visualization, you'll be able to fight whatever holds you back directly. Start today and experience the excitement and meaning true spirituality brings to your life.

Dream Catchers

Dream catchers are hand-made woven hoops, traditionally crafted by Indigenous American artisans and adorned with sacred items such as feathers and beads. They are believed to protect the sleeper from negative dreams.

Cultural Significance: Dream catchers are deeply rooted in Indigenous American cultures, particularly among tribes like the Ojibwe, Lakota, and Anishinaabe, where they hold spiritual significance and are considered sacred objects.

Authenticity: There is a belief among some Indigenous communities that only dream catchers made by Indigenous artisans are authentic and hold spiritual power, while mass-produced versions may lack cultural integrity.

Appropriation Concerns: The commercialization and mass production of dream catchers by non-Indigenous individuals or companies has led to concerns about cultural appropriation and the commodification of Indigenous spiritual practices.

Sweetgrass

Sweetgrass (Hierochloe odorata) is a fragrant grass native to North America, traditionally used by Indigenous American tribes in smudging rituals and ceremonies for its pleasant aroma and spiritual properties.

Cultural Significance: Sweetgrass holds cultural and spiritual significance for many Indigenous American tribes, symbolizing healing, purification, and connection to the Earth.

Appropriation Concerns: Concerns about cultural appropriation arise when non-Indigenous individuals or communities commercially exploit sweetgrass without understanding or respecting its cultural significance, leading to calls for sustainable harvesting practices and cultural sensitivity.

In summary, these "closed objects" hold deep cultural, spiritual, and ecological significance for the communities from which they originate. However, they are also facing endangerment due to over-harvesting, habitat loss, and commercial exploitation, leading to concerns about cultural appropriation and the need for sustainable conservation efforts.

Closed Objects

Objects that carry cultural or spiritual significance for certain communities, emphasizing their value, as well as addressing issues related to their preservation and respectful use.

White Sage
Description: White sage (Salvia apiana) is a sacred herb traditionally used by various Indigenous American tribes in smudging rituals to cleanse spaces, objects, and individuals of negative energy.
Cultural Significance: White sage holds deep cultural and spiritual significance for Indigenous American communities, who have used it for ceremonial purposes for centuries.
Endangerment: Due to over-harvesting, habitat destruction, and climate change, white sage populations are currently declining, leading to concerns about its sustainability and conservation.
Appropriation Concerns: The commercialization and widespread use of white sage by non-Indigenous individuals or communities have sparked concerns about cultural appropriation and the exploitation of sacred traditions.

Palo Santo
Description: Palo Santo is a type of aged wood from the Bursera graveolens tree, native to South America, particularly regions like Peru and Ecuador. It is burned for its aromatic scent and spiritual properties.
Cultural Significance: Palo Santo holds cultural and spiritual significance for Hispanic/Latino communities in South America, where it is used in rituals, ceremonies, and healing practices.
Endangerment: Like white sage, Palo Santo is facing endangerment due to over-harvesting and habitat loss, leading to efforts to regulate its trade and promote sustainable harvesting practices.
Appropriation Concerns: The commercial buying and widespread use of Palo Santo by those outside of Hispanic/Latino communities have raised concerns about cultural appropriation and the unethical exploitation of natural resources.

Haitian Vodou

Haitian Vodou is a syncretic religion that developed in Haiti among Afro-Haitian communities during the Atlantic slave trade. It combines elements of traditional West African religions (such as Yoruba and Fon), Roman Catholicism, and indigenous Caribbean beliefs.

Beliefs: Haitian Vodou is polytheistic, with a pantheon of spirits, each associated with different aspects of life, nature, and human experience. Practitioners believe in the interconnectedness of the spiritual and physical worlds and the importance of rituals, offerings, and ancestor veneration.

Cultural Significance: Haitian Vodou is deeply ingrained in Haitian culture and identity, serving as a source of spiritual guidance, communal solidarity, and resistance against oppression. It is recognized as one of the main religions in Haiti, alongside Catholicism, and influences various aspects of daily life, art, music, and literature.

Historical Context: Haitian Vodou emerged as a survival mechanism and form of cultural preservation among enslaved Africans in Haiti, who faced harsh conditions and brutal treatment under French colonial rule. It provided a means of resistance, empowerment, and cultural resilience against oppression.

Hoodoo

Hoodoo, also known as conjure or rootwork, is a syncretic folk tradition practiced primarily by African Americans in the Southern United States, as well as in the Caribbean. It incorporates elements of African spirituality, Indigenous American beliefs, European folk magic, and Christian mysticism.

Beliefs and Practices: Hoodoo encompasses a wide range of spiritual practices, rituals, and beliefs aimed at achieving specific goals, such as protection, healing, prosperity, and love. It often involves the use of herbs, candles, roots, charms, and rituals passed down through oral traditions and family lineages.

Cultural Significance: Hoodoo has played a significant role in African American culture and history, serving as a means of empowerment, survival, and resistance against oppression. It has influenced various cultural expressions, including music, folklore, literature, and art, and continues to be practiced as a form of spiritual and cultural heritage.

Historical Context: Hoodoo originated among enslaved Africans in the Southern United States, who adapted and syncretized spiritual practices from their diverse cultural backgrounds to navigate the challenges of slavery and maintain connections to their ancestral traditions.

Kemetic Orthodox

Kemetic Orthodoxy is a modern religious movement that seeks to reconstruct and revive the ancient Egyptian religion of Kemet (Egypt). It draws inspiration from archaeological evidence, historical texts, and scholarly research to reconstruct the beliefs, rituals, and practices of ancient Egyptian spirituality.

Beliefs: Kemetic Orthodoxy emphasizes devotion to the gods and goddesses of ancient Egypt, including deities such as Ra, Osiris, Isis, and Anubis. It incorporates rituals, offerings, prayers, and meditative practices aimed at honoring the divine and fostering personal spiritual growth.

Initiation and Training: Kemetic Orthodoxy does not require formal initiation in the traditional sense, but it does involve a process of study, learning, and engagement with the religion's teachings and practices. Practitioners may undertake a series of coursework and rites of passage as part of their spiritual development.

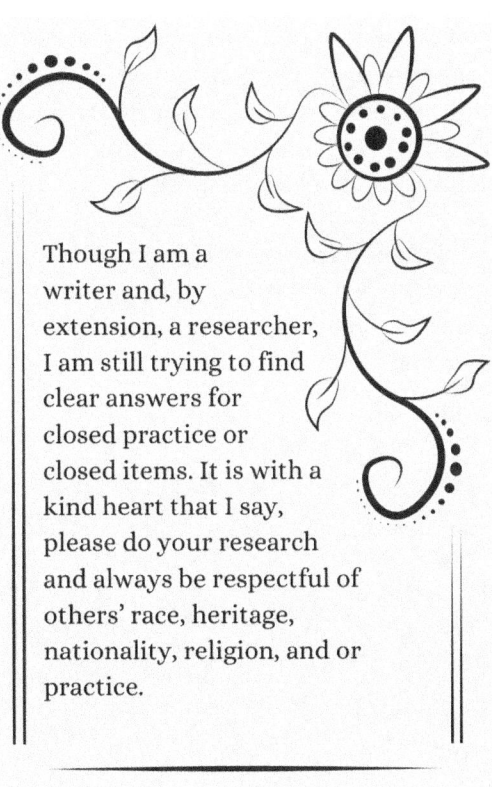

Though I am a writer and, by extension, a researcher, I am still trying to find clear answers for closed practice or closed items. It is with a kind heart that I say, please do your research and always be respectful of others' race, heritage, nationality, religion, and or practice.

Tribal (almost all)

Indigenous tribes or tribal communities exist in various parts of the world, including Africa, the Americas, Asia, and Oceania. These communities often have distinct languages, cultures, traditions, and social structures shaped by their historical experiences and connections to the land.

Cultural Diversity: Tribal societies exhibit remarkable diversity in their beliefs, practices, and ways of life, ranging from hunter-gatherer societies to settled agricultural communities. They may practice animism, ancestor worship, shamanism, or other spiritual traditions.

Connection to the Land: Many tribal cultures maintain strong connections to their ancestral lands, viewing the natural environment as sacred and integral to their spiritual and cultural identities.

Zoroastrianism

Zoroastrianism is one of the world's oldest monotheistic religions, originating in ancient Persia (modern-day Iran) around the 6th century BCE. It was founded by the prophet Zoroaster (or Zarathustra) and served as the state religion of the Persian Empire.

Beliefs: Zoroastrianism revolves around the teachings of Zoroaster, who preached the existence of a single supreme deity, Ahura Mazda (the Wise Lord), and the dualistic struggle between good (truth, order) and evil (falsehood, chaos). It emphasizes ethical conduct, free will, and the pursuit of righteousness.

Practices: Zoroastrian rituals and practices include prayers, purification rites, fire worship, and the veneration of sacred elements such as fire, water, and earth. Death rituals, including exposure of the deceased to scavenging birds (sky burial), are also significant in Zoroastrian tradition.

Inuit

The Inuit are Indigenous peoples inhabiting the Arctic regions of Canada, Greenland, Alaska, and Siberia, known for their resilience, adaptability, and unique cultural traditions.

Spirituality: Inuit spirituality is deeply connected to the land, sea, and animals of the Arctic environment. Beliefs often revolve around animism, shamanism, and a profound respect for the natural world.

Shamanism: Inuit religious practices may involve shamanic rituals, drumming, storytelling, and ceremonies to communicate with spirits, seek guidance, and maintain balance with the environment.

Judaism

Judaism is one of the oldest monotheistic religions, originating in the ancient land of Israel and encompassing a rich tapestry of beliefs.

Rastafari Movement

The Rastafari Movement is a religious and cultural movement that originated in Jamaica in the early 20th century. It emerged as a response to social, economic, and political conditions faced by black Jamaicans, drawing inspiration from various sources, including Christianity, Pan-Africanism, and Ethiopianism.

Beliefs: Rastafari adherents believe in the divinity of Ethiopian Emperor Haile Selassie I, whom they revere as the Messiah (or Jah), and the fulfillment of biblical prophecies regarding the return of the King of Kings. They also emphasize principles such as African liberation, social justice, and the rejection of Babylon (systemic oppression).

Cultural Practices: Rastafari culture is characterized by spiritual practices such as Nyabinghi chants, cannabis sacrament (known as ganja), natural living, dreadlocks, and a distinctive lifestyle focused on unity, love, and righteousness.

Some Parts of African Vodou

African Vodou, also known as Vodun, Voodoo, or Vodoun, is a syncretic religion practiced primarily in West Africa and the African diaspora, particularly in Haiti and parts of the Caribbean.

Beliefs and Practices: African Vodou incorporates elements of African spirituality, animism, ancestor worship, and Christian symbolism. It revolves around the veneration of spirits of loa, divination, healing, and ritual ceremonies.

Variation: Different sects, groups, or families within African Vodou may have variations in their practices, beliefs, and rituals, reflecting regional differences, cultural influences, and individual preferences.

Hinduism

Description: Hinduism is one of the world's oldest religions, originating in the Indian subcontinent and encompassing a diverse array of beliefs, practices, sects, and philosophies.

Diversity: Hinduism encompasses a wide range of beliefs, including polytheism, monotheism, pantheism, and atheism, as well as various philosophical schools such as Vedanta, Yoga, and Samkhya.

Denominations: There are numerous denominations and sects within Hinduism, each with its own theological interpretations, rituals, and practices. Some are open and inclusive, while others may be more exclusive or restrictive in their membership requirements.

Beliefs and Practices: Hinduism encompasses a vast array of beliefs and practices, including devotion (bhakti), ritual worship (puja), yoga, meditation, karma, dharma, and reincarnation.

Hopi

The Hopi are a Native American tribe located in northeastern Arizona, known for their rich cultural heritage, artistry, and spiritual traditions.

Spirituality: Hopi spirituality is deeply rooted in reverence for the land, ancestors, and cosmic forces. Central to Hopi beliefs are the concepts of balance, harmony, and interconnectedness with nature.

Kachinas: Hopi religious ceremonies often revolve around the worship of kachinas, spiritual beings believed to inhabit the natural world and serve as intermediaries between humans and the divine.

Shinto

Shinto is the indigenous religion of Japan, characterized by a reverence for kami (spirits or deities) and a deep connection to nature, ancestors, and the spiritual essence of Japan.

Branches: While Shinto practices vary among different regions and communities, there are both open and closed branches of Shinto. Jinja Shinto, which revolves around the worship of kami at shrines, is one of the more open denominations.

Rituals: Shinto rituals, ceremonies, and festivals are central to communal life in Japan, often involving purification rites, offerings, prayers, and processions.

Druidism (proper, not neo)

Druidism is a modern revival of ancient Celtic spiritual and religious practices centered around reverence for nature, the cycles of the seasons, and the wisdom of the ancestors.

Historical Context: Druidism originated among the Celtic peoples of Europe, particularly in regions such as Britain, Ireland, and Gaul, where druids served as priests, scholars, and custodians of traditional knowledge.

Beliefs and Practices: Druidic beliefs encompass animism, polytheism, and a deep respect for the natural world. Practices may include rituals, ceremonies, meditation, and storytelling, often conducted in sacred groves or natural settings.

Gardnerian and Alexandrian Wicca

Gardnerian and Alexandrian Wicca are two branches of modern witchcraft that emerged in the mid-20th century, founded by Gerald Gardner and Alexander Sanders, respectively.

Beliefs: Both Gardnerian and Alexandrian Wicca draw inspiration from Western esoteric traditions, folk magic, ceremonial rituals, and pagan beliefs. They honor a pantheon of deities, practice magic, and celebrate seasonal festivals such as Sabbats and Esbats.

Initiation: Gardnerian and Alexandrian Wicca typically require initiation into a coven or lineage, with teachings passed down through oral tradition and ritual ceremonies. Each tradition has its own specific rituals, practices, and codes of ethics.

Many African Cultures

African cultures comprise a vast array of ethnic groups, societies, and civilizations across the African continent, each with its own languages, customs, traditions, and belief systems.

Diversity: African cultures exhibit remarkable diversity in their languages, religions, art forms, cuisines, and social structures, shaped by thousands of years of history, migrations, and interactions with neighboring peoples.

Religious Traditions: African religions encompass a wide range of traditional beliefs, including animism, ancestor worship, polytheism, and shamanism, often intertwined with cultural practices, rituals, and ceremonies.

Saami (in Finland)

The Saami, also known as Sámi or Sami, are Indigenous peoples inhabiting the Arctic regions of Norway, Sweden, Finland, and Russia (Sápmi).

Cultural Practices: Saami culture is characterized by reindeer herding, fishing, hunting, and a close relationship with nature. Traditional Saami practices include yoiking (a form of traditional song), handicrafts, storytelling, and shamanic rituals.

Spirituality: Saami spirituality is deeply connected to the natural world, with beliefs in spirits, deities, and the importance of maintaining harmony and balance with the environment.

Santería

Santería, also known as Lukumi or Regla de Ocha, is a syncretic religion that originated in Cuba and later spread to other parts of the Caribbean and the Americas. It combines elements of Yoruba religion (brought by enslaved Africans) with Roman Catholicism and Indigenous American traditions.

Beliefs: Santería worships a pantheon of orishas, or deities, derived from Yoruba cosmology, each representing different aspects of nature, human experience, and divine forces. Practitioners engage in rituals, ceremonies, and divination to honor the orishas, seek their guidance, and cultivate spiritual growth.

Cultural Significance: Santería is deeply rooted in Cuban culture and society, influencing various aspects of music, dance, art, and folklore. It is also practiced in other parts of the Caribbean and the Americas, particularly among Afro-Cuban and Afro-Latino communities.

Historical Context: Santería emerged among enslaved Africans in colonial Cuba as a way to preserve their cultural and religious traditions in the face of oppression and forced conversion to Christianity. It represents a blending of African, European, and Indigenous American influences, reflecting the complex history and identity of Afro-Cuban communities.

Many Native American Cultures

Native American cultures encompass a diverse array of Indigenous peoples, tribes, and nations across the Americas, each with its own unique languages, traditions, beliefs, and practices.

Cultural Diversity: Native American cultures vary significantly in their social structures, spiritual beliefs, artistic expressions, and ways of life, reflecting the rich tapestry of Indigenous identities and histories.

Spirituality: Many Native American cultures maintain spiritual traditions deeply rooted in reverence for the land, ancestors, and natural world. Practices such as ceremonies, rituals, storytelling, and sacred dances play central roles in maintaining cultural continuity and connection to the spiritual realm.

CHAPTER 26

Race and Culture

Race-Locked Spirituality

Race-locked spirituality refers to spiritual or religious practices that are exclusive to individuals of a specific racial or ethnic group. These practices may be rooted in cultural traditions, historical experiences, or shared identities and may involve beliefs, rituals, symbols, or ceremonies that are specific to a particular racial or ethnic community.

Certain forms of African traditional religions, such as Vodou or Santería, are often associated with specific ethnic or racial groups and may be practiced predominantly by members of those groups. Similarly, some forms of indigenous spirituality or Native American religions are deeply connected to specific tribal identities and may be inaccessible to those outside the tribe.

Characteristics
Cultural Specificity: Race-locked spiritual practices are deeply intertwined with the cultural identities, histories, and worldviews of specific racial or ethnic groups.

Ancestral Connections: Practitioners of race-locked spirituality often emphasize connections to their ancestors and draw upon ancestral knowledge, rituals, and teachings in their spiritual practices.

Collective Experience: Race-locked spirituality may arise from collective experiences of oppression, resilience, and cultural survival, shaping the beliefs and practices of the community.

Resistance to Appropriation: Some practitioners of race-locked spirituality may be wary of cultural appropriation and may seek to protect their traditions from outside influence or exploitation.

Debates and Perspectives: Discussions around race-locked spirituality often intersect with debates about cultural appropriation, authenticity, and identity. While some argue for the preservation and protection of cultural heritage, others advocate for greater inclusivity and accessibility to spiritual practices across racial and ethnic boundaries.

In summary, closed communities restrict membership based on specific criteria, while race-locked spirituality involves spiritual practices exclusive to particular racial or ethnic groups. These concepts reflect complex interactions between culture, identity, tradition, and belonging, with implications for inclusivity, diversity, and cultural preservation.

Closed Communities

"Closed Communities" and "Race-Locked Spirituality" are terms that describe cultural or spiritual practices that are exclusive to specific racial or ethnic groups.

Definition: Closed communities refer to groups or societies that restrict membership based on specific criteria such as ethnicity, race, religion, nationality, or other factors. These communities often have boundaries that limit interaction with outsiders and may have strict rules or traditions governing behavior, beliefs, and social interactions within the group.

Examples: Historically, closed communities have included indigenous tribes, religious sects, ethnic enclaves, and cultural groups that maintain a sense of identity and solidarity through shared ancestry, language, customs, or beliefs.

Characteristics
Limited Access: Closed communities typically restrict access to outsiders, requiring individuals to meet certain criteria or undergo initiation rituals to become members.

Strong Group Identity: Members of closed communities often share a strong sense of identity and belonging based on common ancestry, culture, or values.

Preserving Tradition: Closed communities may prioritize the preservation of cultural or spiritual traditions by maintaining strict boundaries and resisting external influences.

Protection and Security: Closed communities may form in response to historical persecution, discrimination, or marginalization, providing a sense of safety and protection for members.

Challenges and Controversies:
Closed communities may face challenges related to inclusivity, diversity, and integration with broader society. Critics argue that strict boundaries can foster insularity, prejudice, and exclusion, while proponents emphasize the importance of preserving cultural heritage and protecting vulnerable communities.

Cultural Appropriation

Cultural appropriation is a complex and contentious issue that involves the borrowing, adoption, or use of elements from one culture by members of another culture. This concept often sparks debate because it can lead to misunderstandings, disrespect, and harm to marginalized communities. Here, I'll explain the concept of cultural appropriation in detail, focusing solely on factual information:

Definition:
Cultural appropriation refers to the adoption or use of elements of one culture by members of another culture, typically by a dominant culture appropriating aspects of a marginalized or minority culture. This can include clothing, hairstyles, symbols, language, rituals, music, dance, art, and more.

Examples:
Fashion: The use of Native American headdresses as fashion accessories by non-Native individuals without understanding their cultural significance or respecting their sacredness.

Cuisine:
Commercializing traditional dishes from various cultures without proper acknowledgment or understanding of their origins and significance.
Art and Music: Sampling or replicating traditional songs, dances, or artworks without giving credit to the original creators or understanding the cultural context behind them.

Religious Symbols:
Wearing religious symbols (such as bindis or crosses) as fashion statements without understanding their religious or cultural significance.

Power Dynamics:
Cultural appropriation often occurs within a framework of power dynamics, where the dominant culture appropriates elements from marginalized or oppressed cultures. This can perpetuate stereotypes, reinforce power imbalances, and contribute to the erasure of the marginalized culture's identity.

Cultural appropriation can lead to various forms of harm.

Diminishing Cultural Significance: Appropriation can strip cultural symbols or practices of their original meaning, reducing them to superficial trends or commodities.

Disrespect and Insensitivity: Appropriating sacred or meaningful elements of a culture without understanding or respect can be deeply offensive to those who belong to that culture.

Economic Exploitation: In cases where cultural products or practices are commodified without benefiting the originating culture, appropriation can perpetuate economic exploitation and inequality.

Appreciation vs. Appropriation

It's important to distinguish between cultural appreciation and appropriation. Cultural appreciation involves respectfully learning about and engaging with different cultures, often with acknowledgment and understanding of their significance. Appropriation, on the other hand, involves taking elements of a culture without proper understanding, respect, or acknowledgment.

Call for Cultural Sensitivity and Respect: Many advocates emphasize the importance of cultural sensitivity, education, and respectful engagement when interacting with cultures different from one's own. This includes listening to and learning from members of the culture, acknowledging sources, and considering the potential impact of one's actions.

Controversies and Debates: Cultural appropriation is a subject of ongoing debate and controversy, with differing perspectives on where to draw the line between appreciation and appropriation, as well as how to address instances of appropriation when they occur.

Legal and Policy Considerations: While cultural appropriation often involves ethical considerations rather than legal ones, some countries have laws or policies aimed at protecting indigenous cultures or traditional knowledge from exploitation or misuse. However, enforcement and interpretation of such laws can vary widely.

In summary, cultural appropriation involves the adoption or use of elements from one culture by members of another culture, often without proper understanding, respect, or acknowledgment. It can perpetuate stereotypes, reinforce power imbalances, and cause harm to marginalized communities. Discussions around cultural appropriation emphasize the importance of cultural sensitivity, education, and respectful engagement with diverse cultures.

Cascarilla Powder

Cascarilla powder is an essential ingredient in protective magic that's easy to make. The powder is made from powdered eggshells and is primarily used for spiritual cleansing and protection. Originating from Hoodoo and Santeria, it has become increasingly popular throughout America due to its accessibility. Cascarilla powder can also help create spiritual barriers similar to salt, add blessings, aid in protection, and make a great nutritional addition for plants in the garden. For added protection, try complementing the cascarilla powder with Florida water.

Tip: To make a higher-quality powder, run the eggshells under a kitchen faucet to remove the membrane before drying them.

Ingredients:
2 dozen eggshells, dried
A food processor or mortar and pestle
½ teaspoon of Florida water (see recipe)
A small glass jar or sealable container

Directions:
Bake the eggshells at 200 degrees for approximately 30 minutes to further dry them. This step allows excess moisture to cook off, making for a more delicate powder. This step is significant if you grind the shells by hand using a mortar and pestle! You might notice the color change slightly if you're using white eggshells. Don't worry - your powder will still come out white.

When the eggshells are dry, grind them into a fine powder using a mortar and pestle or food processor.

Add about 1/2 teaspoon of Florida water and process until you have a fine, sand-like consistency.

Store the cascarilla powder in a jar or pack it into chalk.

For Cascarilla Chalk:
Mix 1 tablespoon of flour and 1 tablespoon of loose cascarilla powder thoroughly.
Add a tablespoon of warm water and mix until the ingredients combine to form a ball in your hands.
Roll the mixture into sticks about 1/2 to 1 inch in diameter and let them dry for 3 to 5 days. Alternatively, you can roll the mixture into balls and place them in a small-pack paper condiment cup.
Store the chalk in a glass, plastic, or metal container to protect it from breaking, and keep it in a cool, dark place.
Note: Be careful not to add too many additional or specific herbs, as this may stop the mixture from sticking together and forming chalk. You can use cascarilla powder in spells and make sigils and magical symbols.

Salt for Magic

Himalayan/Pink Salt - ("purest salt on Earth" because of maturing for 250 million years) is used for love, removing negative blockages and curses, and cleansing.

Hawaiian Black Salt - (harvested from the evaporated water on Hawaiian Island Molokai) is used for its extra strength.

Table Salt - Used for purifying, protecting, and cleansing, and used in culinary recipes.

Kosher Salt - (blessed by a Jewish Rabbi)
Used to draw out negativity or absorb negativity

Black Salt -(leftover ashes or scrapings from cast iron)
Used for banishing and protection.

Alaea/Hawaiian Red Salt - (From iron-rich volcanic clay)
Used for love and sex, blocks negative energy, protects aggressively to defend an area that has been set with or encircled with it, and is used in culinary recipes (high in nutrients 80+).

Sel Gris Sea Salt - Used for blessing.

Celtic Sea Salt - Used for protection and attracting financial abundance.

Sea Salt - (carries the power of the sea and water elements)
Used for purification and cleansing, it helps to balance emotions.

Cyprus Black Salt - (sea water dried in lava beds mixed with charcoal)
Used to evoke properties of the pyramids, energy from heaven, used in culinary recipes.

Rock Salt - Used for return to sender, used to reflect negativity to sender.

Fleur de Sel Salt - (sea salt from France) is a gentler salt used with fairies and elementals.

Gray Salt - (developed in clay pools) Used in liminal workings.

Blue Salt - (sea salt mixed with blue flowers) Used for protection from the Evil eye, justice, and healing. That being said, you can make any color salt by mixing colored herbs.

Herb Infused Salts - (Salt infused with edible herbs)
Choose an herb that aligns with your intentions.

Epsom Salt - Use in the bath to reduce inflammation and muscle pain and to help you de-stress.

Pickling Salt - (purest form, no added agents)
Used for purification, preservation of love, prosperity, etc., and used in culinary recipes.

Banishing Spell

Write down the name of the person or thing you want to banish on a piece of paper. Write your own name over the top of what you want to banish so your name crosses out theirs. Say this chant three times: "I cover you, I cross you, I command you, compel you, [name of person], get out of my life!" Burn the piece of paper with the names on it in the flame of the candle. Dress a black candle with banishing oil and light it. Let the candle burn out completely. Dispose of the remains in the trash as a symbol of banishment.

Banishing Candle Dressing

Mix equal parts of:
Black pepper
Cinnamon
Paprika
Salt
Cayenne pepper
Then add a little vinegar to make a paste.
Rub the paste around the candle to dress it

Door Protection Sachet

Create a small sachet or pouch using fabric or a small bag.
Fill it with protective herbs such as rosemary, sage, and basil.
As you fill the sachet, visualize a protective barrier forming around your home.
Once the sachet is filled, tie it securely with a knot.
Hold the sachet in your hands and focus your intention on protection and safety for your home and those within it.
Place the sachet near your front door or doorstep, either hanging it on the doorknob or tucking it discreetly nearby.
As you do so, recite a simple incantation, such as:
"By earth and air, by fire and sea, Protect this home, so mote it be. May all who enter find peace and light, Warding off darkness with gentle might."
Visualize the protective energy of the herbs surrounding your home like a shield, keeping negativity and harm at bay.
You feed the sachet periodically, refreshing it with new herbs and repeating the spell to maintain the protective energy around your doorstep.

CHAPTER 27

Mabon
Journaling

Journal Prompts for Self-Reflection and Shadow Work

Journaling prompts can be an excellent tool for self-reflection by helping you delve into your thoughts and emotions. Expressing yourself through journaling can be therapeutic and provide clarity and understanding of your experiences without fear of judgment.

The versatility of journaling prompts is a significant advantage. You can customize them to your unique needs and interests and use them to explore any aspect of your life. Whether it's your relationships, career goals, personal values, or simply gaining a better understanding of yourself, there's a prompt that's perfect for you. You're free to choose the prompts that speak to you and follow your authentic path.

Remember, there's no right or wrong way to engage in self-reflection. This is a personal journey, and the insights you gain are unique to you. Embrace the process, trust your instincts, and allow yourself to be vulnerable. Your journaling practice will mature over time, and each entry will bring you closer to a deeper connection with yourself.

Self-Reflections

What are 3 ways I can share of my abundance with others this season

Self-Reflections

Which areas of my life could use some preparation and improvement

Self-Reflections

Why is fall a great time to set some new goals and get clear about your dreams

Self-Reflections

What do you look forward to in the winter months

Self-Reflections

How much have you changed since this time last year

Self-Reflections

What changes would you love to see by fall next year

Self-Reflections

What are 3 ways I can share of my abundance with others this season

Self-Reflections

Fall is the perfect time to think ahead with an open mind. What ideas are bubbling up in the back of your mind, ideas that you would love to give space to

Self-Reflections

What are your three favorite things about life in Autumn

Self-Reflections

What things have you been able to let go of in this past year

Self-Reflections

List the things you're grateful for as you transition into the new season

For the past five years, I have been reviewing books for independent authors under my company, Robin's Review. This experience has allowed me to connect with some truly amazing individuals. If you are curious, feel free to visit my reviewer page at Robinsreview.com for reviews on books spanning various genres. (no shameless promotion intended)

CHAPTER 28

Books
and
Resources

The Voyage & The Return: The Path to Self Discovery

June 4, 2022

The Voyage and the Return: The Path to Self Discovery is a book for women who have been wondering, "Is this all there is?" Sharing the voices from women whose lives were turned upside down—who went through a major upheaval or a life-changing experience. They took that moment as an invitation to find out who they truly are and what is possible for them. Each one of them embarked on a voyage that took them into the unknown.

And, every one returned home with an answer to their most important question:What does my heart most long for?

The Voyage and the Return...
is about taking the first step on your unique path to self-discovery
is about the challenges you might face along the way
is about trust, courage and celebration
is about truly living these next chapters of your life.
is about believing that you can do this.
is for those of you who are ready to explore your edge
is for those of you who know it's time
is a manual for living an extraordinary life
This book gives you tools and stories to help you on your own journey of self discovery.

Robin's Review

Embark on a transformative self-discovery journey with "The Voyage and the Return," a top-rated anthology crafted by a team of talented authors. This inspiring book urges you to take bold steps toward your path, confront challenges confidently, and celebrate progress along the way. It serves as a guiding light for those eager to push boundaries, providing varied viewpoints and wisdom for navigating an exceptional life.

Explore a collection of diverse stories within these pages, each offering a distinct perspective on overcoming adversity. Experience the essence of resilience as contributors share personal tales of facing darkness and discovering newfound strength. Through moving narratives, readers are encouraged to join a shared journey of belief, resilience, and change.

The anthology highlights each author's exceptional storytelling ability, fostering a deep connection with readers through their healing narratives. With a range of voices and experiences, "The Voyage and the Return" presents a tapestry of viewpoints that enhance the reader's exploration of self-discovery. Immerse yourself in this captivating anthology and uncover the strength of collective healing and personal growth. #TransformativeRead #HealingJourney

Ask Yourself.

Understand and Unlock Your Psychic Power
for Personal & Planetary Healing

Rev. Pamela Irene Flowerday

With 22+ years of professional clairvoyant experience in over 8,000 readings for clients around the globe, Flowerday will teach you to:
Understand your subtle energy system and how your chakras are hardwired for psychic perception;
Shed cultural conditioning that undermines your psychic experience;
Navigate your chakras to enter a psychic space and "read" clairvoyantly;

Release your negative patterns and blocks; Manifest transformative change through personal and planetary healing techniques. Based largely on the clairvoyant training model of the late Lewis Bostwick (founder of the Berkeley Psychic Institute), ASK YOURSELF. reminds us that our answers can be accessed directly through our higher chakras. Learn to navigate your energy system, enter a clairvoyant space, and ask yourself what you want to know. Your answers will find you.
Sub-topics covered by this psychic abilities guide & workbook include:
Definition and discussion about ESP and the "5 clairs" (clairvoyance, clairsentience, clairaudience, claircognizance, clairalience) as well as remote viewing, psychokinesis/telekinesis, telepathy and other intuitive gifts.
Cultivate greater subtle energy awareness through practical spiritual awakening meditations and multiple exercises that build one upon the other.
Learn how to read auras and heal chakras of blocks and thoughtforms.
Empaths. You can stop absorbing other people's energy/negativity and reduce your stress and anxiety. Embrace your empathic abilities but learn to build better energetic boundaries with others and your environment.
Techniques for manifesting your desires, a better life, and improved relationships.
Manifest positive change collectively to heal Gaia and support peace on earth.
Taking mindfulness a step farther. Develop more spontaneity and notice a big boost to your psychic perception and paranormal experiences.
Suggestions to cultivate your self love, heal spiritually and emotionally, embrace your intuitive gifts and empower your life.

Robin's Review

Book Reviewing for Independent Authors: A Personal Experience
As part of my company, I have been reviewing books for Independent authors for five years. I've had the opportunity to meet and interact with some really incredible people. One of those individuals was Rev. Pamela Irene Flowerday, who reached out to me with her book, "Ask Yourself: Understand and Unlock Your Psychic Power for Personal & Planetary Healing." Her writing style was absolutely incredible, and I was blown away by the content. I highly recommend this book, and if you're interested, check out my reviewer page at Robinsreview.com for a short Q&A with the author. (sorry not a shameless plug)

The author, Rev. Pamela Irene Flowerday
wrote Ask Yourself: Understand and Unlock Your Psychic Power for Personal and Planetary Healing.

"Ask Yourself" by author Rev. Pamela Irene Flowerday combines her special expertise and techniques to help you along your spiritual path.

The subjects cover a wide range of relevant topics, and the author provides useful exercises and even some pro tips. At first, I was unfamiliar with some of the author's terminology, but after reading this book, I now understand it and find it sensible.

The amount of valuable information contained in this book and its concise style have made it an excellent addition to my metaphysical studies. I highly recommend this book and author and hope to read more books from her in the future.

After completing some of the exercises in the book, I was astounded by the wealth of knowledge I had gained. The book helped me to identify and trust my inner knowing, and I was inspired by Rev. Flowerday's insightful content. With this newfound understanding of my intuitive abilities, I was able to embark on a path of profound spiritual growth and personal transformation.

THE
SOUL
FAMILY
A GUIDE TO KARMIC RELATIONSHIPS, SOULMATES,
SOUL TRIBES, AND TWIN FLAMES

ALEXX SHAW

The Soul Family: a Guide to Karmic relationships, Soulmates, Soul Tribes, and Twin Flames
December 2, 2023

Have you ever met someone that you just couldn't get out of your head? Or immediately disliked someone for no apparent reason? Do you have a longtime friend that you have nothing in common with anymore, but you're still holding onto the friendship? Or do you and your parents continuously fight, never seeing eye-to-eye?

Though seemingly different at first glance, all of these people have something in common...they're part of your Soul Family...and they're in your life for a reason.

This book is about understanding energy by breaking down the Ego and seeing past perceived "reality." It is about remembering who you are, not by who society dictates you to be, but rather your true nature. And it is about learning to see the lessons shown to you by every person playing a role in your life, navigating more easily through your connections, and remaining non-attached as you heal your traumas.

Whether you're struggling with Karmic relationships, Soulmates, Soul Tribe members, or a Twin Flame, Alexx will help guide you through. Utilizing Quantum Physics, String Theory, biology, epigenetics, Samkhya philosophy, energetic healing modalities, astrology, and stories on each Soul Family member, you'll gain a deep comprehension of what lessons you chose to learn in this incarnation, and how they're being presented to you.

Robin's Review

5 ⭐
5 🧠
Profound

As I listen to The Living Years by Mike + The Mechanics
I have to admit that I took a break from reading for a day to digest all the information from just the first few chapters, giving myself time to let the information sink in before continuing. Also, I will be rereading it, and instead of my sticky notes, I will highlight (sorry) and annotate passages throughout the book. It's that good.

"The Soul Family" by Alexx Shaw dives deep into this intriguing phenomenon, shedding light on why these connections occur and what valuable lessons they carry. Shaw's book goes beyond surface-level interactions, urging readers to see past societal expectations and glean insights from each encounter. Whether dealing with challenging friendships, soulmates, or twin flames, Shaw offers practical guidance infused with spiritual wisdom and scientific perspectives. This book is a transformative journey of self-discovery, providing tools to navigate relationships more effectively and heal from past experiences. With clarity and depth, Shaw's exploration of existence, purpose, and relationships challenges conventional notions and illuminates the intricate dynamics of ego, karma, and soul connections. Through insightful reflections on core karmic lessons, readers are empowered to understand the significance of the individuals in their lives and embrace the journey of self-discovery. "The Soul Family" is a must-read for anyone seeking deeper insights into their existence and the connections that bind us all.

If you read only one book in 2024, let this be that book.

I had the pleasure of engaging with author Alexx Shaw. She shared her book, "The Soul Family: a Guide to Karmic Relationships, Soulmates, Soul Tribes, and Twin Flames", which blends practical advice with spiritual insights and scientific perspectives, making perfect sense. I highly recommend this book.

For those interested, visit my reviewer page on Robinsreview.com for a brief Q&A with the author. (Apologies for the shameless plug.)

Alexx Shaw, the author, penned "The Soul Family: a Guide to Karmic Relationships, Soulmates, Soul Tribes, and Twin Flames".

D.B. Earthly's Of Dirts & Earths: A Compendium & Guide to Dirts, Soils, Sands, Silts & Dusts, and Their Use in Witchcraft, Including A Guide to Simple Geomancy
March 1, 2024

D.B.Earthly's Of Dirts & Earths is a unique and comprehensive guide to the use of earth in witchcraft and magical practices. The book delves into the world of various dirts and soils, illuminating their historical uses, properties, and ways to incorporate them into one's own magical workings. From grave dirts to crossroads dirt, to forest and river dirt, this volume brings together an impressive array of dirts which are often overlooked magical literature.

Divided into three main sections, the book firstly introduces readers to general practices, ethics, and the process of collecting and using dirts in ritual work. Included are guides to performing geomancy and communicating with spirits. The second, and largest part, is an encyclopedic catalog of various types of dirts and soils, detailing their uses and associations in witchcraft. The final section serves as a useful reference guide, offering cross-referencing options, bibliography, and an appendix.

Robin's Review

OMG, D.B. Earthly's "Of Dirts & Earths" is a game-changer in the world of magical literature! This enchanting compendium is like a treasure map to the mystical secrets hidden within the earth itself.

Earthly's expertise shines through as they guide readers through the vast and often overlooked world of dirt, soil, sands, silts, and dusts in witchcraft. From the eerie grave dirts to the lively river soils, every type of earth is explored with meticulous detail, revealing their historical uses, properties, and how to harness their magic in your own spellwork.

But this book isn't just a dusty old tome filled with esoteric knowledge—it's a practical guide for both beginners and seasoned practitioners alike. Earthly breaks down the process of collecting and using dirts in ritual work, and even throws in a guide to performing geomancy and communicating with spirits for good measure.

The real magic of "Of Dirts & Earths" lies in its encyclopedic catalog of earth elements, which serves as a comprehensive reference guide for any witch's bookshelf. And let's not forget the thrilling finale—a useful section packed with cross-referencing options, a bibliography, and an appendix for easy navigation.

In short, if you're looking to deepen your connection to the earth and enhance your magical practice, look no further than "Of Dirts & Earths." With its blend of earthly wisdom and mystical magic, this book is a must-have for any witch's library. Trust me, you won't be disappointed! 🌿🪦

D.B. Earthly's Compendium of Magical Ingredients & Curios Vol. I: A guide to herbs, fungi, zoological curios, ritual items, minerals, concoctions, and their use in witchcraft. May 31, 2023

Behold, the wondrous D.B. Earthly's Compendium of Magical Ingredients & Curios Volume I, A guide to herbs, fungi, zoological curios, ritual items, minerals, concoctions, and their use in witchcraft!

A true masterpiece in the realm of magical items and properties. This splendid compendium spans over 400 pages and contains more than 200 extraordinary items of power, each more wondrous than the last...

Learn the uses of items from the most obscure and ancient traditions, to folklore and legends, to modern esoteric uses. Every facet of magic is represented within these pages. This is no mere book, but a veritable cornucopia of magical ingredients and curiosities!

From the darkest corners of the occult to the ancient protective magic of our forests, rivers, woods, and gardens, this compendium is the ultimate guide to the ingredients and curios of witchcraft!

Delve into the obscure folklore and ancient traditions of the past alongside modern esoteric practices. Every facet of witchcraft truly is represented within the pages of this remarkable compendium. With the utmost attention to detail and a reverence for the ages-old ways of the occult, this tome is the pinnacle of reference books in the field of witchcraft ingredients and magical properties.

Robin's Review

A remarkable find, truly enchanting! 🌟 D.B. Earthly's Compendium of Magical Ingredients & Curiosities is a masterpiece in the realm of magical objects and properties. With over 400 pages, it presents more than 200 extraordinary items imbued with power, each more captivating than the one before. From ancient customs to contemporary mystical practices, this book encompasses all facets of magic. It's not just a book; it's a treasury of magical ingredients and curiosities! 📚 ✨

This compendium acts as the ultimate manual for witchcraft ingredients and curiosities. Explore common folklore and age-old practices alongside modern techniques. Every aspect of witchcraft is intricately explored within the captivating pages of this exceptional compendium. 💀🌿

Crafted with meticulous attention and deep reverence for ancient occult traditions, this book serves as the essential guide for witchcraft ingredients and mystical properties. #MagicalDiscovery #WitchyWisdom 📓

Colby Parrish

(727) 831-8077

Facebook: The Wondering Fool - Spiritual Advisor
Instagram: Thewonderingfool333
TikTok: TheWonderingFool333

Hours of Availability
Tuesday through Saturday 11 am - 8 pm EST

Service Menu
General Psychic Readings
30 min/$60
45min/$90
60min/$120

Tarot - Oracle - Lithomancy
3 Card Single Message
Pull/ $20
Couples Readings
40min/$80
Personal Monthly
Forecast/$120
Numerological
Chart/$150

Available for private parties and events!

He is my spiritual adviser, so I highly recommend him and his services!

Jamie Wareham

www.lightworkerpath.com
Email: lightworkerpathsite@gmail.com

Service Menu
Reiki + Sound Healing Sessions
Soul Coaching Sessions (spiritual life coaching)
Intuitive Development
Mentorship Programs
Reiki Level 1,2 & 3 Attunement
Certification Courses
Spiritual/Energy Development Classes

She is a fellow writer who co-authored "The Voyage & The Return: The Path to Self Discovery." Moreover, I've taken her classes, and they were interesting and helpful. She's super knowledgeable about energy work, angel spirit guides, meditation, and reiki healing.

Here is a profound quote from her book "Some of the best teachers are ones who have journeyed into the heart of darkness and come through it all like the powerful Phoenix they are! A rebirth into something else, something stronger, something that yearns to help others through their own forms of darkness."

Mystic Mind Community

Why Join The Mystic MindCommunity?

We bring together spiritual people who are seeking more connection, the ability to share their own experiences, and learn from online Challenges, Live Events, Courses, and each other!

The concept for building this Spiritual Social Network is so we can grow together in a supportive, inclusive, and fun Spiritual Metaverse covering a wide range of spiritual resources.

The Mystic Mind Podcast

The Mystic Mind Podcast is a creative exploration to help support you in your intuitive and spiritual development journey and add a little fun!

I mean, we have to have fun on this journey, right?

As a professional Energy Healer and Spiritual Teacher, I share some of what I've learned along the way during my spiritual development journey for over a decade. In this podcast, you will find shows on Intuitive Development and/or reflections, Angels, Divination, Energy Work, special guests, interviews, and more.

Also, have you joined our Mystic Mind Community?
Mystic Mind is available on
Spotify
Anchor fm
Amazon Music
Apple Musi
DCNW Podcast:
Spotify:

Elemental Magic

For all of your metaphysical needs

elemental-magick-inc.myshopify.com
948 4th Avenue Coraopolis, PA 15108
Phone Number: (412) 741-1428

Facebook Group Elemental Magick
Instagram Elemental Magick Inc

We are a women-owned metaphysical business that has been operating since 2015! Located in Coraopolis, Pennsylvania, we provide some of the best quality crystals in Pittsburgh with a personal service guarantee every time you shop. Our products include candles, books, incense, and items from local artisans, including Gaias Grace.

Hours of Operation
Sunday: CLOSED (Sunday Funday Facebook Live 7:00 pm EST)
Monday: CLOSED
Tuesday: CLOSED
Wednesday: CLOSED (Witchy Wednesday Facebook Live 7:00 pm EST)
Thursday: 12 pm - 6 pm
Friday: 12 pm - 6 pm
Saturday: 12 pm - 6 pm

Odie's Curiosities

Handmade High-Quality Jewelry Available on Facebook

Discover beautifully crafted handmade items, including reiki-charged jewelry that is hand-strung with care. With a specialty in Mala beads, this Facebook store offers stunning and unique pieces you won't find anywhere else.

Contact through Facebook Messenger

Whimsical Cauldron and Crafts

www.whimsicalcauldronandcrafts.com
Email: Whimsicalcauldron2019@gmail.com
Facebook: Whimsical Cauldron and Crafts, LLC

They sell crystals, minerals, specimens, jewelry, herbs, sage, etc.
They also feature other vendors and their merchandise.

I have purchased almost everything they have for sale and can confidently say they are a great small business for high-quality crystal needs. They have always been kind and patient, especially when I first learned about crystals. If they didn't have something I was looking for, they would get it for me.

Emerald Coast Alternatives

emeraldcoastalternatives.com

Welcome to Emerald Coast Alternatives, your online herbal tea shop. We aim to provide accessible, effective, and affordable herbal tea blends that help you feel better and enjoy life more. Our teas are delicious and effective in managing symptoms of anxiety, PTSD, PMS, insomnia, inflammation, and headaches. We donate one Herbal Tea "Care Package" monthly to a Recovery Center in the USA. Thank you for choosing Emerald Coast Alternatives as your trusted herbal teas and self-healing tools source.

Follow them and learn more about what their products can provide on TikTok @freespirit.beauTEA

Enhance your Health with The Plant Cemetery Herbal Subscription Box!
MONTHLY HERBAL HEALTH & BEAU-TEA SUBSCRIPTION BOX
$10 OFF YOUR FIRST BOX with Code: PlantBox10
FREE SHIPPING ON ALL PRODUCTS!

Although I am not typically a tea fan, I absolutely adore the tea from this company. I purchase it frequently and have even signed up for their monthly subscription box.

Reference

A History of Magic, Witchcraft, and the Occult DK

The Modern-Day Witch (11 books) by Shawn Robbins, Leanna Greenaway, Lisa Chamberlain

Witchcraft for Daily Self-Care: Nourishing Rituals and Spells for a More Balanced Life by Michael Herkes

The Untamed Witch: Reclaim Your Instincts. Rewild Your Craft. Create Your Most Powerful Magick. Lidia Pradas

Paganism: Pagan holidays, beliefs, gods and goddesses, symbols, rituals, practices, and much more! An Introductory Guide by Riley Star

Buckland's Complete Book of Witchcraft   Raymond Buckland

The Modern Witchcraft Spell Book: Your Complete Guide to Crafting and Casting Spells (Modern Witchcraft Magic, Spells, Rituals)
by Skye Alexander

Scott Cunningham—The Path Taken: Honoring the Life and Legacy of a Wiccan Trailblazer by Christine Cunningham Ashworth

Herbalism for Witches: 3 Books In 1-Guide to Herbal Apothecary and Plant Witchery+Magical Herbs for Spiritual Healing and Sacred Heart+Manifest Your Spiritual Wellness with Spells and Herbal Magic
by Ruby Goldwin

Protection and Reversal Spells: The Witch's Self-Defense Guide Against Curses, Hexes, Negative Energies, Harmful Spirits, and Psychic Attacks. Create Your Own Shield with the Most Powerful Magic!
by Alyssa Vera

Reference

The Complete Book of Correspondences Sandra Kynes

The White Goddess Graves, Robert Guiley, Rosemary Ellen. The Encyclopedia of Witches and Witchcraft

The Complete Grimoire: Magickal Practices and Spells for Awakening Your Inner Witch by Lidia Pradas

Heal the Witch Wound: Reclaim Your Magic and Step Into Your Power by Celeste Larsen

Cunningham's Encyclopedia of Magical Herbs (Llewellyn's Sourcebook Series) (Cunningham's Encyclopedia Series, 1) by Scott Cunningham

Psychic Witch: A Metaphysical Guide to Meditation, Magick & Manifestation Mat Auryn

Llewellyn's Practical Magick (11 books)

Encyclopedia of World Mythology and Legend

The Encyclopedia of Celtic Mythology and Folklore Monaghan, Patricia. Astronomer's Stars Moore, Patrick

Self Care for Witches: The Art of Healing and Self Love through Witchcraft by Blair Blackmore

The Door to Witchcraft: A New Witch's Guide to History, Traditions, and Modern-Day Spells by Tonya A. Brown

Seventy-Eight Degrees of Wisdom: A Tarot Journey to Self-Awareness (A New Edition of the Tarot Classic) by Rachel Pollack

Everyday Tarot: Unlock Your Inner Wisdom and Manifest Your Future by Brigit Esselmont

The Ultimate Guide to Tarot Card Meanings by Brigit Esselmont

Intuitive Tarot: 31 Days to Learn to Read Tarot Cards and Develop Your Intuition by Brigit Esselmont

Everyday Tarot: Unlock Your Inner Wisdom and Manifest Your Future by Brigit Esselmont

I am deeply grateful for your continuous support. It has been a pleasure sharing all of this with you, and I hope you have enjoyed it as much as I have. Your likes, follows, shares, and reviews mean the world to me. If you feel inclined, please spare a moment to share your thoughts by leaving an honest review to help promote my book! Together, we can make a positive impact on the world. Once again, thank you from the bottom of our hearts.

Thank you!!
Robin

Embark on a world of possibilities with KIPS Publishing LLC. Books have the power to transform lives and expand horizons. We are excited to introduce you to a range of captivating, enlightening, and inspiring books that exceed your expectations. By scanning our QR code, you can immerse yourself in a diverse collection of KIPS books and discover top-quality content. Seize this exciting opportunity to enhance your reading journey. Scan now to open the door to a realm brimming with wisdom, imagination, and inspiration!

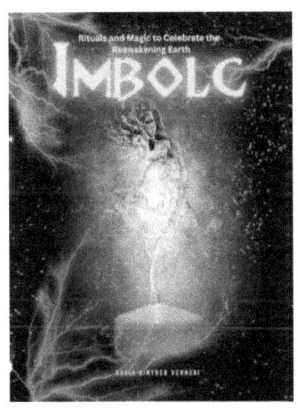

 Scan here for the latest release
from Robin Ginther Venneri and
KIPS Publishing

If you found this book enjoyable, please consider leaving a review on Amazon and sharing your thoughts on your social media platforms, and don't forget to tag me.

Thank you very much!

Sending blessings to you and your loved ones,
Robin Ginther-Venneri.

For any questions, concerns, or ideas, feel free to reach out to KIPSPublishingllc@gmail.com.

How to Support Indie (Independent) Authors

Review their books;
Like & comment on their posts;
Share their in-story or about pages;
Preorder their books. You know you are going to buy them anyway!
Recommend them to other readers;
Email or message about a book of theirs you loved;
Follow them on social media.

www.ingramcontent.com/pod-product-compliance
Lightning Source LLC
Chambersburg PA
CBHW082006140626

46553CB00020B/2446